ASK YOUR HUSBAND

A Wife's Guide to True Femininity

MRS. TIMOTHY J. GORDON

Publishing services provided by Archangel Ink | archangelink.com

Paperback ISBN: 978-1-950043-44-6
Hardback ISBN: 978-1-950043-45-3

Acknowledgements

Dedicated to my husband, Timothy Gordon, who inspired the creation of *Ask Your Husband* when he asked if he could be mine. Concerning the closeness of our marriage, Emily Brontë put it best, "Whatever our souls are made of, his and mine are the same." Also, to the memory of John Moorhouse, who knew just what to say to a first-time author to give her confidence to write her first book, and whom to ask to convince her write it.

And, of course, to the Most Blessed Virgin Mary who gave the greatest answer ever to the greatest question ever asked.

Stephanie Gordon,
Hattiesburg, Mississippi
Valentine's Day, 2021

Contents

1

The Basics: Do Whatever He Tells You (Even Writing Books)

The most profound wisdom spoken by any woman, in any time, was the Virgin Mary's response at the Cana wedding feast: "Do whatever he tells you."[1] Our Lady, of course, spoke in deference to her Most Holy Son. Such deference constitutes the precise topic of this book, in the arena of the Christian household: the husband is the head of the wife in "all things not inconsistent with Christian piety."[2] This plainly means that the husband can order his wife in all ways, except to sin.

Mary, deferring to her Son, used these words to respond to a wedding attendant's request. Note: she responded not with silence—which we might mistake for perfect deference—but by opening her mouth and thereby diverting all authority to her Son.

That, is, she said *something* rather than *nothing*.

I would expect that if a woman writes a book, she "speaks her mind" by it. Life after the advent of feminism frequently insinuates the false alignment of absolute silence with perfect deference. This proposition—usually true enough—proves false when uttered or received categorically. I caution my reader: the opposite of the opposition's

---

1 John 2: 5. *The Holy Bible: Revised Standard Version, Catholic Edition, Translated from the Original Tongues, Being the Version Set Forth A.D. 1611, Old and New Testaments Revised A.D. 1881-1885 and A.D. 1901 (Apocrypha Revised A.D. 1894), Compared with the Most Ancient Authorities and Revised A.D. 1952 (Apocrypha Revised A.D. 1957).* San Francisco: Ignatius, 1994. Print.

2 *Catechism of the Council of Trent.* 1st ed., Baronius Press, 2018., Duties of a Wife.

credo is not always true. That is, feminists falsely claim that more female voices are needed; yet calling such a proposition "false" does not require the anti-feminist never to speak. After all, the Virgin Mary navigates the middle course, whereupon a woman speaks *and thereby defers to a man.*

This book will aim to do just as Mary did. One might even say this book recommends that women defer to male headship *by* its very expression (instead of remaining silent).

An editor who is a friend of my husband requested that I write this book because my former Twitter handle, *@AskYourHusband,* proved to be a salty laywoman's nod to Our Blessed Mother's great wisdom offered at Cana. And I humbly accepted this call. (In reference to my Twitter account, I say "former" because I quickly found that Twitter was hardly the place for a lady. The year I spent on "Catholic Twitter" proved one too many.)

When a woman speaks, she ought to direct her listeners to the wisdom of her husband. After all, the husband is the priest of the home, the Domestic Church. He is in turn accountable only to Christ: "For the husband is the head of the wife as Christ is the head of the church, his body, and is himself its Savior."[3]

On this note, I must contend honestly with the question: how does the writing of an anti-feminism book square with the same book's narrative that women should never hijack leadership roles? Also, isn't the authorship of a book by a married woman, by definition, an exercise of one form or another of feminism?

These questions will be thoroughly answered through my first few chapters. But the short answer is, "no." The Patriarchy instituted by Scripture (or Catholic Tradition) and nature does not require complete silence from women. What it *does* require of women is knowing *when* to speak. After all, silence is not an integral part of womanly humility and obedience for no reason. Contrary to those who hold out female

3 Ephesians 5:23.

silence as *inherently good*, it is primarily good on account of the opportunities it furnishes wives for listening to their husbands. If one's house is on fire, wouldn't it be imprudent not to shout "fire!"?

Feminism has, from its inception in the mid-nineteenth century, set the Christian world ablaze. Accordingly, the need for traditional-minded women to speak out—to speak out on behalf of silence!—is long overdue.

We have permitted feminists—like the one below—to direct the conversation on the Patriarchy for far too long:

> Ancient intellectual greats like Plato, Hippocrates, and Aristotle laid the foundations on which centuries of sexism were built. Although these Greek authors did not invent sexism, their writings contained ideas and arguments that were used to rationalize a particularly virulent form of misogyny. Once these ancient trend-setters devised arguments for female subjugation in the name of a divine good, it became self-confirming in the sense that women were taken to be naturally inferior to men, treated differently from birth, and trained to subjugate themselves, which itself further supported views about female imperfection and the disempowerment that entailed.[4]

So, here follows the proverbial poke in the feminist eye: a housewife writing a book to recommend to her readers the longstanding wisdom of the Patriarchy (i.e. Christianity). More specifically, I direct my female audience to the wisdom of their own husbands. If they are half-decent Christian men, then they have only Christ as Judge of their familial headship.

God bless the Patriarchy, the foundation of Western culture for 2,000 years.

In a society beset by the moral putrefaction of feminism, celebration of the Patriarchy is certain to summon a host of nasty responses

---

4 Mercer, Christia. "The Philosophical Origins of Patriarchy." *The Nation*, 2019, Web. 25 Apr. 2021.

(hence my departure from Twitter). I know whereof I speak: I am the vocally supportive wife of a public, conservative, Catholic alpha-male who built his career upon, among a few other items, the restoration of the Christian Patriarchy. The insults are bountiful, and I've read them all: "you're brainwashed"; "you hate fellow women"; "don't you know this is 2021?!"; and my personal favorite, "your husband probably makes you think this way!".

The notion of the happy Christian marriage wherein the wife "knows her place"—and is honored for it—shocks the modern feminist's imagination, even her "conscience." After all, up is now down, and notions of justice are considered scandalous and even illicit. Unfortunately, my detractors condemn what they should praise and vice versa. They have no idea what it's like for a real man to treat them in accord with their God-appointed femininity. Indeed, it is a prize to be treasured and protected and, for that matter, heeded (though this part is a little trickier; more on that later). Their "shock" at the simple description of Christian marriage tells the true narrative of what feminism has done to the popular view of men and women.

Christian Marriage Is Shocking

Let's investigate briefly why a basic, Christian, marital relationship is so shocking to everyone in 2021: because...feminism...is... everywhere.

The husband who kowtows to his wife is much like the push-over father who allows his petulant child to walk all over him. This means that feminist-friendly households harbor hen-pecked, unhappy, bitter husbands and officious, unhappy, bitter wives. The unhappiness and bitterness of husband and wife prove to be reciprocally arranged: each party craves the sexually derived behaviors in his spouse which he commandeered. Wives want leaders and husbands want followers, which spells—when granted—the sexual joy of Christian complementarity.

Since they lack it, nowadays, both husband and wife prove to be under-sexed, unpleasant denizens of the failing feminist city.

There are only so many hours in a day. Under the new feminist arrangements, this old fact proves to be more of "novelty" for women than men. For obvious reasons of arithmetic, these freelance, half-time wives are spread far too thin, having to squeeze household duties into a short window after work and before bed. As we all know, doing two jobs poorly instead of one job well is a recipe for disaster. No wonder the modern wife has become an unpleasant, nagging, over-taxed, under-sexed *roommate*—a very poor surrogate for the cheerful heart of the happy home, which is precisely what she was designed to be.

Most feminists assume that submissive wives, who hold no tangible final authority, fail to enjoy a conspicuous place of honor as the single source of sacramental counsel to the head of the household. They're scandalized and shocked by a wife who is not boss. According to nature and history, this is the sheerest nonsense. Although the Catholic wife doesn't make the final decisions for the family, she does submit her wisdom for review by an often-heeding husband who *does*.

Certainly, even the most open-minded Catholic husband will fail occasionally to employ his wife's advice or counsel when it is offered. But among parties of good will, a wise wife's word will be heeded when needed. Further, it is fallacious to assume that a second opinion fails to shape what it does not replace. Most Christian men take great care to ask for their wives' opinions on important family matters. Presumably, a prudent man asks his wife for counsel neither to heed categorically nor to reject unthinkingly what she proffers. A faithful wife trusts this, no matter how often she's not indulged.

But the point remains that wives are not designed to be family bosses any more than they are suited to be society's bosses. And this shocks the modern conscience *more than anything*.

Full disclosure: this was precisely the case when that same friend (viz. the late acquisitions editor)[5] approached me through my husband, to request this book. Tim respectfully laid out the conditions under which it could be accomplished. Again, how might a married Catholic woman author a book in accord with the Church's insistence on her domesticity—which carries the presumption that her homely duties are not compromised by outside endeavors, except in cases of extreme need? (This books' later chapters will reveal *that* the Church clearly supports this belief.)

Chapter Two will also thoroughly respond to this charge of hypocrisy which could be leveled at its author. Let us again return to the paradigm instance. At Cana, the Virgin Mother spoke to empower her son, and she did so with His permission. The feminists, in all their anger and vileness, forget or disregard that in Our Lady's deference, she became the perfect model for all women and for all times. Of all her many virtues, her deference proves the highest. Thus, not surprisingly the Church expects all women to honor her example: *deference by communication*. Imagine the terrible power of a God-fearing mother who directs her children to listen to their father. The next chapter will unpack this notion thoroughly.

The Church's Marginalized Teaching on Wifely Duty

In 2020, citizens across the world were asked to comply with government mandates because of Covid-19; many people followed blindly. Now, in 2021, it is time for wives to comply with their husbands' governance, not based on blindness but reason and truth, which will be spelled out throughout this book. I cannot overstate my next point: I never received this basic advice to comply with my husband from any of my female elders. Never. Ever. I didn't receive it from the Catholic female "leaders" teaching RCIA when I entered the Church, during early adulthood. Nor did I get it from the priests' homilies even though

5 The former acquisitions editor at TAN, John Moorehouse, to whom this book is partially dedicated.

many households were utterly broken and needed most especially to hear it. Prior to becoming Catholic, I didn't receive it from my secular relatives or friends. Neither before nor since being married have I received it from my Protestant friends. Why not?! Because few know about it, and few are courageous enough to live it.

The reason few know about this teaching, and embrace it, is that the Church and the world refuse to preach it boldly. In fact, the Church teaches it, but she seems embarrassed by her own teaching and refuses to promulgate it in anything more than a whisper. I'll tend to that defect below, and more specifically in Chapter Five.

In other words, in order for you to read this, someone must have written it. I thought, why not me? It veritably seems that no one else will.

After all, the basis of this Christian teaching is the basis for this book. Consider the *Catechism of Trent–the only definitive catechetical statement by the Church on the matter*—on the duties of the wife:

> On the other hand, the duties of a wife are thus summed up by the Prince of the Apostles: Let wives be subject to their husbands, that if any believe not the word, they may be won without the word by the conversation of the wives, considering your chaste conversation with fear. Let not their adorning be the outward plaiting of the hair, or the wearing of gold, or the putting on of apparel: but the hidden man of the heart in the incorruptibility of a quiet and meek spirit, which is rich in the sight of God. For after this manner heretofore the holy women also, who trusted in God, adorned themselves, being in subjection to their own husbands, as Sarah obeyed Abraham, calling him Lord. To train their children in the practice of virtue and to pay particular attention to their domestic concerns should also be especial objects of their attention. The wife should love to remain at home, unless compelled by necessity to go out; and she should never presume to leave home without her husband's

> consent. Again, and in this the conjugal union chiefly consists, let wives never forget that next to God they are to love their husbands, to esteem them above all others, yielding to them in all things not inconsistent with Christian piety, a willing and ready obedience.[6]

The most controversial portion of the above segment says, more or less, this much: ladies, **your husband is your boss,** plain and simple. If you don't care for the concept "boss," take it up with God. The *Roman Catechism* uses much less flattering imagery. Ladies, reread the above passage, and ask yourselves: who is the boss, husband or wife, that is, who sounds like the head and who sounds like the subordinate? Facts, as they say, have no use for your feelings…or terminological preferences, for that matter.

Ask yourself: why should the husband *not* be treated with the highest deference? Is he not the head of the household, sacramentally appointed by God Himself? For God is not some out-of-touch, out-of-date watchmaker who assigns mandates according to the changing cultural fashions of the day. His Word is eternal. What higher authority would today's liberated and open-minded women require on this subject? *Cosmo Magazine*? Sadly, many Christian women defer more readily to filthy, pagan tabloids than to basic Christian teaching.

On a simple, emotional level: is the husband not the one who is duty-bound to lay down his life for the protection and sacralization of his family? Like a medieval king, a husband is indebted with the protection of his subjects, and his credit is their honor. Heavy is the head who wears the crown, and the wearer of that marital crown is owed obedience. Being called "boss" is the cheapest honorarium we can pay him.

Across the board, the feminist movement chiefly centers upon women having the "right to choose." Instead of the evil misdeeds that

---

6 *Catechism of the Council of Trent*. 1st ed., Baronius Press, 2018.

motto usually insinuates, the Church too says women have the right to choose…their husbands. According to historian James Hitchcock:

> The first Christian wedding liturgies made their appearance during the fourth and fifth centuries, their relative lateness perhaps reflecting the belief that a true marriage was brought about not by the action of the priest but by the mutual vows of the couple.[7]

If you are a woman in the married vocation, you chose not only the man, but also the duties that came with him. In our day, it is even *shocking* to hear something as banal as that our major decisions and choices—like whom to marry—have real consequences.

Needless to say, the Church is not pro-choice in the standard feminist ways, such as the "choice" to murder one's offspring or to use artificial birth control. But as part of the Church's embarrassment of its (correct) perennial teaching about the sexes, it has camouflaged a subtler, third feminist "choice" issue. This particular one has embedded itself more furtively into the fabric of the popular culture: the "choice" by husband and wife to swap vocational duties.

The Church Is Not Pro-Choice About Vocational Duties

Many readers are, at this point, thinking: "but we prefer to run our households according to our feminist preferences—and even our husbands agree." Neither wives nor husbands may tell God they know better than He how a marriage ought to be structured, which is a precursor for transgenderism. Above, we saw that the Church is "pro-choice" about the woman's right to select her own husband; this was a historical novelty unique to Christianity. Yet the Church is not pro-choice as to the functional hierarchy of the Christian household, which means that your husband cannot give away the duties he holds in trust. Neither can the wife.

7 Hitchcock, James. "History of the Catholic Church: From the Apostolic Age to the Third Millennium." San Francisco, Ignatius Press, 2012, pp. 67.

Simply put, they are not really allowed to "swap."

Many women today say, "I will not serve," which is the exact opposite of the most humble and obedient woman to ever live, Our Lady, who said, "Amen." As a corollary, the twenty-first century husband's motto—knowing as he does that his wife would probably resist his authority anyway—seems to be, "I will not *require* her to serve." In this way, her noncompliance inaugurates his (and eventually, their children's). The bitter result is a familial rebellion against God, initiated by the mom. By capitulating to his noncompliant wife, via agreeing to "swap" duties, the husband more or less guarantees that no one in his domestic church will serve God, since he is the household's irreplaceable priest.

By refusing to submit naturally and supernaturally to their appointed familial roles, such "Christian" couples will never know the beauty and goodness of a life of serving each other and their family, the Church in miniature. Accordingly, they will never recognize their marriage as their vocation, their path to Heaven.

The Church is not pro-choice concerning a wife's duties outside her home, her daily whereabouts, though there is some prudential latitude in this arena. As the *Catechism of Trent* clearly states above, a Christian wife must "never presume to leave home without her husband's consent." Yes, gals, this teaching is still true today. If the woman is under her husband's headship and if she is to "love to remain at home," why should her husband contradict this fundamental teaching by compelling her to "go out?" Further, the Church rarely tells us what we must *love*, aside from Christ and one another and virtue. Hence, she must be teaching something of great importance, and we ought to heed this instruction—that is, to *love* being at home (which further insinuates that we must make it a highly pleasant place to be!).

Even non-feminists grapple with this teaching. Many Christian women today assume it's almost an abusive practice for the husband to be managerially aware of his wife's goings on throughout the day.

But at some level, intimate couples—even if they don't consider themselves hardcore anti-feminists—already function to some degree in this manner. Common sense, rather than a control-freak husband, dictates that the gentler sex must be cloistered, at some level. My husband and I have always been in communication during the day, which is not atypical. This much makes sense even to my non-anti-feminist friends. And when I've had to leave home, I've nearly never been "disallowed" from doing so. (I say "nearly" because occasionally, my judgement was lacking, by suggesting running an errand to a bad part of town. In such rare cases, I praise Jesus for the protective and loving husband He gave me.) Contrary to popular assumption, the *Roman Catechism's* passage on wifely duty is not an anachronism.

To contextualize the above information: Our Lady's life was defined by her humble and obedient service to the Patriarchy. Her service began at the Annunciation with the words "Behold, I am the handmaid of the Lord; let it be to me according to your word."[8] And it continued with her wisdom at Cana, at the beginning of her Son's service: "Whatsoever he shall say to you, do ye." Note her calm, quiescence, submission, and self-possession...which she willed and propagated in her goodness. In other words, she began her role in the greatest tale ever told by affirmatively submitting to the Lord's will. At Cana she tells every Christian woman to do the same.

This is the *only* time in the Gospel in which Our Lady approaches evangelizing, as if to say, "I submitted to the Lord's will, so should you."

If married women were to begin seriously tracking the Blessed Virgin as our Morningstar and Eveningstar—the Lord clearly asks that we do—then her simple wisdom at the Annunciation and at Cana ought to be enough for us to "know our place": viz. the home, at the service of our husbands and children. Simple prudence dictates as much. So does nature.

Ladies: never presume that you deserve more than—or even as much as—Our Lady did. Never presume that you know better than

---

8 Luke 1:38.

God which spouse ought to run the household. The Lord chose one perfect woman to bear and raise the one perfect man, the Son of Man. None of us is she.

A brief cautionary word on exceptions: as they say in court, *exceptions make bad law*. Since you may be wondering, daily spousal tasks and chores *can be* fungible. In this way, small tasks of each spouse can be lovingly traded or volunteered for, unlike the general mantle of male leadership, which must be the husband's. For example, my husband helps me not infrequently with some of my wifely chores. Admittedly, the ones he helps with are always those which he tends to enjoy, and *never* include doing the dishes, which he hates. Similarly, I help him with many of his husbandly chores which prove enjoyable to me. What's the difference, you ask, between this and the household, role-swapping feminism decried above? Only this: between my husband and me, chore-swapping is *never* expected or demanded. We always appreciate each other's help. So doing keeps it pleasant and pleasantly surprising when the help shows up.

G.K. Chesterton once prophetically proclaimed on feminism, which "is mixed up with a muddled idea that women are free when they serve their employers but slaves when they help their husbands."[9] These words are more important than ever.

God's Expectations Are Timeless

Our Lady was a simple, uneducated housewife. Yet she was destined to become the greatest woman in the history of the world, not to mention the Queen of Heaven. This contrast between expectations and facts should not be understated. Of all possible ages, of all possible women, God chose her.

It's impossible to overstate the importance of her "underwhelming" resume for her female Christian emulators. Feminists—both the secular brand and the confused "Christian" ones—will certainly ponder why

9 Quote attributed to author G.K. Chesterton.

the Lord chose an unworldly teenager above all other imaginable candidates. Why Mary of Nazareth rather than an "accomplished" boss-lady pulling in the big bucks, or at least a boss-like thirty-five-year-old Nazarene "with her life together" prior to pregnancy?

Unfortunately, we are told, the boss-lady is the perfect embodiment of what every woman ought to be. The female exemplar of our age is one that can "have it all," and only later add (or not) the cherry on top—i.e. a child. Wrong. God's choice of Mary seems to indicate exactly the opposite. For He exalted Our Blessed Lady out of all women (in all eras) to give us the perfect representation of what a woman should strive to be: a perfectly loving mother and a ceaselessly docile wife. This much is true in season and out of season.

Mary didn't "go out and see the world," "get real-work experience," or "date around" before she was entrusted to be the mother of Jesus Christ and the wife of St. Joseph...*in her teens*. Women of today recur to Mary's feminine inactivity and inexpressiveness—two of her leading virtues—as excuses *not* to emulate her. Today's women aim to be active and expressive. Clearly, if Mary is the mother of God, then young women should imitate her holy example. Conversely, if young Christian women cannot look to Mary's life and "resume" as the most perfect example of true femininity, then we should question whether we believe her to be the mother of God.

No academic degrees or professional careers were necessary for the fulfillment of her holy calling. In fact, such things would have been *barriers* to her duties as wife and mother. Although Christ came into the world in circumstances unbefitting of a king when he was born in a manger, the Virgin Mother's simplicity and purity more than made up for what was lacking. She dutifully served Him like no queen has ever served a king, like no mother has ever loved a son. At His birth and at His death, her tender arms became the throne of God.

In our sad, anti-Mary times, many women scoff at the relevance of this most blessed of women. As a result, they favor an old charge of anachronism: "that was *back then*." Feminists would say: "It's twenty-first century: I don't take a donkey to work." This is an important rejoinder. It's true, if Mary were to live today, she'd use a car and not a donkey. Yet one's means of transport is an *accidental property* of life in one's era. On the other hand, if Mary were alive today, she would take neither a car nor a donkey to work, because full-time homemaking is an essential property of her ageless vocation. Prudence lies in distinguishing essential properties of wifeliness—like not working outside the home—from accidental properties thereof—like what one rides to the market (unicycle, roller blades, donkey, automobile).

The moral order is immutable,[10] a fact that always disappoints radicals and feminists. As if God expects us to follow His natural and supernatural moral order any more or less depending on such arbitrary things as advancements in technology. Whether we travel from point A to point B on a donkey or on the much-anticipated hovercraft, God requires from us the same things He always has. The Lord is aware of all things in all eras, and He chose Mary (and her era) for the birth of Christ. God's words are perennial: then, now, and always.

Every woman in every generation must wrestle with the decision to follow God, just like the humble Virgin did two thousand years ago. We can choose the blessing or the curse (See Dt 11:26–28). So which way, western woman, will it be? Mary's heavenly way or the culture's worldly way? We are ceaselessly told that unless we support ourselves through careerism, as a man does, we are but a leech upon society (and even upon our husbands who may provide for our needs, but begrudgingly). This is a lie from the devil. The way of the world is *neither* Christian nor even practical. As will be seen in later chapters, household labor specialization and single-income households are *both* Christian and practical.

I'd be willing to wager that the Lord doesn't view childrearing by daycare and public school as an alternative to that of a loving mother

---

10 Gordon, Timothy. *Catholic Republic: Why America Will Perish without Rome*. Manchester, NH: Crisis Publications, 2019, Chapter Zero.

attending the hearth of the home. Can you even imagine the Blessed Mother dropping off the Christ-child at daycare, in order that she could pursue a trifling career in nursing or marketing or retail management or education (of *other* people's children)?[11] In this horrific scenario, the great Madonna artworks would, instead, depict her in a pantsuit at the office without the infant Jesus beside her. He would instead be somewhere else, mistaking another woman for his mother. How absolutely absurd is this scenario. Consider ruefully, dear reader, that this passes as acceptable and even advisable by the "experts" who have imagined into reality such a pitiful situation for millions of children today.

Make no mistake, the greatest achievement a Catholic—or any—laywoman can attain is being a faithful wife and mother. Simple housewives beneficently alter the course of history by raising the next generation. Abraham Lincoln once declared, "All that I am, or hope to be, I owe to my angel mother." This is always the case. From his youth, Jesus' mission was molded by His mother's gentle attention.

With God's grace, simple, yet faithful housewives *do* accomplish sublime things —even and especially those who have no formal education, marry young, and submit themselves to the Christian Patriarchy every day of their lives. This is what the Lord asks of us. The path to faithfulness involves following Our Lord and our husband's lead, not our own foolish pride.

Conclusion

It cannot be overstated that *Mary, the Mother of God, loved the Patriarchy*. She joyfully submitted herself to it every day of her blessed life. And remember, the Patriarchy simply means the Christian priesthood, which was established under two fonts, that of the clergy and of the lay household. By serving and preparing the way for her blessed Son, she submitted to the clerical Patriarchy, whose priesthood

---

11 Gordon, Timothy. *The Case for Patriarchy*. Crisis Publications, 2021, Footnote 105.

emanates from Christ's. By obeying and honoring her husband, St. Joseph, she submitted to the lay Patriarchy, a priesthood of the home.

This is not complicated, and yet we seldom hear this fundamental truth. Few priests proclaim this simple truth because cowardice often silences them when they ought to speak. Fortunately, some faithful priests are willing to risk their popularity to preach the unpopular (yet obvious) truth. Father Isaac Mary Relyea is one of those priests:

> That's why I tell the feminists, you're all a bunch of miserable, miserable beings because you won't accept your role. The greatest person on Earth that was created is… a woman! It wasn't a man. The Blessed Virgin Mary. What are you complaining about? And then, what did she do in the eyes of the world? She cooked, she cleaned, and she prayed. I tell you; you think you're better than the mother of God. And that's why you're miserable! I tell women—normally speaking—women shouldn't be working, if you're married. Now, people say "what do you say, you know, I'm a single parent…" Of course, you have to work then. But, the Devil twisted everything and [you no longer recognize] your role as a mother is to imitate the mother of God. And you belong home with your children, in the kitchen cooking and cleaning. Yes, it's beautiful. Sweeping the floor. According to the world, what did Our Lady [actually] do? They say, "nothing, she was a simple handmaid of the Lord." What'd she do? She cooked, she cleaned…and in that life she's holier than all the saints and angels.[12]

In other words, the modern woman has turned her back on that for which God designed her. Yes, she continues to eat of the forbidden fruit rather than accept her irreplaceable role in salvation history as another handmaid of the Lord. Accordingly, she is now more inexplicably miserable than any other demographic in any other time in history. To

---

12 Relyea, Father Isaac Mary. *Only She Can Help Us; Our Lady and the Spiritual Life* Speech at Our Lady's Army of Advocates, Seattle, 5 Aug., 2019.

wit, according to the 2009 article, "The Paradox of Declining Female Happiness:"

> We will show, in this paper, that women's happiness has fallen both absolutely and relative to men's in a pervasive way among groups, such that women no longer report being happier than men, and, in many instances, now report happiness that is below that of men. Moreover, we show that this shift has occurred through much of the industrialized world.[13]

The same paper continues and the plot thickens:

> Alternatively, women's lives have become more complex and their well-being now likely reflects their satisfaction with more facets of life compared with previous generations of women. For example, the reported happiness of women who are primarily homemakers might reflect their satisfaction with their home life to a greater extent compared with women who are in both the labor force and have a family at home. For these latter women, reported happiness may reflect aggregating over their multiple domains. While this aggregation may lead to lower reported happiness, it is difficult to know whether this reflects a truly lower hedonic state.[14]

Note the undeniable implications of Wolfers's conclusions:

> This is all a way of saying that whatever's making women sadder may merely be aggravating what's already in their heads. And that's where the gender wars come in. Some critics believe that by convincing females they could succeed in the workplace without sacrificing family life, the women's movement set up the vast majority for disappointment; whether

13 Stevenson, Betsey, and Justin Wolfers. "The Paradox of Declining Female Happiness." *American Economic Journal: Economic Policy*, vol. 1, no. 2, 2009, http://www.jstor.org/stable/25760045. Accessed 13 Apr. 2022. pp. 190–225.

14 Ibid.

> you're talking hormones or spare time or fatigue, they're just not equipped to handle what the feminists envisioned. It's a theory so freighted with controversy that Wolfers jokingly calls it the "Rush Limbaugh interpretation," implying as it does that women were better off when they were barefoot in the kitchen. "Did the women's movement make things worse? Unattainable? Plausibly, yes," muses Wolfers.[15]

The women's movement has indeed set women up to fail. If Christian women were to meet their full potential by accepting their domestic duties by returning to their place—the heart of the home—then society would radically change for the better.[16] Peace and happiness would reign in our marriages, in our children, permeating to our fallen world. It is hoped that the unintentionally obstinate woman will embrace the Creator's call for obedient wives and dutiful mothers. That her converted heart will enthusiastically shun the devil's lies to abandon her wifely and family duties in the name of worldly successes and goods.

If, in my off time from my own duties, as my children rest or play, I can help to convert even one of my fallen-away sisters, it will have been time well-spent. I will thereby have emulated—imperfectly yet sufficiently—Our Lady when she instructed her audience to "do whatever He tells you."

If the heart dies, so does the body…and so it is with the heart of the home.

---

15 Intini, John. "Men Are Getting Happier (and Women More Miserable)." *The Canadian Encyclopedia*, 11 Dec. 2007, https://www.thecanadianencyclopedia.ca/en/article/men-are-getting-happier-and-women-more-miserable.

16 Incidentally, happiness in the sense of pleasure, isn't the point of life (contrary to what the feminist modernists would have you believe). However, true happiness does follow upon doing what God created us for—getting over our pride to accept truth is another matter. As James A. Garfield once said, "the truth will set you free, but first it will make you miserable."

2

Why This Book Isn't a Performed Contradiction

Mother, First; Hobbies, Second

Given the above information, it's fair for a reader to ask more specifically: how can a wife and mother find the requisite time and focus to write a book? As Marge Simpson hilariously puts it: "I spend twenty-three hours of the day here [home]." Like Marge, I am a "full-time" wife and mother and, admittedly, writing a book is a monumental task. As I will repeat time and again, not all monumental tasks (e.g. authorship) are off-limits to married Christian women, just as not all incremental or "part-time" tasks are allowable (e.g. ostensibly "minimal" outside work for twenty weekly hours). To wit, for a married, Christian woman of usual circumstances, twenty-one hours of post-bedtime book-drafting *is* perfectly harmless while twenty weekly hours of toil at even a non-stressful retail job outside the home *is not*. By no means is this my standard, but rather it is the Catholic standard. Amid such high stakes, a married woman must know therefore what standard she is to be judged by.

There's no point in circumventing the issue. Answering the question thoroughly requires that we specify the obvious: *working a job does not qualify as a pastime*. As noted, earlier, I never desired to join my female counterparts in their futile search for outside "fulfillment" via careerism. Thus, I cannot claim that I commiserate the "loss" of permission to work an outside job. Irrespective of personal biases, it is safe to say that mothers seeking refuge and fulfillment in outside work renders them "freelance moms." In their case, the pastime immediately swallows the true vocation. Such women are reduced to tacking on mothering before and after their paid shifts.

Tragically, most children (and husbands) today only have access to their mothers (or in the case of husbands, wives) in the evening. And during that brief window of time, such women must fit in all their mothering, housework, cooking, recreation, and husbandly attention. Although some readers embrace this hybrid lifestyle, over time it proves to be taxing on the entire family. Thus, I must begin by distinguishing how and why, "going to work at a job," is *never* a valid wifely answer to the question, "what do you do in your spare time to refresh your enthusiasm for your marital vocation?"

Conversely, seeking fulfillment in appropriate pastimes not only *fails to harm* but even *enhances* our mothering. It is necessary. Accordingly, this chapter will help the reader to understand and distinguish good from bad wifely pastimes.

How I Almost Slipped into the Fallacy

Full disclosure: in my initial married years, I held a few part-time jobs. Guilty as charged. But to be fair, the brief time I *did* work in my pre-child marriage comprised just two short stints. The first was a stint when I was first married and in college; I "went back to school" at the community college at which my husband taught, mostly during the hours of his courses. I never earned a degree. When he stopped teaching there, I stopped attending, but instead got a neighborhood part-time job. My second marital working stint occurred when we lived in Rome: after my husband began teaching English to Italians in order to fund his studies of graduate philosophy, his agency offered me work at mostly the same locations and times. Both of my marital jobs were very part-time, and very proximate to home and husband, it should be noted.

Even prior to my conversion to the faith, I intuited that even part-time work proved detrimental to the harmony of my home—even childless as it was then. Moreover, before I *recognized* it, I sensed it: there was simply too little time for being a proper wife. Despite working only part-time in non-career roles, the trivial stress grew insidiously. Imagine the comparative toll it takes on married women who nurture and covet their full-time careers after having children. The physical and spiritual harm increases exponentially. Looking back, my husband wasn't treating me unkindly by permitting me to work in our early marital years. Unfortunately, we learned through trial and error by haplessly believing the crypto-feminist fallacy that part-time labor qualifies as healthy recreation. And the results were far from what we expected. The chores built up; we had less time for each other (and, childless, we had no excuse for having any less than much time together); my prayer life suffered; most meals were eaten out.

Although this represents a brief time before our children, I was nevertheless spread too thin. In what should have been an easy introduction to marital time management during those first couple of years, we borrowed trouble. Only after we began practicing the last, "inconvenient" tenets of the faith, a few years after marriage, did we both finally understand why the Church teaches the woman is to be the practically ever-present "heart of the home": the house (or apartment) is simply *not* a home when the woman is absent from it. It's simply a structure, a home without a heart. Like St. Thomas Aquinas says (in a different context), four walls and a roof do not make a home, without more.[17] Since then, we have been thriving as a single-income household, and we've never looked back. Indeed, we never wanted to. Turns out, the Church knows best.

The recurring premise of this book—in all its disparate chapters—is that the humble and obedient wife belongs in the home. From within its four walls, she directs her own corner of the world—much like Mary

17 Nevitt, Turner C. "Aquinas on the Death of Christ: A New Argument for Corruptionism," *American Catholic Philosophical Quarterly 90*, no. 1, 2016, pp.77-99.

did at Cana—to the longstanding wisdom of the Christian Patriarchy. Like Mary, a godly wife does so without regrets. As Hyman Roth says in *Godfather Two*: "this is the [vocation] we have chosen: I didn't ask who gave the order, because it had nothing to do with business!" I wanted to serve my God, who gave the order. Since I wasn't called to the convent, my vocation as wife and mother presented itself plainly. Many of you can relate to this calling—a calling no less worthy of God. And yet, at the same time, we experience great tension as to how best to use our precious free time. Unlike a convent's daily schedule providing predictability and structure, a married women's day often varies moment by moment.

To do anything well, "downtime," rests, and breaks are utterly necessary. Hence wisely selecting the most appropriate hobbies and pastimes from among competing ones is key. Even though certain activities enhance and strengthen our vows, our fulfilment ultimately comes by means of our vocation as wives and mothers. Still, to avoid vocational fatigue, we require rest for our weary souls. And in the world of refreshing recreation, not all pastimes were created equal.

Egalitarianism of every sort is a sham. Gardening, crafting, writing, painting, sewing, knitting are vastly superior eventide refreshments to married women than part or full-time labor. They are on a different level: one renews the body and soul, the other tears it down. One builds up the family, the other destroys it. For those who believe my reasoning to be "subjective," we can ask ourselves the following questions to determine whether a prospective hobby is beneficial.

First, does each of the pastimes, through its creative productivity, enhance not only the woman's mood, but also her overall family's while being enjoyed with children and/or the husband? Second, does each of the pastimes occur within immediate proximity to the home? Third, does each of the pastimes *actually* relax the participant?

None of these justifications apply to part or full-time work. The stresses of one job do not ease the stresses of another—only hobbies and rest do. As men regularly say about their favorite pastimes, such as hunting and fishing: "the worst day of hunting and fishing beat the best day of work." It's a human axiom.

Apparently, everyone except feminists understood the punchline being expressed by the truthful jest. Instead, feminists claim that labor gets them away from the home and thereby relaxes them. This insanity represents a confused blend of equal-parts *sex revolution*, on one hand, and *Puritan work ethic*, on the other, as my husband argues in his book *Catholic Republic.*[18]

As articulated by the commonsense standards above, a good wifely hobby proves to be productive and creatively enhances the household mood; proximate to the homeplace; relaxing to the female hobbyist. Every part or full-time work outside the home fails to answer two or all three of the questions above. Any hobbies that are truly praiseworthy will refresh the household woman for the following day's responsibilities. For me, writing accomplishes these things, although other women will select different pastimes from my list and others not mentioned.

How the Hobby of Writing Aids My Vocation

The written word affords wives—who require shelter from notoriety—a unique opportunity to privately express the public word. More specifically, authoring books is arguably the most appropriate means for a traditional Catholic woman to exercise her voice while tending to the home. During my children's naps, play time, or bedtime, I wrote this book. The homeschooling of our seven children continued unabated. Dinners were cooked. Cookies were baked. None of my duties as a wife or a mother suffered since my priorities are straight. The care and attention to the household comes first—both chronologically and on my list of importance. As a result, my vocational duties were never outsourced to another woman as an expense of completing this book.

---

18 Gordon, Timothy. *Catholic Republic: Why America Will Perish without Rome.* Manchester, NH: Crisis Publications, 2019, pp. 209-254.

As noted above, authorship qualifies as a great *hobby.* From the comfort of my own dining room table—during spontaneous "openings" in the daily household schedule—I get to exercise any productive intellectual impulses I entertain throughout the day. Honestly, such impulses are frequent; most of my book ideas occur and get processed and shaped throughout the doing of my daily chores. Like my other good hobbies, writing thereby affords me "the best of both worlds": my "wifing" and mothering sharpens my desire to write for an opportune hour or two, and vice versa.

In addition, writing enhances my mood and the mood of those around me. Accordingly, the authorship of this book answers the first of three questions above. I refuse to write a single word from anywhere outside my home—or at least, anywhere outside the presence of my family. It also resolves the second question. You'll have to take my word on the third question. Writing after a day of rote housekeeping simultaneously relaxes and enlivens my mind in the simultaneous action known as "refreshment."

As insinuated above, the same principle also operates in reverse: after my brain becomes addled from several hours of writing, I enthusiastically return to my chores, which provide a much-welcome thoughtless physical activity. Such is the ebb and tide of the intellectual and physical virtues, which work best in tandem.

I've gone through my checklist here not so much to justify myself—I already did this privately before consenting to write this book and thereby jeopardize some portion of my privacy—but rather as a sort of illustrative exercise as an important part of this chapter's content. In brief, a wifely pastime can be objectively scrutinized as good or bad for the home.

When I considered the prospect of writing this book, I also harbored concerns of being "too public." Typically, authors grant interviews, speaking tours, and promotional events, which would contradict the precept that a woman should be chiefly in the privacy of the home. Although Scripture paints Mary with Jesus and His Apostles on a few instances, she likely did not travel with them to the hostile parts of Palestine. After her Son died, she did not accompany the Apostles to the ends of the earth spreading the Gospel. Such publicity would have exposed her to incredible danger, which is possibly why Christ didn't choose female disciples. On the rare occasion that Mary had something to say, she did so from a place of feminine safety.

A counterexample to the healthfulness of book-authorship presents itself. On my former Twitter account, I learned the hard way how uncivilized the world proves to be to women who foray into the public, notwithstanding the geographic privacy that it affords. My husband had to enforce new rules which led me to delete most of my social media accounts. Twitter was the most obvious social platform on the chopping block. The "take away" principle here is that certain pastimes—not only getting a job, but also interacting on Twitter and the like—contradict or threaten to contradict the private vocation of the Christian woman. Notwithstanding the fun I had poking the feminist "bear" on Twitter, the fights it provoked and the time it wasted was not worth the privacy I lost.

When we identify one of these bad habits in our daily routines, no handwringing or garment-tearing is needed; simply, we must root it out. Such is the life of a Christian. Note that I share my own failings in these areas to reinforce the Aristotelian proposition that life is a series of trials and errors.

The virtuous are not virtuous because they were born perfect; rather, they are virtuous because over time they've habituated the reverse of their vices.

Writing a book such as this within the protection of the home is the best medium for safeguarding the private principles of my household while expressing them to the public. I get to publish my anti-feminist point of view without the social media catfights. It is truly the best of both worlds. Arguably—and I'm still less than perfectly convinced on this score—I bear a duty to speak *because* I am a simple housewife: I enjoy the luxury of having the type of "job" from which I can never be fired for saying true, thus controversial things. No one can call my boss to try to get me terminated. My boss explicitly approves of the project. Not only did he give me permission to take it on, but he has been an aid in its completion. Most men today cannot say these things, even if it is most veritably their duty to say them (since it is the birthright of men, not women, being hijacked).

Now that we've established *that* a traditional Catholic woman may engage the hobby of authorship without contradicting her vocation, what renders one (specifically me) *qualified* to do so?

The credentials for *writing a homemaking book* and for *being a homemaker per se* prove to be identical. And to be qualified to write such a book, a woman need not to have passed a home-economics course or reached a certain mature age. Rather, God has implanted a desire within her heart to share the wisdom of her vocation and nothing more. Sometimes God even chooses women like me who are far from being "credentialed," in the world's eyes. Like many of you, my childhood experiences fell utterly short of informing my vocation—theologically or even practically. I was raised in a divorced, secular home but with God's grace, I became a Catholic, traditional wife.

The latter sentence proves to be the most understated portion of this book, upon which I shall not elaborate much. Suffice to say, I was born to teenaged parents who divorced a few years after my birth. The next seventeen years of my world-weary, military step-childhood proved to be trying and faithless (but not entirely without its joys and charms). One final caveat to my gentle reader: however distant you may assume your early childhood placed you from your eventual vocation, it can scarcely be farther than mine placed me from the loving Christian model of matrimony and sacrifice. But placed me it did.

Thus, my transformation was a stark one. As you will see, everything I have learned about being a submissive wife first came from answered prayers to God and then from…asking my husband. It turns out that much of what he taught me (and in some cases, that which we learned together), I may hereby pass onto women who may be craving—and lacking—what I was formerly missing. The point is this: given my earliest beginnings, if *I* can turn up where I did, then anyone can.

Ask Your Husband...To Teach You the Faith

I knew almost *nothing* of Christianity until I met my husband, Tim, at eighteen. I was born to an unwed, atheist, teenaged mother. As Providence would have it, she was also devoutly pro-life and never considered an abortion when she became pregnant in high school. God bless her for that: although she gave me no instruction in the faith, she gave me precious life.

It would be my husband, years later, who would instruct me in the faith. I have no college degree to speak of, although I was earning decent grades through two years of college. The closest thing I bear to formal theological education would comprise my time in Rome when I would sit in and take notes (when Tim was sick or working) on his graduate philosophy and theology courses at two renowned pontifical Roman universities: the Gregoriana and the Angelicum. This happened somewhat frequently since we lived so hand-to-mouth in the ancient city, and since Tim could not afford to miss any course material. In fact, we sold most of our possessions to afford the move to Rome, where Tim worked almost full-time while being a full-time student.

Since the wife is the husband's helpmate—and since those two medieval universities were so fascinating and alluring—I was happy to assist him in any way I could. And as a result, I found that by assisting my husband, God was forming me both spiritually and intellectually. As a recent convert to Catholicism—one who had "crossed the Tiber" less than a year before literally relocating near it (and then delivering my first child in the middle of it.)[19]—I had a long educational road to hoe. And yet I was honored to learn technical aspects of the faith in such a city, inspired by my proximity to Christ's relics, tombs of the

19 My eldest daughter Abigail was born on Tiberina Island at Fate Bene Fratelli Hospital in Rome, Italy.

greatest saints, churches older than the first ecumenical council, and magnificent artworks at literally every corner.

As enjoyable as it was grabbing coffee at Roman cafes and sipping it as I walked into the center of Rome to attend class at a university twice as old as the American republic, it didn't constitute the extent—or even the majority—of my "home-spun" education.

As a young Catholic wife, I was eager to invite Tim's classmates, many of whom were priests, to our small Roman apartment to try the new Italian recipes I was learning. (I introduced many of them to American classics like pumpkin pie—which, incidentally, cost about twenty bucks per pie to make since the ingredients were so hard to find in Rome. They also first tasted Thanksgiving turkey and stuffing at our place.) Most of these priests were South Americans and Africans foreign to Europe, home-sick, and accordingly quite eager to enjoy a home-cooked meal and friendly conversation. Our dinner table was frequented almost every week by a diverse group of young men who were studying philosophy and theology alongside Tim.

In exchange for the many meals I prepared, my educated guests (along with my husband) taught me the fundamentals of the Catholic intellectual tradition. Many hours were spent by faithful Catholic men, gathered around my tiny kitchen table recalling the day's lectures discursively. These men would debate, ask questions, and read texts aloud…until the wee hours of the morning. Fortunately, I recognized the unique opportunity before me, and soaked it all in. Catholic graduate education is remarkably affordable in Rome, but I received mine for even cheaper than the low cost of Rome's pontifical university tuition: the cost of a few home-cooked meals.

We often wonder if, during those golden days, we hosted any future bishops in that cramped little apartment in the bustling San Lorenzo neighborhood of Rome.

As a child of divorced parents, one who was raised entirely outside of the faith, I had much to learn from my cradle-Catholic husband on the workings of a properly run Christian household (and the tenets of the faith itself). I am thankful that the Lord provided me with an eager disposition which allowed me to learn the foundations of Catholicism in this way.

Unlike my lost opportunity to attain a degree at the Gregorian Pontifical University in Rome, I did not miss the in-house educational opportunity afforded to me by my husband and his dinner guests. During and immediately after our sojourn to Rome, as my husband "came into his own" with his own Catholic writings, cultural commentary, and inchoate apostolate, I found myself engaging with increasingly profound teachings of Catholicism. In very much the same way parents teach their child a native tongue, I learned the language of the Church from my husband, who speaks it fluently.

While my education was unusual, it should not be surprising. After all, it is proper for a wife to learn from her husband and from his adventures. Within the domestic hierarchy, the husband is "priest of the home," meaning he is duty-bound to prepare his family for heaven by instructing them in the faith. As a consecrated priest is to the larger Church, the husband is to the miniature Church, the family.

As we spelled out the duties of the wife, let us now consider the *Catechism of Trent* on the duties of the husband:

> It is the duty of the husband to treat his wife generously and honourably. It should not be forgotten that Eve was called by Adam his companion. The woman, he says, whom thou gavest me as a companion. Hence it was, according to the opinion of some of the holy Fathers, that she was formed not from the feet but from the side of man; as, on the other hand, she was not formed from his head, in order to give her to understand that it was not hers to command but to obey her husband. The husband should also be constantly occupied in some honest pursuit with a view to provide necessaries for the support of his family and to avoid idleness, the root of almost every vice. He

> is also to keep all his family in order, to correct their morals, and see that they faithfully discharge their duties.[20]

Few women are blessed with a similar situation—a learned husband who takes time to instruct her. For those who aren't, however, the good news is that you can start to "learn from Him" by reading the Bridegroom's words in the Holy Bible, and Holy Church's interpretation of their meaning. Also, a multitude of texts written throughout Church history by philosophical and theological geniuses are widely available with commentary breaking them down for beginners. For example, within the *Catena Aurea* by St. Thomas Aquinas, the Gospel commentaries of the Church Fathers are masterfully assembled into four volumes.

For women who simply don't have the time to read expansive texts due to the constraints of homemaking, I've found the resources online conveniently edifying. (There exists a multitude of YouTube and online radio channels, for instance, where a housewife can tune in as she does her household chores.) But even primary and secondary sources from the Catholic tradition are insufficient for replacing instruction by the loving head of a household. Realistically, most of my readers find themselves in precisely this situation. The title of this book, *Ask Your Husband*, applies even in the lives of such wives: they must ask their husbands to teach them. Of course, for this to happen, such husbands nascent in their knowledge of the faith may have to *learn with their wives at first.* Later, they may become husbandly instructors. But before one can walk, one must crawl.

As my sex dictates, most everything I've learned about the faith has come from the tutelage of men: my husband, his fellow students, Church Fathers, and of course from the male writers of Scripture.

20 *Catechism of the Council of Trent*. 1st ed., Baronius Press, 2018.

When Women Should Speak (and When They Shouldn't)

The Church teaches perennially—up until a recent silence on the matter—that married women are to submit themselves to the authority of their husbands. As part of a larger twentieth-century apostasy, unfaithful churchmen abandoned the longstanding teaching of Holy Mother Church regarding proper sex roles. Last century, at the hands of Marxists, secularists, and feminists, the very notion of Christian "Patriarchy"—which bears two components, clerical and lay[21]—grew unpopular. Instead of proclaiming the truth about the sexes "in season and out of season" as the Church requires of itself, weak churchmen of the twentieth century opted not to jeopardize their own personal popularities secured by telling married women what they wanted to hear. The charge of the faithful shepherd consists instead in telling his flock *what they need to hear.* For married women, their vocation itself dictates that what they need to hear is virtually always in conformity with obedience and fealty.

If you are shocked by this teaching on the proper hierarchy of the home, *it is not your fault*–not initially anyway. You were deliberately not told any of this. It was withheld from you to spare your "feelings." Modern churchmen deem married women so fragile that simply hearing Our Lord's path for them—obedience—might break them. As a matter of fact, the Missal has even been edited with brackets around the inerrant or free from error words of St. Paul which proclaim, "Wives submit to your own husbands, as you do the Lord."[22] Revoltingly, those words may now be *omitted* by the attending priest during the Holy Sacrifice of the Mass if he wishes (and most of them do). Regarding the Holy Word being censored, altered, and memory-holed at the Holy

---

21 The Church's bi-millennial tradition has always taught a two-prong Patriarchy: an all-male episcopate and presbyterate, in one vocation, and a male-led household, in the other.

22 Miletic, Stephen Francis. "'One Flesh': Ephesians. 5.22-24, 5.31: Marriage and the New Creation." *Pontificio Istituto Biblico*, 1988.

Sacrifice of the Mass, Benjamin Wiker of *National Catholic Register* perhaps too honestly writes:

> You've been there, sitting uncomfortably in the pew, waiting for the lector to read the dreaded Ephesians passage, the one that speaks the culturally anathema, "Wives be subject to your husbands…" Sometimes you notice that the offending passages have been delicately bracketed, so that only St. Paul's admonitions to the husband are going to be read, "Husbands, love your wives as Christ loved the church…" The lector gladly takes the hint, and you sigh in relief. Yet, sometimes the entire passage is read while everyone looks uncomfortably downward, counting the seconds until it's over. Once it's over, you know you're home free. Happily, no priest will ever preach on the whole passage, but will slip into the culturally comfortable preface, "St. Paul says to all of us, 'Be subject to one another out of reverence for Christ,' and so we see…" Then follows a warm meal of platitudes served on a boilerplate, perhaps with a side of nervous humor.[23]

The effeminate cowardice of the modern Church knows no limits: putting the words of the Holy Bible in brackets—what an accursedly cautious time in which we live. Priests complicit with radical left "newspeak" like Scriptural redaction and replacement understand only too well that oppressive feminism visits furious anger upon even the most meager dissenters. And these cowardly priests behave accordingly. Moreover, informing women of their proper place does nothing to gain parishioners, donations at collection time, or episcopal appointments. So again, these spineless leaders remain mum, knowing full well that the married women in their flock are failing in their vocations.

Yet silence does not abrogate the truth; it simply disregards the truth.

---

23 Wiker, B. D. (n.d.). *The Key to the Dreaded Ephesians' Passage*. NCR. Retrieved 19 Apr. 2022, from https://www.ncregister.com/blog/the-key-to-the-dreaded-ephesians-passage.

The ambiguity and silence from the pulpit have resulted in an unprecedented time of complete marital discord, vocational confusion, and vice. In lieu of proper, top-down Church teaching and culture, books like this and my husband's *The Case for Patriarchy* try to fill the void left open from our shepherds' derelict instruction. The duty to teach the faith and morals falls, in the first place, to the bishop and the priest, not to the layman (and especially not to the *laywoman,* as we will recall with the words of St. Paul below). The layman, as the priest of his house, is ordinarily responsible for teaching in a secondary way, *reiterating* and *putting into practice* what his wife and children heard at Church. Because of the abandonment by our shepherds, more and more households today are being led by fathers who fill both roles: the role of the priest *and* the household priest, which is an onerous charge. Still, men who spiritually lead their wives and children are the minority.

Roman Catholic priests honor a lifelong vow of celibacy for several reasons. Of these, the most relevant to feminism is the reason that, unmarried priests can more efficaciously defend the faith, even to the death. Since by design, they lack a wife and children to provide for, the priestly sacrifice of their entire life—and if necessary, death—remains most readily available to men without dependents. And yet, the easier choice is to preserve their lives and popularity by refusing to teach the Church's hard saying, which many continue to do. As a result, Catholic laymen have had to fill this moral void, courageously exposing themselves (and their families) to possible retribution by teaching "hard truths" to a society gone mad.

Uncoincidentally, the most important of these abandoned teachings today happen to be the most controversial. Thankfully, even if churchmen no longer *speak* on the wifely obedience issue, inerrantly inspired churchmen once *wrote* on it in a saner age in such a way as to be perennially binding. It is a saving grace, indeed, that the laity can still access the Church's many documents and sources regarding the proper hierarchy of the home. For, even if truth is rarely spoken these days, it is always relevant because truth never changes! But as I insinuated above, the written word is a dead letter unless it is read and heeded. Leadership must point household wives to these wise words.

A woman should happily accept her role as "second in command," assisting her husband as he faithfully discharges his duties as the head of the domestic church—just as Mary did for her Son at Cana. However, being second in command carries more ambiguities than being first in command does. The present ambiguity to be worked through centers on this question: "how *much* and how *authoritatively* should the household's second in command speak?"

The answer is simple, but not easy. Since the woman is under the authority of her husband, everything she says and does is an extension of his headship. Accordingly, I must reply to the above question with the somewhat unsatisfying answer: a wife should speak as much as is necessary for her household. But who renders this qualification? The husband does. It is a prudential call and as such it is his to make. Prudence is called by Aristotle the "special ruler's virtue,"[24] since it involves the kind of authority exercised in snap decision making and subsequent decision-enforcing. If lieutenants held the prudential authority, then they would rule over their generals. Regarding the specific question about how much and how authoritatively they ought to speak, wives should...ask their husbands: "how much do you need me to help articulate our way of life to the children? Am I presently doing it too much, too little, too loudly, too quietly, etc.?"

A quiet husband might prefer a slightly more assertive wife—but then again, a quieter man might see increased female assertiveness as a threat to his household's order. Many factors will influence each householder's decision in this arena. *What's important is that each household wife applies no pressure, guilt, or manipulation such as to engineer a desired response from her husband.* And the salient point is that prudential judgment calls, such as this, admit of disparities among households

---

24 Aristotle, and H. Rackham. "Aristotle: Politics." *Aristotle: Politics*. London: Heinemann, 1959, III. 4.

only in small degrees. Notwithstanding the many temperaments of all the household leaders, their commonalities should vastly outweigh their differences. All Christian households must have male headship in common: i.e. quiet, effusive, or moderately assertive husbands who lead their wives and children in manners which leave no doubt as to who the head is.

All Christian wives must actively embrace their own passivity and encourage their husband's preferences in regard to their own wifely voice. Each faithful Christian husband's answer is good enough to suffice. And while St. Paul refrains from answering the precise question at issue, he provides an appropriate set of answers related to female authority.

> As in all the churches of the saints, the women should keep silence in the churches. For they are not permitted to speak, but should be subordinate, as even the law says. If there is anything they desire to know, let them ask their husbands at home. For it is shameful for a woman to speak in church.[25]

To the "Christian feminists"[26] out there, why else would this be taught by inerrant Scripture, if my characterization of women as "second in command" wasn't true? Once more, we are not permitted to teach—except perhaps as a kind of "teacher's aide" to our husbands—because teaching implies headship.

As a related matter, the notion of a woman speaking in Church and writing a book may be connected. As such, St. Paul's instruction to women on consulting their husbands with questions of theology was particularly meaningful to me. As a female author on the topic of a wife's proper role in her vocation, I am especially called to "ask my husband" for guidance. Female authors ought not to usurp the male right of leadership. Authoring an anti-feminist book, from a woman's

25 1 Corinthians 14:33-35.

26 Feminism is incompatible with Christianity. This chapter ought to prove that proposition.

perspective, would be consistent with Scripture only with her husband's active guidance and approval.[27]

On this note, St. Paul also writes,

> A woman should learn in quietness and full submission. I do not permit a woman to teach or to assume authority over a man; she must be quiet. For Adam was formed first, then Eve. And Adam was not the one deceived; it was the woman who was deceived and became a sinner. But women will be saved through childbearing—if they continue in faith, love and holiness with propriety.[28]

Pope Leo XIII adds the following gloss to St. Paul's words above: "teachers of Sacred Scripture are not to be appointed at hap-hazard out of the crowd; but they must be men whose character and fitness are proved by their love of, and their long familiarity with, the Bible, and by suitable learning and study."[29]

Where this book differs significantly from my husband's feminism book is that I do not presume to teach men how to run their households. My objective is to help guide my sisters in Christ to humble themselves to their husbands' authority.

---

27 A Christian husband ought not needlessly criticize his wife, especially on trivial matters, to flaunt his authority. Rather, if there is an instance where a wife needs correction, whether in real life, or on the page, he must do so with Christian charity. Recall that the husband, according to the *Catechism of Trent,* is "to treat his wife generously and honourably" and to "keep all his family in order, to correct their morals, and see that they faithfully discharge their duties".

28 1 Timothy 2:11-15.

29 Leo XIII. *Providentissimus Deus (November 18, 1893): Leo XIII,* 1893, Retrieved 19 ip 2022, from https://www.vatican.va/content/leo-xiii/en/encyclicals/documents/hf_l-xiii_enc_18111893_providentissimus-deus.html, Section 11.

Teaching Women to Read and Write a Good Thing?

In the previous chapters, I have defended the importance of female non-leaders' (such as myself) published written words, especially in this book's domain of anti-feminist encouragement. From time to time, it is important for wives to receive instruction from other wives. Accordingly, there must be some female authors. This raises yet another important inquiry.

Many feminists contemplate the following question: if a woman is to be primarily in the home after she is married, what use is there for her to understand academic disciplines like philosophy and theology? Why pursue a "worthless" education she will not use? Perhaps with good reason, this is a favorite feminist rhetorical question. It is worth addressing in full.

Like most leftists, feminists claim to think that education is "priceless." Yet apparently, education is worthless to them unless economically profitable. And this is key to understanding the feminist lie about the connection between education and career.

Remember, it was Catholicism that gave the world the library, the grade school, and the university system. These endowments by the Church carried the tacit notion that education is *primarily* for enhancing the moral and intellectual virtue of the human being, which literally makes humans better at being human. In sum, educating people is good for their *souls,* not their pocketbooks.

The Church has historically, but not exclusively, focused on the education of young men. After the medieval period, during which higher education was reserved almost exclusively for priests, laymen increasingly received university education. More recently, young women began to enroll at universities.

But only in the twentieth century did a university education—traditionally reserved for the highest studies like theology, philosophy, and mathematics—become increasingly mistaken or misused as a sort of glorified trade school. Simultaneously, only recently have university degrees been popularly received as "accreditation" for the job market. This represents a complete paradigm shift in the popular understanding about *what an education is.* Prior to this change, true education, constituted by study in disciplines like theology and philosophy, was its own end and its own reward. An inverse correlation exists between the highest, "speculative" academic disciplines and the lower, practical disciplines which have only recently been added to university catalogues: the most important are the least "useful."

This carries interesting implications for the feminism question. In this domain—unlike many others this book will touch upon—I can offer the female university student encouragement rather than discouragement. (But my encouragement comes with a caveat: a virtuous wife does not need a university education.) In fact, a faithful young Christian woman in the twenty-first century society enjoys, on the average, greater latitude for studying the speculative disciplines than her future husband does.

Before a woman becomes the helpmate to her husband and a nurturer to his children, she has a unique opportunity to grow in virtue through the study of subjects which middle-class males typically cannot (since most men must now take practical degrees as to provide for a family).

As will be outlined more thoroughly in Chapters Four and Five, a Catholic woman properly prepares for her married vocation differently than the world, which does so by means of a careerism. Consider the words of Pius XI:

> In the first place, the worker must be paid a wage sufficient to support him and his family. That the rest of the family should also contribute to the common support, according to the capacity of each, is certainly right, as can be observed especially in the families of farmers, but also in the families of many craftsmen and small shopkeepers. But to abuse the years of childhood and the limited strength of women is grossly wrong. Mothers,

> concentrating on household duties, should work primarily in the home or in its immediate vicinity. It is an intolerable abuse, and to be abolished at all cost, for mothers on account of the father's low wage to be forced to engage in gainful occupations outside the home to the neglect of their proper cares and duties, especially the training of children. Every effort must therefore be made that fathers of families receive a wage large enough to meet ordinary family needs adequately.[30]

So, unlike men, women bear no pressure to attain practical degrees oriented at high-salaries—leastways, they *ought* not to experience this pressure, anyway (although most parents nowadays unjustly apply feminist-type pressure on their daughters to do so). Faithful future-wives who do attend college ought to pursue degrees in the Christian classics which will aid them in their own edification and their expected vocational duties of eventual mothering, homemaking, and homeschooling. Rather than pursuing veritably useless degrees that would fetch a certain dollar amount while conferring little true wisdom, like most of their husbands must do, most women can actually attain degrees to deepen their faith and to assist the formation of their children.[31]

As implied above, many parents of college-aged daughters find it absurd to pay for an education that "won't be used." (This really means that it won't be used *in the workplace*.) Parents who face this dilemma are

---

30 Pius XI. *Quadragesimo Anno* (May 15, 1931), 1931, https://www.vatican.va/content/pius-xi/en/encyclicals/documents/hf_p-xi_enc_19310515_quadragesimo-anno.html, Section 71.

31 Regrettably, I passed on such an opportunity when we were young and child-free in Rome. I didn't understand the importance of such an education at the time since we were without children and hadn't even begun considering how to educate them. As I mentioned, education is inexpensive in Rome and many of their fine universities are remarkably easy to get admitted into. Even so, I questioned spending time and money on a degree that I "wouldn't use," not understanding that I would find that ridiculously foolish years later as I homeschool my seven children. Which is why all of the theology I reference here had to be learned in an informal way. This can be successfully done if one has an in-house teacher, like I do.

those with daughters who have proper views on the married vocation. They also tend to be the ones with daughters who are honest (read: brave) enough to tell them they won't be working after getting married.

What *is* absurd is the notion that money spent on classically training one's mind would be money wasted. Sometimes, one invests money on things that better the soul and mind without expecting one dollar in return.

Here I must repeat the warning that female education in the Catholic tradition is permissive, not mandatory. And if done, faithful Catholic women should be educated in one of the classical, not practical, disciplines. In the case of the classically trained young woman who accepts the Catholic sex roles, she will not only be bettering herself by these studies, but also preparing herself to educate her future children. As the *Catechism of the Catholic Church* states:

> Parents have the first responsibility for the education of their children. They bear witness to this responsibility first by creating a home where tenderness, forgiveness, respect, fidelity, and disinterested service are the rule. The home is well suited for the education in the virtues.[32]

Also consider:

> Through the grace of the sacrament of marriage, parents receive the responsibility and privilege of evangelizing their children. Parents should initiate their children at an early age into the mysteries of the faith of which they are the "first heralds" for their children. They should associate them from their tenderest years with the life of the Church. A wholesome family life can foster interior dispositions that are a genuine preparation for a living faith and remain a support for it throughout one's life.[33]

---

32 Catholic Church. *Catechism of the Catholic Church*. 2nd ed., Our Sunday Visitor, 2000, #2223.

33 Ibid. #2225.

Even if one is fortunate enough to find a traditional, Catholic school to properly teach children, the responsibility to educate chiefly belongs to the parents. Since the mother and the father are *primarily* responsible for the educating of their children, shouldn't they be educated enough to do so (whether they decide to homeschool or not)?

Catholic professor Anthony Esolen once said classical curriculums focus on the "whole human being, not disembodied chunks of him."[34] He continued to say of graduates of classical studies:

> Gabriel Marcel said long ago that it was the duty of the sane man, the Christian man, to set himself apart from the mass society and against it, because the mass society bids fair to devour humanity itself. Every family you raise against that mass society is a castle of sanity and health in an age of confusion and disease. And from out of those sane graduates, there may arise some who will actually be what the mass-educators claim to produce: leaders in thought, art, public affairs, and the Church.[35]

After all, the importance of teaching the classics was once widely acknowledged:

> From the Middle Ages until the late 19th century, knowledge of the classics thus provided educated people the world over with a common frame of reference. Physicians wrote their prescriptions in Latin; scientists still often published research papers in Latin to ensure a worldwide audience of fellow professionals. Lawyers buttressed their arguments with Latin phrases. Artists flattered their subjects by painting or sculpting them in togas. Architects designed buildings in the increasingly fashionable

---

34 Smith, Peter Jesserer. "Anthony Esolen in His Own Words: 'Why I Left Providence College for Thomas More,'" *National Catholic Register*, 4 May 2017, https://www.ncregister.com/blog/anthony-esolen-in-his-own-words-why-i-left-providence-college-for-thomas-more.

35 Ibid.

> Greek Revival style that we sometimes call "Federal," its Doric, Ionic, and Corinthian columns providing an idiom of dignity and rationality to a variety of American structures, including plantation homes, courthouses, banks, and churches. The United States was self-consciously constructing itself as a modern version of a classical republic.[36]

What if a married woman did not pursue an education in her single days? The good news is that she can still be a student of the classics in her "off-time." It is appropriate for a young, single woman to spend some of her day with her nose buried in books, but a married woman has to squeeze in these pursuits in her off-time. Remember, a woman's time is no longer her own after she is married.

However, the good news is that even the busiest mother can find time throughout the day to improve her mind. Prior to this book, I occupied my spare time by supporting my husband's writing as his research assistant. When I wasn't doing that, I spent my off-time reading up on important texts deliberately overlooked by my public-school education. Eventually, I began to write my own articles on feminism, which led me to author this book.

Perhaps, some readers prefer an author with multiple degrees. If so, I'm sorry to disappoint. But it would be quite contrary to my thesis if I had spent much energy attaining such credentials. Closely interrogate the fact that the only way to speak authentically on this topic would inhere in "practicing what I preach."

The Union of Work and Study in Religious Life

To better understand the married vocation, especially as it pertains to wifely duties, it is important to examine the life of a religious sister, the bride of Christ. In the context of the other female vocation,

---

36 Howe, Daniel Walker. "Classical Education in America," *The Wilson Quarterly*, 19 Dec. 2014, www.wilsonquarterly.com/quarterly/spring-2011-the-city-bounces-back-four-portraits/classical-education-in-america/.

working and studying means something a bit different. But given its analogous import, it bears mention in this book on the marital life. Religious sisters spend much of their off-time on their studies. Like housewives, the education religious sisters receive is used entirely for enhancing personal virtue, not worldly riches.

Nestled in the mountains above Tehachapi, California is a small convent of cloistered sisters, the Norbertine Cannonesses of the Bethlehem Priory of Saint Joseph. When I lived in California with my husband, we occasionally took our daughters there. Merely observing the sisters shows the observer that a life devoted to study, service, and prayer is an even nobler option than the married vocation.

The Norbertines "live off of" the land they plow, sow, and harvest. The sisters have little down-time, but they still devote a great deal of it to their studies. Curious, I once read their daily schedule on their newsletter. Instructive even to married laywomen, here is the rigorous daily schedule of the Norbertine Cannonesses of the Bethlehem Priory of Saint Joseph:

12:00 am Matins (Office of Readings) Bell
5:20 am Rise and Breakfast
6:00 am Lauds (Morning Prayer) followed by the Angelus
6:30 am Chapter
7:15 am Exposition of the Blessed Sacrament followed by Terce (Mid-Morning Prayer)
8:15 am Benediction of the Blessed Sacrament
8:30 am The Holy Sacrifice of the Mass
10:00 am Classes/Study/Work
11:45 am Sext (Midday Prayer), Angelus, and Rosary followed by Dinner
1:00 pm Nones (Mid-afternoon Prayer)
1:30 pm Solemn Silence
2:30 pm Work
5:15 pm Vespers (Evening Prayer) and Angelus

5:45 pm Lectio Divina
6:30 pm Supper
7:00 pm Recreation
8:00 pm Compline (Night Prayer)[37]

From morning until night, the sisters stay busy cultivating their land, their community, and their own minds. On their site, NorbertineSisters.org, they have an apt quote describing their study hours:

> The goal of formation is to help the candidate to respond faithfully to her divine vocation, so that she may grow harmoniously into a mature human and Christian person… that she may sincerely develop a sense of Christian responsibility and may learn to dedicate herself, her qualities, and her talents to her sisters and to the Church in apostolic activity.[38]

Concerning their rigorous program of studies, they write: "The morning hours after the time of Holy Mass are dedicated to classes and study for the sisters in initial formation, as well as to work. In addition to academic formation in Latin, Spirituality, Chant, Philosophy and Theology, formation also includes the learning and developing of various work and artistic skills. Sisters learn building and farming skills, as well as sewing, cooking, property maintenance, animal care, cheese-making, bee keeping etc."[39]

Who would dare accuse the Norbertine Sisters of a "worthless education" simply because they don't enjoy a financial gain, but rather "just" the spiritual enhancement? Since the time people studied by candlelight to the present—when people do so beneath fluorescent lighting—the properly trained mind achieves salvation, one at a time. Those infected with modernism only see the value in endeavors which afford wealth and creature comforts.

---

37 "Norbertinesisters.org." Web. 16 Apr. 2021.

38 Ibid.

39 Ibid.

Rather than a slew of fancy credentials, your author can offer only a combination of her home-study and experience in service of wifely submission. If the many hours I've spent studying at home inspires women to reclaim a devotion to the married vocation, I will consider provident my dinner-table education in Rome those many years ago.

3

An Obedient Wife Is *Actually* Man's Best Friend

Aristotle: Husband and Wife Are a Friendship of Unequals

Husbands and wives were designed by God to be best friends. They were not designed to be equal in rank. How does the former proposition square with the latter? By examining some very basic teachings of Aristotle on the natural law,[40] this chapter will show the following: why and how a husband and wife are true, best friends, notwithstanding their disparity of rank; their mutual relation is "glued" by the attractive and attracting virtue in each, which fit together like the pieces of a puzzle. From there, it will become clear why a woman is *most truly feminine* under a just husband's headship.

Marvel, dear reader, at this unbelievably handy assemblage of Scripture verses establishing man's Christian headship over his wife—please keep in mind, this is by no means an exhaustive list of instances in Scripture wherein the role of married women are clearly laid out:

> The husband is the head of the wife (Eph. v: 23), the woman being made for the man and not the man for the woman (1 Cor. xi: 8); therefore, the woman is not to usurp authority over the man (1 Tim. ii: 12), but to be obedient (Tit. ii: 5; 1 Pet. iii: 6), submitting herself (Col. iii: 18), with reverence (Eph. v: 33), and in subjection to her husband (1 Pet. iii: 5); while the

40 The natural law is the basic moral precepts written on the hearts of human beings. Christians and non-Christians alike share the capacity to understand the natural law.

> husband is to love his wife as his own body (Eph. v: 28), even as Christ loved the church and gave himself for it (Eph. v: 25), and he is especially to honor his wife because of her weakness and dependence (1 Pet. iii: 7).[41]

Even though there is a difference in power, nature, and responsibility, the relationship between husband and wife is designed to be a best friendship. *Believe it or not, the difference in rank between man and wife adds to their intimacy rather than detracts from it.*

You heard that right: a man's closest male friend is an intimate peer of equal rank, who at the same time is likely the head of his *own* household. Using Aristotle, I will show how even the most virtuous peer friendships (e.g., these two close male householders) will fall short of the intimacy between a husband and his wife, provided that the marriage in question is properly ordered. In other words, rightly ordered rank *strengthens* rather than *weakens* intimacy.

The modern reader might be thinking, *how in the world can the most intimate human bond come from a hierarchical friendship?* Our post-Enlightenment obsession with egalitarianism has infected our ability to make and understand intimate relationships. Isn't equality the first necessary feature in truly intimate friendships? A reading of Aristotle answers the question definitively in the negative.

But this is clearly wrong because a *properly intimate* Catholic marriage constitutes an intimate sacramental version of something that Aristotle called the "friendship between unequals." Aristotle sheds light on how friendships between unequals work.

Though unequal in rank, the bond between husband and wife is intended to be closer than bonds shared between persons of equal rank. Saint John Chrysostom confirmed this in a homily,

---

41 Fulton, John. "The Laws of Marriage; Containing the Hebrew Law, the Roman Law, the Law of the New Testament, and the Canon Law of the Universal Church: Concerning the Impediments of Marriage and the Dissolution of the Marriage Bond." New York: E. & J.B. Young & Co., 1883, pp. 15.

> A certain wise man, setting down a number of things in the rank of blessings, set down this also in the rank of a blessing, 'A wife agreeing with her husband.' (Ecclus. xxv. 1.) And elsewhere again he sets it down among blessings, that a woman should dwell in harmony with her husband. (Ecclus. xl. 23.) And indeed from the beginning, God appears to have made special provision for this union; and discoursing of the twain as one, He said thus, 'Male and female created He them' (Gen. i. 27.); and again, 'There is neither male nor female.' (Gal. iii. 28.) For there is no relationship between man and man so close as that between man and wife, if they be joined together as they should be. And therefore a certain blessed man too, when he would express surpassing love, and was mourning for one that was dear to him, and of one soul with him, did not mention father, nor mother, nor child, nor brother, nor friend, but what? 'Thy love to me was wonderful,' saith he, 'passing the love of women.' (2 Sam. i. 26.) For indeed, in very deed, this love is more despotic than any despotism: for others indeed may be strong, but this passion is not only strong, but unfading. For there is a certain love deeply seated in our nature, which imperceptibly to ourselves knits together these bodies of ours. Thus even from the very beginning woman sprang from man, and afterwards from man and woman sprang both man and woman.[42]

In Book VIII of the *Nicomachean Ethics,* Aristotle describes the rapport between husband and wife as an example of friendship between unequals. He perfectly captures the essence of the leader-follower, husband-wife relationship in the following words:

> There is a different kind of friendship, which involves superiority of one party over the other, for example, the friendship

42 Chrysostom, John. *The Complete Works of Saint John Chrysostom,* 33 Books with Active Table of Contents, Kindle Locations 120365-120377, Kindle Edition, Homily XX.

> between father and son, and generally between an older person and a younger, and that between husband and wife, and between any ruler and the persons ruled.[43]

The modern woman and man might recoil from such a "bold" expression of misogyny, shouldn't they? Even many faithful Catholics, who mostly reject the modern world, will grapple with this quotation. Such faithful Catholics, no doubt, will counter by citing the *single* way in which the Catholic Church proves to be egalitarian: the equal dignity of persons.[44] They assume it requires ranklessness and an attack on all hierarchy. It does not. Marital dignity consists in virtuous hierarchy.

Aristotle is not denying the terms of human dignity by affirming that husband and wife are not equals. Rather, he is dealing in the differential terms of male and female *station* and *funct*ion, which the Church has always affirmed in a teaching more recently called "complementarity." The modern *Catechism of the Catholic Church* explains the term indirectly: "Physical, moral, and spiritual *difference* and *complementarity* are oriented toward the goods of marriage and the flourishing of the family life. The harmony of the couple and of society depends in part on the way in which the complementarity, needs, and mutual support between sexes are lived out."[45] While the Church's more recent *Catechism* announces the requirements of complementarity with less vigor than its Tridentine precursor, the two catechisms in tandem make for a clear teaching to the effect that enhanced female dependency—and loving male protectiveness—spell a satisfying and lasting marital bond.

Pre-Christian Aristotle gives a more gratifying description of complementarity than even the 1992 *Catechism,* by examining what naturally motivates each party—man and wife—to perpetuate and

---

43 Aristotle, W D. Ross, and Lesley Brown. *The Nicomachean Ethics*. Oxford: Oxford University Press, 2009, Books VIII, viii.

44 Aquilina, Mike. *The Social Doctrine of the Catholic Church, Didache Series,* James Socias, Downers Grove, IL., 2013.

45 Catholic Church. *Catechism of the Catholic Church*. 2nd ed., Our Sunday Visitor, 2000. #2333.

deepen their mutual friendship. Unlike friendships between equals, the bond between husband and wife is sealed and strengthened by differing motivations, corresponding to the differing roles played by man and woman:

> Such friendships [between or among unequals] also vary among themselves. The friendship between parents and children is not the same as that between ruler and ruled...nor that [intimate affection] of husband for wife as that of wife for husband; for each of these persons has a different excellence and function, and also different motives for their regard, and so the affection and friendship they feel is different.[46]

In friendships between peers, the two friends give and receive the same prize; in friendships between unequals, the two friends give and receive disparate prizes to one another. However stark it sounds—here or anywhere else in his writings—Aristotle is simply and clearly stating natural truths about human relationships, and then extracting their logical conclusions.

In this way, Aristotle's natural law conclusions can simply be called the arithmetic of desire, or the heterosexual logic of sexiness. The puzzle-like "fit" between man and wife extends even more to temperament than it does even to anatomy. Contrary to popular opinion regarding marriage, properly ordered heterosexual attraction is nine parts psychological to one part anatomical. The *Catechism* calls this natural fact "difference," meaning that the male and female psychology lack and crave one another in all ways.

Who would deny that, when a husband holds the door open for his wife, the excellence and the gratification exercised by each party differs? Certainly, the courteous husband exercises the excellence of his physical prowess and expects in return an affectionate glance or gesture from his wife; the wife reciprocates his courtesy mostly through

---

46 Aristotle, W D. Ross, and Lesley Brown. *The Nicomachean Ethics*. Oxford: Oxford University Press, 2009, Books VIII, viii, 1.

her beauty and grace, and she expresses this through some small or subtle transmission of her affection. Again, in this simple, customary transaction, the two parties involved are neither giving nor getting the same thing out of the transaction. They are each giving and getting completely different things...*complementary* things.

Aristotle explains why the logic of intimacy works this way: even as best friends, the two spouses are parties to a friendship between unequals. Like peers, part of their attraction is amicable, because it is based on moral likenesses; unlike peers, the predominant part of their attraction is sexual, because it is based on functional differences of ability, temperament, and anatomy which correspond to well-ordered males and well-ordered females. And this latter fact of nature constitutes my book's most inflammatory truth.

Most people already know that nature designated the husband the leader on account of his alpha psychology and his superior physical strength (which is why he holds open the door), even though they do not like the implications. In fact, God christened men as servant-leaders. Modern women gladly receive the fruits of the latter while denying the fact of the former. It is utterly illogical. We cannot be the more beautiful, dainty, pampered, and receptive sex unless there exists a more assertive, stronger, and expressive sex on the other side of things. Aristotle makes this painfully clear:

> Now in these unequal friendships, the benefits that one party receives and is entitled to claim from the other are not the same on either side: but the friendship between parents and children will be enduring and equitable, when the children render to the parents the services due to the authors of one's being, and the parents to the children those due to one's offspring. The affection rendered in these various unequal friendships should also be proportionate: the better of the two parties, for instance, or the more useful or otherwise superior as the case should be, should receive more affection than he bestows: since when

> the affection rendered is proportionate to desert, this produces equality in a sense between the parties, and equality is felt to be an essential element of friendship.[47]

There is a world of meaning in the three words used above by Aristotle: *in a sense.* Marital complementarity between husband and wife—who are not equals—produces equality *in a sense* between them. But equality "in a sense" is not equality proper. The latter means mathematical identity. The former simply means *intimacy* or *attractive interdependence* in the context of the mysterious, unequal, sexually charged best-friendship between husband and wife (the restoration of which will save most of the world, and lead it back to Christ's sacramental Church).

Ionic and Covalent Bonds[48]

In an analogy from Catholic social teaching, Pope Leo XIII in *Rerum Novarum* rejects artificial, imagined social equality and favors instead the natural inequality among persons in society, which leaves intact a disparity of their talents.[49] In other words, this inequality is a good thing because it produces a kind of affection and interpersonal needfulness among strangers. This mild-moderate attraction between strangers in society is likened to a covalent bond—it binds stably yet loosely—and is called "solidarity." We need each other *because* of our different strengths and weaknesses.

Think of St. Catherine of Siena, writing of God's hierarchical creation: "I could easily have created men possessed of all that they should need, both for body and for soul. But I wish that one should have need of the other, and that they should be my ministers to administer the

47 Ibid. Books VIII, viii, 2.

48 These comprise two disparately strong types of chemical bonds.

49 Leo XIII. *Encyclical Letter Rerum Novarum, May* 15, 1891: *Apostolic Letter Graves De Communi,* 18 Jan. 1901, [on Christian Democracy], 1891.

graces and the gifts that they have received from me."[50] She continues further down the page: "See then, that I have made men my ministers and placed them in diverse stations and various ranks in order that they may make use of the virtue of love."[51]

Pause. God so loved the hierarchy of unequal persons within His Creation that love emerges from the very fact of their inequality. And this is just between strangers. How much more then would St. Catherine's stark connection between love and inequality apply to the matrimonial bond where it only gets *stronger*.

Spousal intimacy equals the highest human bond, more ionic than covalent: it binds more stably and more strongly. Yet at a higher level, it works on the exact same basis: the attractiveness of opposites. Imagine how Rocky describes his intimacy with his wife, Adrian: "We fill gaps in each other, I guess."[52] (Also, recall Adrian's more specific characterization of the relationship: "my mother told me, 'you've got no body, so you better develop your mind'." She says this right after Rocky tells her that his mind is poor, so he developed his body.) This mutual dependence—a much stronger, sacramental species of solidarity—creates not only a feeling of need, but also a feeling of attraction. In the "ionic" bond of matrimony, this special kind of solidarity is called *complementarity*.

While the friendships between peers may involve gap filling to a certain extent, the Church would never describe such bonds as complementary. This designation exists only for the marital bond. Why are virtuous rank-friendships (i.e. husband and wife) more optimally intimate than peer-friendships (i.e. male best friends)?

---

50 Siena, St. Catherine. *A Treatise of Divine Providence.* Trans. Algar L. Thorold, Scotts Valley: *CreateSpace Independent Platform*, 2014.

51 Ibid.

52 Stallone, Sylvester. *Rocky Balboa.* Metro-Goldwyn-Mayer (MGM), 2006.

True Friendships Are Based upon Virtue

In Book VIII of Aristotle's *Nicomachean Ethics*, he lays out the basics required for a true friendship: "To be friends, people must 1) feel good will towards each other, that is, wish each other's good; and 2) be aware of each other's good will; and 3) the cause of their good will must be one of the loveable qualities mentioned above."[53] Applying Aristotle's analysis to the highest form of human friendship—that between spouses—and thereby answer the question posed at the end of last section.

The "lovable qualities" to which Aristotle refers include three possible bases for the human bond: utility, pleasure, and virtue. He stipulates:

> There are accordingly three kinds of friendship, corresponding in number to the three lovable qualities...when people love each other, they wish each other well in respect of the quality which is the ground of their friendship. Thus, friends whose affection is based on utility do not love each other and themselves, but insofar as some benefit accrues to them from each other. And similarly with those whose friendship is based on pleasure: for instance, we enjoy the society of witty people not because of what they are in themselves, but because they are agreeable to us. Hence, in a friendship based on utility or on pleasure men love their friend for their own good or their own pleasure, and as not being the person loved, but as useful or agreeable. And therefore these friendships are based on an accident, since the friend is not loved for being what he is, but as affording some benefit or pleasure as the case may be.[54]

Utility proves an even more superficial—and less personal—basis for friendship than pleasure does. Aristotle calls each of these two types

---

53 Aristotle, W D. Ross, and Lesley Brown. *The Nicomachean Ethics*. Oxford: Oxford University Press, 2009, Books VIII, viii, 4.

54 Aristotle. *The Nicomachean Ethics*. Books VIII, iii, 1-2.

"accidental forms" of friendship. In the case of "friendships" of utility, think for example of the nerdy, unlikeable kid down the block who you played with just for use of his ping pong table. In the case of "friendships" of pleasure, think for example of the funny or interesting kid in middle school who got you into a lot of trouble. In the latter case, you at least *believed* you liked the likable mischief-maker, whereas in the former case—even at the time—you never believed you cared for the kid whose toy you wanted to use.

But the third, and only the third, type of friendship qualifies for Aristotle as a true one. He writes: "the perfect form of friendship is that between the good, and those who resemble each other in virtue. For these friends wish each alike the other's good in respect of their goodness, and their good in themselves."[55]

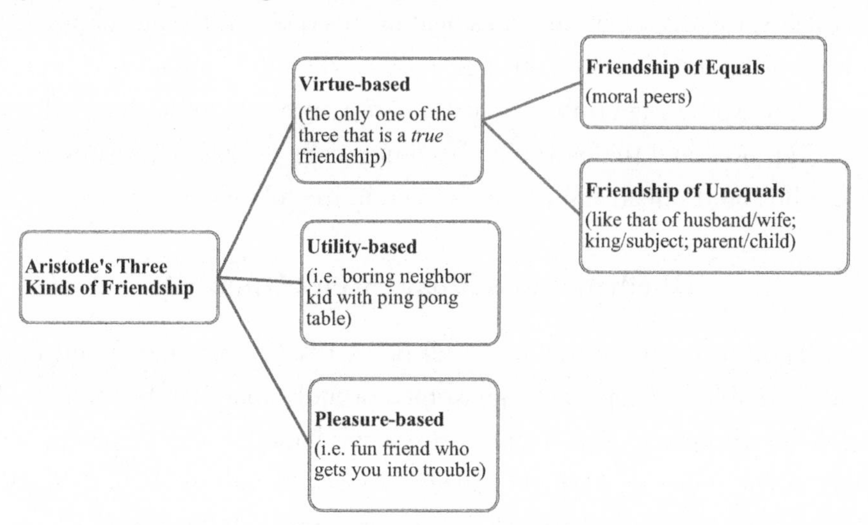

Now, here's the important part for spousal friendship: the single true form of friendship—one based in mutual virtue—can designate either the peer-friendship (between equals) or the rank-friendship (between unequals). This is where things get really interesting. What Aristotle stops short of articulating specifically is that a certain type of rank-friendship proves truer and more intimate than all the other forms

55 Aristotle. *The Nicomachean Ethics*: Book VII., iii, 6.

of rank-friendships and friendships between equals. That certain type is the husband-wife friendship. Aristotelian thinkers of the Catholic Church like St. Thomas Aquinas, basing their reasoning upon the sacramental theology of matrimony, correctly made this diagnosis—mostly unexpressed as it was in Aristotle.

It's this simple: virtue is the strongest binding force of human friendships. Therefore, the most intimate friendship enables and requires the cultivation of virtue. Holy matrimony equals that most intimate friendship. Without the natural male-female hierarchy of marriage, neither party will advance in virtue as quickly.

For example, imagine when one friend of the same-sex takes it upon themselves to play the role of the moral teacher. An argument will likely transpire. Equals in friendship tend to jealously guard their equality. On the other hand, in a healthy marriage, where the hierarchy is preordained, no power struggle ensues when the man takes charge, and the woman's natural docility encourages her to follow his lead.

It is no secret that a woman becomes more truly feminine under a just husband's headship as will be seen in the following sections.

Obedience and Moxie Aren't Opposed

Feminism is besetting us on all sides. It's "in our faces," and we seem unable to escape it. Many women proudly abandon their families for the workplace; girls' "sports" are being hailed as legitimate entertainment; widespread single and even married mothers claim to head households; politics are in all corners fraught with "iron ladies"; on the stage and screen, girls regularly masquerade as comedians; meanwhile, many men live lives of quiet desperation by the motto, "happy wife, happy life"; etc. What a sharp contrast to Aristotle's refreshing commonsense teachings!

Society has fallen apart because the family fell apart.

One more, somewhat subtler marker of feminism quietly dwells amongst the more pronounced grievances and indications named above; its advocates and exponents seem to be the most vocal adversaries of a traditional lifestyle. Nothing embodies the feminist mentality, "what's mine is mine, and what's yours is… also mine" quite like the hyphenated surname.

What's the big deal? Isn't a hyphen just a stupid little line? Make no mistake, the widespread use of a hyphen is *far* more toxic to society than you might assume. It is an outward, if muted, symbol of feminism's chief goal: to generate as many rifts as possible between men and women. Not unlike contraception, feminists use the hyphen to separate that institution which ought to be superlatively unitive. A woman takes her husband's name because she assumes one flesh with him. Have you ever met a woman who uses a hyphen and simultaneously conducts her life with a proper understanding of femininity? I haven't.

Nowhere is the hyphen more predominant than it is in the author lines of articles and commentaries in "enlightened" woman's magazines and weblogs. (If you currently don't read such robust claptrap, don't waste your time. I have and I can tell you that they can easily be summed up as: all woman ought to be free to choose *any* lifestyle they desire….so long as they don't choose lives celebrating the Patriarchy.

In my estimation, the hyphen is *the* scarlet letter betraying an illogical, emotional female. It makes no difference how educated such a woman happens to be. I know instantly when a woman introduces herself with a hyphenated surname that she and I will have nothing important in common. Typically, such a woman holds the nonsensical belief that it is demeaning—read "Patriarchal"—to accept her husband's last name. (Well, patriarchal, yes; demeaning, no. Long live the Patriarchy!)

If adopting a man's surname demeans us, then why cling to an original surname *given to us by our literal patriarchs?* So much for slighting the Patriarchy, gals. And since "choice" is the feminist's favorite word, shouldn't she be delighted that a woman is free to choose her mate and to some extent, her surname—inasmuch as she chooses the man and the name that comes with him. Hilariously, these warriors against the Patriarchy end up adopting *two* male surnames instead of just one like the rest of us simpletons. Literally every objection these tortured souls try to build against the Patriarchy seems to be built on sand. Such is the nature of feminist "logic," without which they would have no logic at all. But they won't stop there.

Articles in modern women's blogs and magazines are full of dreadful stories about how traditional women lack the spice of life. The authors of these articles posit that traditional woman prefer, instead, to live out their uninspired lives one playdate at a time. Here's the thing: I attempt to cede ground wherever I deem it fair. To some extent—in this limited area—those hyphenated women may have a point.

We make it far too easy for those hostile to tradition to characterize Christian women—and Christians in general—as lacking moxie and a healthy dose of enjoying life. I'm sad to say that many Christian women (and sometimes willingly) perpetuate this stereotype. That is to say, I've noticed that moxie, the "spice of life," does seem to be in short supply among women with whom I might otherwise match, as a potential friend. I've too rarely met other women within the ranks of tradition-minded Catholicism who share my love for both the one true faith *and* an amusing conversation offset by belly laughs.

Here we come to the point: being a Christian doesn't mean we have to be bland or boring. Properly disposed, our Christianity actually requires us to be daring and interesting. One is not made "holier" than his neighbor because he listens to Christian rock or because his wife refuses to wear make-up. (Christian rock, incidentally, is an abomination against the auditory system.) We are specifically called as Christians to be in the world but not of it. For instance, secular entertainment such as sports, movies, books, and music—and even Halloween (gasp)—are permissible as long as they don't cause you to sin and violate your duties. There is no duty to consume exclusively Catholic content.

Somewhere down the line, someone spearheaded a Ned and Maude Flanders version of Roman Catholicism, and sadly it's taken off like wildfire—especially among American Catholics. If you're unfamiliar with Ned and Maude Flanders, from *The Simpsons*,[56] I'll leave you with a perfect example of what I mean: in an early episode of the series, the Flanders (the bland, nerdy Protestant family who live next door to the Simpsons) babysit Bart and Lisa Simpson as their mother, Marge, is in labor at the hospital. Ned kindly offers the Simpsons kids an afternoon snack: nachos. But Bart and Lisa's delight quickly fades into disappointment as Ned delivers what he calls "Nachos, Flanders style," which consists of cucumbers topped with cottage cheese.[57] The Flanders have no spice of life—even on their food. Henceforward, Bart and Lisa begin to characterize—the way secular families usually typify Christian families—the Flanders as the most flavorless, insipid family on the block. The Flanders hurt their own case by creating and strictly abiding needless rules—like making gratuitously healthful snacks—above the rightful and needful rules of Christianity.

People may hate it, but stereotypes usually prove true: that's why they're funny. The American Catholic seems today to have borrowed the trouble described above from the Protestants who surround us. As a result, their "salt" has lost its flavor as Our Lord declared (See Lk 14:34) just like many of the Protestants surrounding them. In other words, the reason the secular left has been so successful at characterizing Christians as insensible, fun-haters because *we* provide them with all the requisite material for the assumption.

We ought to renounce the Puritan-like expectation for a one-size-fits-all approach to personality. Women who have interests outside of Catholicism, passionate personalities, and a good sense of humor offer their husbands a most suitable friend. An interesting

---

56 Groening, Matt, James L. Brooks, Sam Simon, Alf Clausen, Dan Castellaneta, Julie Kavner, Nancy Cartwright, Yeardley Smith, Hank Azaria, and Harry Shearer. The Simpsons., 2007.

57 "Home Sweet Home Diddly-Dum-Doodily." The Simpsons. Created by Matt Groening, Performances by Dan Castellaneta, Julie Kavner, Nancy Cartwright, Yeardley Smith, Hank Azaria, and Harry Shearer, Season 7, Episode 3, 20th Century Fox, 1 Oct. 1995.

personality is not in tension with a passionate zeal for the faith and devotion to God.

For a proper balance between piety and joyful spontaneity, the best rule of life is that which Cicero expresses to Maximus in *Gladiator*. Maximus asks: "Do you find it difficult to do your duty?", to which Cicero responds: "sometimes I do what I want to do; the rest of the time I do what I have to."[58] This is a keen, and even an admirable, approach to the Catholic life—especially if we interpret strictly those many duties which we cannot fail to do.

Moreover, in the realm of our first duty to our husbands, which involves being his best friend and cheerful helpmate, Cicero's rule plays a heightened role since men are especially sensitive to the "domesticating" and "civilizing" influence women tend to wield, which most men oppose to their sense of marital freedom and fun. The husband jealously guards both of these two things. As much as all Christians need to be on the watch against being characterized as, "sticks in the mud," Christian *women* need to be doubly so, especially around their husbands. I will revisit this point in Chapter Six, but it bears repeating once more here: a wife *must* have fun with her husband, lest she lose her status as his best friend. Once this status is forfeited the husband will seek his male friends for fun on the weekends, away from his home. He becomes the "weekend warrior." If the home is not made into a place of enjoyment, the husband will often seek his entertainment *out with the guys*. Be both responsible and fun for him. Nothing is sexier to a man.

My husband and I frequently quote John Hammond's euphemism for people who have passionate, expressive personalities—we say they "suffer from a deplorable *excess* of personality."[59] It's no secret that this is a shared trait among Gordon family members. Each one of us is riddled with it, including my six daughters, who are forging the path alongside their mother for "big-obedience-big-personality acceptance" within female traditional Catholic circles. I daresay, my daughters are

---

58 Scott, Ridley. *Gladiator.* DreamWorks Distribution, 2000.

59 Spielberg, Steven. *Jurassic Park.* Universal Pictures, 1993.

making immense progress within our home-spun movement by their sheer volume (in both senses of the term).

Obedient, traditional-minded woman can also have moxie. In fact, they must have moxie in one way or another, even if they are the more reticent types. Basically all of our most cherished saints—male and female—were brimming with it. The trick for the modern woman is making sure that moxie doesn't morph into belligerence.

This chapter does nothing to diminish the importance of the naturally quiet, reserved female reader out there. Women who possess such traits are already popularly acknowledged for their adherence to traditional femininity. My aim is to stick up for virtuous women with moxie out there who are oftentimes acknowledged *in spite* of their passionate demeanors, and not *for* them. All of our greatest female saints lived, spoke, and died enthusiastically for Christ.

How Do You Solve a Problem Like Maria?

Ladies with a deplorable excess of personality might prefer the kinder term "enthusiastic expressor." Enthusiastic expressors (such as your author) speak, think, laugh and even *gesture* audibly. In situations where silent gesticulation is required to convey a message, we can't help but to throw in a few claps and finger snaps.

For my part, I've been told my laugh could be heard through walls—across the street. Growing up in a secular home I had no idea that a vow of silence was an actual thing. I thought the expression's sole use was to cheekily tell someone that they needed to take one. After I met my husband, I learned taking a vow of silence wasn't limited to a funny retort or some Hollywood depiction of piousness. Instead, it's a literal vow that some of the stricter religious orders practice.

I never considered becoming a nun like the heroine Maria Von Trapp did in the classic film *The Sound of Music.*[60] This is partly due

60 Wise, Robert. *The Sound of Music.* Beverly Hills, CA: Twentieth Century Fox Home Entertainment, 2005.

to the fact that I converted to Catholicism after my marriage, but I'm certain I chose the correct vocation God outfitted me for. I would never have made the cut in religious life, especially in an order with a vow of silence—even if I had been given a realistic opportunity by my upbrining to consider it.

Like Maria in *The Sound of Music,* I often wondered if my larger personality precluded me from "pious ladyhood," for lack of a better term. In the year leading to my conversion, I seldom met Catholic women who shared my penchant for "enthusiastic expression." Most of the wonderful Catholic women I met were temperamentally shy, a quality that seemed more in line with traditional femininity than my way of expression. I only settled comfortably into my own shoes after I asked myself the question characterizing the section above: *is it possible for pious Catholic women to balance obedience and moxie*?

In fact, this was something I pondered frequently before converting to Catholicism. At times, I struggled with committing myself to a faith that I wasn't a natural fit for. During these moments of doubt, Maria brought me much solace.

Like Maria, whenever I've been fortunate enough to be surrounded by very pious women, I've often felt like I didn't quite fit in. I don't mean to imply this was at the fault of these kind and welcoming women. It certainly was not. I just felt like a black sheep. Maria loves and admires her demure sisters in her Salzburg convent, even though she is not cut from the same cloth. Accordingly, Maria's character became a great comfort to me—having providently seen *The Sound of Music* for the first time during my conversion to Catholicism.

Maria is simultaneously obedient, yet fun. She prayers fervently at Vespers (if a tad tardy), and yet she knows how to cut loose and have a good time. She is not a nag, yet she knows how to respectfully challenge her superiors: Mother Superior and, of course, Captain von Trapp. Almost as important as her balanced relationship with her husband, Maria masters the delicate art of having fun with the children, while being their teacher and guardian.

Applying the logic of the above section, Maria earned the admiration and love of Captain von Trapp not in *spite of* that delicate balance, but *because* of it.

Having lived most of my life not in the Old World's Salzburg, but rather in communities of the American South and West—"the frontier land"—I've noticed that southerners often confuse big personality for sassy defiance. So, I'll take a moment to make the following disclaimer: sassiness is superlatively unbecoming in women and should be absolutely avoided, especially in marriage. If the two words (sassiness and moxie) sound a bit like synonyms, again, *ask your husband*: they're not. They are as different "as lightning and the lightning bug,"[61] as Mark Twain once wrote. Sassiness, for lack of a better term, is a euphemism for disobedience and accordingly, depletes from spousal intimacy and friendship; moxie, on the other hand, enhances spousal relations because by it, a woman uses her determination to obey and aid her husband. Maria von Trapp constitutes a paradigm example of a woman who delivers good-humored replies to her eventual husband, bordering on *without being* sassy. Note how she pays Captain von Trapp far greater heed as his wife than she does as his employee. Even her good-humored ribbing from the beginning of the film (when he was her employer) would have counted as "sassy" after he became her husband (at the film's end). This is why her behavior in his presence changes so drastically.

I daresay if Maria had practiced the sort of sassiness celebrated in the South, she would have been sent packing back to the convent in the first act of the film. Posterity would have forever lost a classic tale depicting how men and women gain happiness by accepting their natural roles and complementing each other. Despite the movie's great success within left-leaning circles, the social commentary on traditional sex roles is plentiful throughout the entire movie. Just look to the lyrics Liesl sings to her beau Rolf in, "Sixteen Going on Seventeen":

---

61 Partial quote attributed to author Mark Twain.

I am sixteen going on seventeen
I know that I'm naïve
Fellows I meet may tell me I'm sweet
And willingly I believe
I am sixteen going on seventeen
Innocent as a rose
Bachelors, dandies, drinkers of brandies
What do I know of those?
Totally unprepared am I
To face a world of men
Timid and shy and scared am I
Of things beyond my ken
I need someone older and wiser
Telling me what to do
You are seventeen going on eighteen
I'll depend on you.[62]

The entire song could be a Traditional Dating Anthem (as well as the honorific title of this book): "Tell Me What to Do, I'll Depend on You."

From *a* Maria to *the* Maria

Fictional examples only get us so far. As a Catholic woman, one need only look to the ideal, Our Virgin Mother, for a real-life female exemplar. What is "proper?" Whatever she did. Since we don't know much about the Virgin Mother's personality outside of the essential Scripture passages portraying her saintly obedience and heroic willingness to serve, we are left to abstract the more lighthearted aspects of her personality. But she lived a life of courage and audacity: such moments were certainly common in her life.

When I was a new convert to the faith, I frequently lamented the

62 Wise, Robert. *The Sound of Music.* Twentieth Century Fox Home Entertainment, 2005.

fact that the authors of the Gospels—especially St. John, who dwelt with her as he authored the fourth Gospel—failed to give us more information on the Virgin Mother. Presently, I better understand why that may have been the case: in the Gospels, Mary was always pointing us to Him. She never points to herself. Her role is to glorify the Son of Man and one can't do so effectively without total focus on Christ. So, it makes sense that the Gospels follow suit. Yes, the Gospels are a perfect tribute to her and her spouse, St. Joseph's mission that their heroic lives be overshadowed by their Son's.

Much like the curiosity of an adopted child, obsession over the traits of Our Mother must be obviated, however natural. As normal as it may be for daughters of absent mothers to get lost in wonderment about genetic similitude and intergenerational inclination, our confidence must be placed in the clear indicia we *do* have. This is especially the case when your mother happened to be the greatest woman in the history of the world, and the Queen of Heaven.

Did my Mother have a good sense of humor? Did she joke lovingly with her Son? What were her hobbies? Those of us devoted to Mary—all good Catholics—sit on dozens of questions like this.

Fortunately, fiction can help us to familiarize and imagine the otherwise unknowable. *The Passion of the Christ* depicted a touching scene, wherein Jesus playfully splashes the Virgin Mother as he washes His hands before a meal—eliciting a hearty laugh from Our Lady.[63] And why would a such moment not have happened between them? Such playful rapport between a mother and her son represents the artistic realism to be appreciated in the film. As a mother, that scene proved as true to me as the one in which Our Lady runs to the Christ Child after He suffered a fall.

After all, Jesus and Mary were the two most joyful people, ever. It's quite simple: the ideal Man and the ideal woman represent the only two perfect humans to have ever lived, having mastered every honorable human excellence. They were probably the only two humans (along

---

63 Gibson, Mel. *The Passion of the Christ*. Newmarket Films, 2004.

with St. Joseph, perhaps) to achieve what Aristotle had described above. They cannot have been other than joyful. Joy is offset by laughter. Like her Son's, Mary's joys were not as renowned as her sorrows, but there is no doubt that she had both.

Even if we assume Our Lady was joyful and laughed often, could we go so far to say that she had a passionate personality? No one but a passionate handmaid of the Lord would answer "yes" at the Annunciation. What a sublime responsibility, the most important task in the history of humanity, i.e., to be charged with mothering God Himself! Imagine the most stalwart, fearless person you know; now imagine how his most profound challenge pales in comparison to Mary's teenaged dilemma at the Annunciation. It is unequivocal: the answer to our question as to Mary's fervor is yes.

Mary's fiat ushered in a long line of female saints, who were as much shrinking violets as they were shrieking violets. Each one of them wanted to imitate their Mother. Saints like Zelie Martin, Therese of Lisieux, Mary Magdalene were known for their audacious, feminine fidelity. Each was strong and *therefore*, very obedient. *Obedience requires strength; female strength is exercised through obedience.* Never forget St. Teresa of Avila, who once joked to her brother, "Let us go to Africa immediately and beg them to cut off our heads there." She longed to serve the Lord so much that she prayed for martyrdom after joining the Carmelites, among whom she spent her time in both amicable, sisterly conversation and impassioned prayer.[64] Note how none of these feminine exemplars were "sassy," "Southern," or surly.

Just as Our Lady experienced great joys and sorrows, there is a season for every mood. Yet faithful daughters of the King—those of us with audacious or peaky temperaments—must carefully mind the burden we carry in and out of season: at all cost, we must never be obnoxious.

---

64 Johnna, Angela, Ginny Kochis, Hope, Marissa, Katie, and Ellen Smith. "5 Saints Perfect for Strong-Willed Girls and Their Moms." *Not So Formulaic*, 25 Jan. 2020, Web. 19 Apr. 2021.

Less Cowbell

Much like a great musician picking the right instant to play—adding the right notes at the perfect time to contribute to a great masterpiece—so should woman pipe up in only the appropriate moments, which are rare.

This is especially true in marriage. Spousal relations used to be more like a beautifully timed ballad, each spouse playing his part well: the man leading; the woman following. Today, by contrast, the world awoke to find itself feminist.[65] Everywhere, males are beset by the unfunny equivalent of the hilarious *Saturday Night Live* "more cowbell"[66] skit: women prompted and encouraged to sound off relentlessly, annoying everyone within earshot and ruining something that was formerly well orchestrated and enjoyable.

For anyone unfamiliar with the legendary skit, its hilarious premise of historical fiction involves the *Blue Oyster Cult* song, "Don't Fear the Reaper."[67] In the actual song, someone in the band infamously plays the cowbell throughout the entire track (low, yet clearly audible in the mix). In the reimagined history of the SNL skit, Will Farrell's character is the band's cowbell musician who is repeatedly (and bizarrely) encouraged by the band's record producer—"*the* Bruce Dickinson"—to add "more cowbell." Dickinson repeatedly breaks into the band's studio recording session inexplicably to demand more cowbell from Farrell. In conformity with the impassioned demands of Dickinson, what ensues is more and incrementally more obnoxious cowbell that overshadows the other musicians, destroys the song, and disrupts the formerly extant harmony of the entire band.

As the skit relates to feminism today, "Bruce Dickinson" appears to be—well—almost everyone in society, beggaring *more* and *louder*

65 This is a spinoff on the old Church history saying, attributed to St. Jerome, of Arianism that the "The whole world groaned and woke to find itself Arianist."

66 Ferrell, Will, Donnell Campbell, and Erika Perez. "More Cowbell." *Saturday Night Live*. NBC. New York, New York, 8 Apr. 2000, Television.

67 Roeser, Donald, Blue Oyster Cult. (*Don't Fear) The Reaper*. Columbia, 1975.

cacophony which was inexplicable and gratuitous in the first place. Read: cowbell equals female bossiness, sassiness, shrillness, imperiousness. Who wants or needs *any* "cowbell" in the family or society—much less *more* of it? A sweet-sounding song needs no cowbell at all; even low in the mix, one puzzles over the motives and the judgment of those who suggested the addition.

And yet, they keep begging for more cowbell: "lean in"; "believe all women"; "me too"; "womankind worldwide"; "ban bossy"; "amen and awoman"; "time's up"; etc. Cowbell morning, noon, and night. Cowbell when one watches sports; cowbell when one watches the news; cowbell sounding off in the military; cowbell bouncing off the walls of the workplace, in our parishes, and even in the home (the few twilight hours of each day that women aren't cow-belling at the workplace). The secular left has deified the shrill.

What is the solution? Silence your bells, ladies. Mute them entirely. Beautiful rock ballads are better without any cowbell. Trust the men you married and do as they instruct. Your marriage will experience true harmony.

The shrewd reader has by now figured that cowbell is not *speaking per se*, but rather criticizing. Calm, honest expression, it turns out, fast becomes one of the natural strengths of the well-ordered wife (after she has changed her bad habits). Because marital intimacy is critical, my husband and I recently shot a two-hour video together discussing the common pitfalls affecting marriages.[68] We concluded that the lack of post-feminist marital intimacy accrues to the pandering to women. In turn, this entails too much ineffective bandying and too little obedience and efficient communication. For example, even if a good husband gives a command that a good wife finds imprudent, she (unlike the children) bears the right to petition him in wifely piety at an opportune moment, perhaps at the end of the day. She thereby practices

---

68 Gordon, Timothy, and Stephanie Gordon. "9 Secrets of Catholic Marriage." *Rules For Retrogrades.* YouTube, Mississippi, Retrieved from https://youtu.be/Wkf_kzvo8XY, 14 Sept. 2020.

obedience and continues to do so even if her husband persists in his command. But in any case, she can make a rational, timely request for clarity or redress.

Unfortunately, the present culture commands that woman should never exercise restraint—especially over her feelings, but instead hum to the ceaseless tune of, "more cowbell, baby!" Far from being humorous, this cacophony is causing damage. Even the church in miniature, the Catholic family, suffers from this baffling encouragement of more cowbell.

A Woman in Combat

Christian wives must master the art of restraint. Even women who detest *any* shade of feminism, like me, still have to rein it in sometimes. Being a traditional Catholic we know that both sexes have different natures—and therefore roles—in marriage. The husband is the head, and the wife is the heart.

There is no quarter for a "transgenderism" ideology within Catholicism which insinuates the falsehood that wives can lead households. Utter nonsense. Even in unfortunate situations where a woman *must* take the lead of her family (i.e. if her husband has died or falls very ill), she cannot ever replace him—even if she labors admirably to properly fill the void of her husband's absence.

All this is just to bespeak something we already know: men and women are different. Women with "stronger" personalities border on proto-transgenderism if they don't master the art of restraint, properly ordering their dynamic energies. There's a fine line between having a colorful personality and allowing it to color you badly. Anyone who followed me under my former Twitter handle @AskYourHusband knows I *occasionally* crossed the line: at times, moxie became obnoxiousness. This was *one* of the many reasons I de-activated the account.

Something vexingly obvious eluded me during the quarrelsome year I spent on social media: women on Twitter is a bad idea. That is especially the case for women of my temperament who are more naturally combative. This particular social media platform famously elicits improper and unnecessary bellicosity in nearly all who use it. This much is doubly true for the platform's female members (who by their God-given natures ought not to be engaging in fights or, worse yet, starting them).

My allergic response to "the herd" has come a long way with the help of Christ and a good husband, that's for sure. What was once combativeness, in youth, has been christened (most days anyway) as an extra source of Christian resolve and even obedience, in my middle age. In high school, for instance, a female peer of mine (hereinafter: "Ginny") decided to make me the target of her taunts and insults, which always took place in the same hall on my way to English class. Ginny would wait for me to take my regular route to English class and shout insults at me every day for an entire week.

This was when big, foam, platform sandals were all the rage in the late nineties. The reason for which I mention this will become apparent in a moment.

Since I always enjoyed a righteous confrontation, I began scheming how to deal with her from the moment she arbitrarily painted a target on my back.

There were two halls that led to my English class and Ginny always waited for me in the same one. Accordingly, I leveraged her predictability to my advantage by biting the bullet and subjecting myself to her daily taunts in that same hall as to ensure she'd be exactly where I needed her.

At last, Ginny's day of reckoning was at hand. Instead of taking my regular path, I purposely went down the adjacent hall. From where I approached, I could see from afar Ginny's backside as she waited to ambush me, in those ridiculous nineties foam sandals. Her gaze was focused on where she anticipated I would shortly emerge. As with all high-school jerks, Ginny was perennially accompanied by a large group of her cliques. On this particular day Ginny's friends gleefully anticipated the scheduled entertainment of the day: my mortification.

It ended up being Ginny's.

From where I stood, the mere sight of Ginny waiting deliberately and patiently to cruelly taunt me stiffened my jaw and set me into an all-out sprint toward her. *No one saw me coming.* Immediately before impact, I raised and stiffened my arms, which sent her sprawling several feet, right out of her ugly foam sandals. Bear in mind: this was in full view of her adoring crowd, two teachers, my entire English class, and the Good Lord. Helpless, she catapulted forward as I nearly ran her over trying to slow down and readied myself for the anticipated counterattack I expected (from Ginny or from any one of her friends). Instead, everyone just froze and stared at me, dumbfounded. Skirt, books, nineties sandals, and limbs askew, Ginny's face was beet-red as she clumsily composed herself on the ground. She tried fruitlessly to hide her tears with her hair as she glared up at me and screeched: "what is wrongggggg with you?!"

I actually felt bad for her in that moment: I had fully expected her to try to retaliate instead of laying on the ground asking me senseless questions. I was also somewhat embarrassed because my home economics teacher witnessed the whole thing and was, along with everyone else, looking at me as if I had lost my mind. Having taught me the dainty feminine arts such as sewing, cooking, balancing a checkbook, my teacher was a respected motherly figure. Naturally, I felt like I had betrayed her tutelage, and the look on her face confirmed it.

My English teacher seconded Ginny's enquiry and escorted me to the principal's office, where I was swiftly issued several weeks of detention. (According to the principal's characterization of my punishment, she actually took it easy on me because she recalled that I had been one of the school's only volunteers to escort the special needs kids around campus to collect attendance.) To further my embarrassment, my home economics teacher had recently asked me to assist her adapted course for special needs kids; according to her, I was "patient and understanding." Luckily, witnessing me stiff-arm a bimbo didn't dampen her high view of me (as I had feared), and I was permitted to continue working in her classroom.

And so, we come to the point of this section: the Good Lord provided me a fighting spirit and I'm *really bad* at reining it in sometimes.

Fighting real-life bullies is one thing. Fighting "fake-name-cowards"[69] on the Internet is quite another. Learning who and when to fight turned out to be something I learned late in life. Embarrassingly enough, I learned no small portion of that lesson on Twitter, in my late thirties. And so, as an adult, I left Twitter and have not looked back.

High school misadventures aside, virtue and a fighting spirit often work together—under the proper circumstances. Most people do not appreciate being pushed around.

But here's the problem: what to do when the culture *intentionally* blurs the lines between a devoted Christian husband who faithfully executes his God-given role as boss of the house, and a bully who must be put in his place. It's precisely *this* confusion which has created a generation of women who fight their husbands—as they would a bully—for merely doing what he is supposed to: being the head family.

Like most survivors of parental divorce, I had to learn this lesson well after I had married. Like most people these days—even those hailing from non-divorced households—I was raised in a home where the woman was the master and feminism ruled the day.

My upbringing combined with a natural fighting spirit made it slightly tougher to embrace God's and nature's hierarchy of the male-led household. Add that to the fact that I was raised by an atheist and bore no idea that God had established a social hierarchy to begin with. My first few years of marriage were quite the learning experience.

Using one's "fighting spirit" has a proper time and place, though never in the home with one's husband. As mentioned earlier, spouses

---

69 A term Patrick Coffin coined to describe social media users who post under a fake name.

are meant to be best friends, despite being unequal in rank. Sadly, I see women treat their husbands less like best friends and more like children.

If your immediate response is, "I treat my husband like a child because he acts like a child!", I'll remind you: your boss, then, is a child. You're the one that picked the child-boss and vowed before God to serve that child-boss. Get ready to serve up some all-candy dinners and keep a larder of Capri Suns handy, sister. In the race to the bottom, never one-up his childishness by fighting him…or worse, by being a nag.

The Nag. Don't Be One

Remember famous Netflix series *Stranger Things's* Eleven's simple aphorism on friendship: "friends don't lie"? She's right. But, in the context of wives-as-best-friends-to-husbands, we should add the following to Eleven's axiom: "friends don't nag." Ask any man. Males are wired to avoid shrill or vexing noises, especially *critical* ones. Nagging only drives men away. And yet it is so common today. I witness women taking after their husbands in public *all the time.* It's never the other way around, not once. A liberal family member once told me that she thought my marriage wasn't normal because she never saw me reprimand my husband for behavior she deemed reproachable. Mainly those "offensive behaviors" amounted to respectfully disagreeing with his wife (me) about a course of action the family ought to take and then executing his own judgment on the matter. This was once called "being a man." I wanted to reply to her, "that's one of the reasons you're thrice divorced." But that would have been mean. True, but mean.

At times, I have expressed my concerns to my husband—an indispensable expression which must happen in healthy relationships from time to time. But there is a proper way to do so. Firstly, it should always happen privately. Discretion is the better part of valour, isn't it? Secondly, it should happen infrequently (that is, carefully choose your battles). Less is more: I've noticed that husbands who heed their wives the most frequently have wives who speak up the least frequently. Thirdly, once you have respectfully given your opinion (outside of serious safety issues or something that affects his salvation), drop it. A counselor's primary rule is that all advice is tendered without guarantee of execution. Or in other words, don't be a nag.

Even St. Thomas Aquinas says women ought to be passive. He writes on the subject:

> In every act of generation there is an active and a passive principle. Wherefore since wherever there is distinction of sex, the active principle is male and the passive is female; the order of nature demands that for the purpose of generation there should be concurrence of male and female.[70]

My husband once took heat for a video he did[71] discussing wifely nags in public. In the video, he painfully recalled our family visit to Disneyworld, whereupon we witnessed an especially mouthy, ungrateful wife (actually, we witnessed several at Disneyworld) who formed the perfect antithesis to all three of the points above.

While enjoying a fine (and a not inexpensive) day at "the Happiest Place on Earth," Tim decided to get us all a snack, for which we were all grateful. What happened next lives in Gordon family lore, traumatizing my husband and me to this day. A grateful wife and grateful daughters met their soda-guzzling antithesis that day. Standing in line was a grown woman giving her husband a scathing tongue-lashing because he—get this—didn't purchase her preferred beverage. As he petitioned her to keep her voice down with desperate urgings, she crossed her arms like a bedeviled three-year-old and snapped a new demand for a straw. Also, she complained that he wasn't honoring her

---

70 Aquinas, Thomas. "Summa Theologica." *Summa Theologica*. New York: Benziger Brothers, 1948, Pt. 1, Q. 98, Art. 2.

71 Gordon, Timothy. "Timothy Gordon, The Matt Fradd Show Ep. 11." Interview by Matt Fradd, *Pints with Aquinas,* YouTube, Georgia, Retrieved from https://www.youtube.com/watch?v=jE3b_1EmYKQ, 7 Aug. 2019.

demands sufficiently quickly. The hapless man attempted several different angles of rehabilitation, but his badly habituated wife continued to carp loudly. Eventually, they left. All this, as one would imagine, without a single "please," "thank you," or, perhaps most importantly: "I apologize for acting like a petulant child and publicly disgracing our family name *over such a trifling matter as a creature comfort of my choosing.*"

I later joked with my husband that I should have turned to her and said, "excuse me madam, you're not nearly attractive enough to pull off this sort of misbehavior." Few are. Nagging is ugly even out of the most beautiful mouth.

What appears above is, as far as I can tell, a plain, commonsense, axiomatic characterization of wifely ungratefulness (crossed with no small amount of petulance). I haven't ventured too far out in presuming that such behavior squarely conflicts with the Christian model of the wife. And yet, in our feminist culture today, many faithful and even conservative Catholics might take issue with my (or my husband's) strong repudiation of it. For example, in July 2019, Tim appeared on Matt Fradd's show and told this precise story—complete with colorful commentary in the fashion I just offered—on air. It produced some backlash. (We travelled directly to Matt Fradd's place straight from Disneyworld, meaning Tim's recounting of the story was especially fresh and accurate.) Whether or not the story was even true—it was—isn't the point. Even if he had told a hypothetical cautionary tale, many of the angry comments in the commentary box still would have exposed a robust double-standard in our culture: men can be nagged, demeaned, and criticized until everyone is blue in the face; but if one counter-criticizes the nagging, demeaning, or criticizing woman, then he just broke the eleventh commandment. More than this, any and all critique of a woman places one at violent odds with society.

Some women wrote that Tim was being unjust to the woman because he didn't know if the husband was first a jerk to his wife, thereby meriting a just rejoinder to *his* earlier (imagined) bad behaviors we didn't witness—as if that would have excused her to respond in kind.

It would not have done so. As the saying goes, "two wrongs don't make a right," especially as between unequals: none of these women would presumably have responded to their employers with a small dose of vitriol or childishness, had their employers been grouchy to them. Not to mention, the scene we witnessed was sufficiently well-developed on its own merits: the husband politely proffered a refreshment to his wife, who rebuked his offer harshly. This is categorically wrong, even if he had left the toilet seat up in the hotel room earlier that day.

Other commenters, mainly women, suggested it was insensitive for Tim to joke—or rather, to reference my joke—about a woman's appearance. Firstly, it was *my* joke and I stand by it. Secondly, even if you don't care for my taste in jokes and agree it was mean, surely you can see the point underlying it: women have become far too comfortable publicly deriding their husbands. Frequently, in the popular culture (think of commercials, for example), wifely critiques of husbands include but are not limited to: his appearance, tastes, work-ethic, fathering, etc.—but don't you dare do the same to them. After all, they reason, doing so would be "unchivalrous." Thirdly, my generation made a sport out of making fun of absurd things—which is why we didn't have dudes dressing up like girls in class (or trying to use their pronouns, bathrooms, or gynecologists). The "shame culture" reified by this habit bore inarguably healthier social consequences than the present lack of shame culture: the ubiquitous acceptance of wifely public (and private) temper tantrums is as—or more—stark evidence for this claim as the widespread existence of men in dresses.

We live in a world with "thin skins and strong stomachs," as my husband likes to say. As such, we have strong stomachs for anything that brings us illicit pleasure and thin skins for anything that gives us offense. Modern husbands would rather keep a strong stomach and keep mum about nit-picking in order to avoid the thinnest skin of all women: their wives' wrath. And certainly a feminist wife loves a weak husband, so she can not only nag him, but dominate him.

The nagging wife's toxic behavior often spills outside of the home, especially if she works. One would think nags would have a difficult time respecting *anyone* in authority. Think again. One would just have to look at how they treat their superiors at work. More women than ever before work outside the home.[72] The obvious rule of thumb is that women should nag their husbands *less* than they would nag a boss at work, or even better, women should nag their husbands and their boss precisely the same amount—since these ought to be one and the same person.

"Giving your best" to anyone other than your spouse is a sure mark of modernity. This is to say: it's a sure mark of marital failure. It is an especially egregious modern paradox that most women today behave more civilly to the man signing their paychecks than to the man who co-signed their marriage certificates.

This notion is particularly crass because it imposes a material emphasis (financial gain/success) over a holy one (the vocation of being a wife). Can't a woman give her best to her husband and her employer?

She cannot because her heart and her time will always be divided. The next chapter, "Unplugging from the Culture of Lies," will explain why married women should not work.

---

72 Ridout, Annie. "More Women Are Working Than Ever Before, Even If They Have Kids." *Forbes Magazine*, 11 Jan. 2021, Web. 19 Apr. 2021.

4

Unplugging from the Culture of Lies

Married Women Shouldn't Work

Anyone who has followed my husband's apostolate knows that we get *a lot* of heat regarding married women in the workplace. The reason for this is because we affirm the Church's teaching that, in ordinary circumstances, married women shouldn't work outside the home. Herein lies this book's most controversial topic.

We argue that one of the devil's greatest achievements was to lure women outside of their homes in pursuit of financial and personal gain. This may initially sound dramatic. It is not. In this chapter, we will take a look at the state of the Christian family. In a collective egress women left their homes in droves and madly dashed into the workplace. Since the devil is actively seeking, since the time of the Original Sin, to destroy the Christian family (for obvious reasons), the more that women remain in the workplace, the unhappier they become—and the more havoc is wreaked upon their families.[73]

A sure mark of modernity is the sudden reaction you might be experiencing to my words. Perhaps you feel tempted to list several exceptions, geared to rebut my claim that married Catholic women shouldn't work. Let's address the pointed exceptions, of varying validity, which I hear most often.

---

73 Gordon, Timothy. *The Case for Patriarchy*. Crisis Publications, 2021, pp. 114.

Objection #1: What about widows, single mothers, or women with gravely sick husbands–don't they have to work?

A woman who no longer has a husband to provide for her and her children must take up the mantle and find employment to meet the needs of her family. *The Catechism of the Catholic Church* clearly states that: "The wife should love to remain at home, unless compelled by necessity to go out; and she should never presume to leave home without her husband's consent."[74] In these unfortunate cases there exists an obvious necessity for the woman to work (and no husband whom to ask). In these unfortunate situations the mother must provide for her in children in light of her husband's absence. She cannot replace him any more than a babysitter or day-care professional can replace her, but she has no option lest her family starve.

If you have ever spoken to a widow (or a woman who has been abandoned by her husband) they will tell you that a large part of their grief comes from the fact that, try as they might, they cannot fulfill the specified roles that only a man can offer.

For different reasons, the exceptions which apply to widows apply with the same force to single mothers and wives of gravely ill husbands. The former, like widows, have no husband from whom to seek permission. The latter, of course, will secure a presumptive permission from their bedridden husbands, depending upon how ill the husbands are.

Objection #2: What about single women who are not yet married?

This woman doesn't have a husband to provide for her, so obviously she has to provide for herself. Some traditionalists argue that single women should remain under their father's care until they are married, but this is an issue of prudence. If they choose to leave the home, single women can provide for themselves until the moment they become married. After marriage they ought to give up their occupation and serve their families.

---

74 *Catechism of the Council of Trent.* 1st ed., Baronius Press, 2018., Duties of a Wife.

Objection #3: What about women who are married and don't yet have children? What about women whose children are grown and out of the home?

These women still have a husband to serve and a household to keep, so the requirement of remaining in ordinary circumstances at home still applies to them. After their grown children have left the home, they will certainly be far less occupied versus when their children lived with them. But the Church's teaching still applies because both household and husband need a woman's gentle touch and near constant ennobling presence. It is a bitter fruit of modernity that so many faithful Catholic women stay home only to care for small children but not for husbands—a motivation which presumes that the service of a husband is not the primary task of the wife. It is. As St. Paul writes in 1 Corinthians 11: 7: "man is the image and glory of God, and woman is the glory of man." This prominent point is far too often overlooked. In this context, the concept of "glory" indicates the role of helper, aid, or handmaiden. The wife's primary duty is to help the husband in the home, which explains—whether or not small children inhabit the home—why in all ordinary circumstances, she is to remain there, beautifying and readying it for his return from work.

For whatever reason, some traditional Catholics have deemed that staying at home to raise children is acceptable, but staying at home to serve the husband is unacceptable. The latter, they reason bizarrely, is beneath a woman's dignity. Neither Scripture nor Catholic Tradition support the false distinction they make: both Scripture and Tradition make it perfectly clear that wives must ordinarily be at home *for the sake of their husbands.*[75]

Cooking, cleaning, intimacy, conversation, mending, nurturing, gardening, making things generally beautiful—all signs of being the wifely heart of the home—take place to accommodate the husband. Even if a woman finds herself at home and all of the above is accomplished, she

75 In the next chapter, the teaching on this topic from Scripture and Tradition will be examined in detail.

ought to use her spare time in the pursuits of bettering herself. Many women learn a new craft around the home or pursue home studies.

Objection #4: Aren't you working right now on this book, Stephanie Gordon?

Fair question. Not in the way that matters according to the teaching of the Catholic Church. In other words, I am at home, writing this book in my off-time, and none of my duties to my household are being neglected or put aside. I've not depended upon anyone to do any of my duties while I've pecked away on my keyboard. I'll admit that I would probably have gotten this book out much sooner if I had.

Moreover, the Church does not forbid a woman to pursue interests or hobbies as long as she is not putting them over her wifely vocation. But even hobbies can become problematic if the woman neglects her duties to the home in their pursuit. If I were to choose to write this book instead of making meals for my husband or teaching homeschool for the day I would be remiss; even without leaving the home, I can still neglect it. In short, the duties of the home come first, and a woman is free to choose how she spends her free time as long as she has discharged these duties. There were many weeks I didn't have time to write because my household duties were particularly demanding.

If a husband, for instance, neglects his work duties and instead plays golf, he is doing a great disservice to God and his family. He is, however, permitted to golf when he has accomplished providing for his family for the day. The same goes for a woman's hobbies and interests: obviously, leaving the home for a scheduled workday relegates the household duties to a distant second place since "working wives" fit in their *vocations* (or not) around their *work schedules.* As Our Lord taught, no one can serve two masters.

Countervailing upon the errant view that married women cannot turn a profit from home, there are instances in Scripture where, licitly, married women indeed make a small wage from their home-spun handicrafts.

Objection #5: If most women are not permitted to hold occupations, why are nuns and religious women allowed to work?

Nuns and religious women aren't married so this rule doesn't apply to them. Similarly, the religious vocation has an altogether different set of rules that doesn't apply to married women. For example, all nuns take vows of chastity and some take vows of poverty. Actually, it's the women religious who once filled positions in the workplace that—as we are constantly reminded—required a "woman's touch" and I'd argue that this practice should be reinvigorated. Unfortunately, a universal decline[76] in religious vocations has left society bereft of female-preferred positions—nurses, midwives, governesses, elementary teachers—that were once filled abundantly by women religious.

Objection #6: Haven't there been examples of married, female saints who have worked, like Saint Gianna Molla?

This is my favorite "gotcha" question from Catholic feminists, and I dedicate an entire section to it after this one.

Objection #7: What about volunteer work or helping a husband with a home business?

As far as volunteer work goes, please see the answer to Objection Four. Let's investigate working in a home-business. I, for instance, help my husband with his writing; I edit all his videos; and I help him to run the technological and administrative aspects of his apostolate. When I help him in this way, we both make sure that I am not neglecting my household duties. But, as a Christian wife, being my husband's helpmate is *also* an integral part of my vocation. So as long as I am keeping up with my duties to the household, I am supposed to help my husband with his ventures if and when it becomes possible. A husband

76 The number of U.S. priests has dropped by almost a third in the last 50 years, from about 37,300 in 1970 to about 25,800 according to this study from the Center of Applied Research for the Apostolate: CARA, cara.georgetown.edu/frequently-requested-church-statistics/.

also has an obligation to make sure he is not demanding too much of his wife's time so that her other duties are not neglected. But *even if he does not do so* and the wife's other duties suffer, it's on him. That is, the wife—because she is under her husband's headship—is not responsible to God for "letting the house go" whenever she has taken orders to do so from her head.

When in Scripture there is a reference to women's "work," it is almost always used in reference to chores and duties around the homestead or in the assisting in a family trade near the vicinity of the home or neighborhood (like farming, gathering food for widows, crafting, etc.).[77]

Objection #8: Working women can simultaneously be excellent employees and wives and mothers!

Unless you have the miraculous gift of bilocation, you will always find yourself choosing workplace over home, or vice versa. Once again, no one can serve two masters: one can either choose to do one well, or to be mediocre at both.

In casual conversation, if I drop the "m" word ("mediocre") I'm usually in for a slew of anecdotes about how such-and-such working mother was as brilliant at work as she was at home. To illustrate the absurdity of this point, I ask them rhetorically if they remember when Michael Jordan made history in 1993 by simultaneously being the greatest player in the NBA *and* playing in minor league baseball.[78] An event which never did happen because it's physically impossible (even if it were, Michael Jordan was no good at baseball). Again, working mothers can't be in two places at the same time—which is precisely what it would require to be a top-notch mother and a top-notch employee. Accordingly, such mother-employees shouldn't get full credit for *either* job done halfway by someone else.

---

77 Once again, this is treated of specifically in the next chapter.

78 Michael Jordan abruptly retired from the NBA before the 1993-94 season to pursue a career in Minor League Baseball. He returned to the NBA in 1995.

Because people nowadays are obsessively predisposed not to hurt anyone's feelings—particularly women's—we now regularly fabricate simple conditional claims such as: "*if* a mother is away from the home at work, *then* she cannot raise her child."

We falsely believe that childrearing by day-care strangers is just as good as childrearing by a loving mother at home. Other times, we tell the lie that stay-at-home-fathers are just as maternal as stay-at-home mothers (which is basically a soft form of transgenderism).

Firstly, without some set of emergent circumstances, childrearing by strangers (or even extended family members) is disordered. Secondly, even a father cannot replace a young child's mother. Men and women bear different roles and virtues, which is why God outfitted each sex for different tasks within the hierarchy of the Christian family. Thirdly, children don't cease to need their mother's attention after they have finished occupying their mother's wombs. As a matter of fact, they *begin* to need their mother's attention at that point. Fourthly, a myriad of professionals could replace you at work: the only place where you're irreplaceable is in your home, ladies. Make no mistake, no one could ever replace you at home, where your role is utterly precious.

If you foolishly claim that your work is so vital to humanity that you cannot be replaced, then you are blinded by a trifling and vainglorious ambition. Everyone foolish says this of their work. I believe I once had a *hairdresser* tell me this. I'd counter that *nothing* is more important to God than *your* training of *your own* children for Heaven while tending to *your* wifely vocation. Nothing could be more personal. The presumed (and usually exaggerated) good of "humanity" does not excuse you from the duties to your own family.

Rather than reacting defensively, all mothers ought to be *immensely proud* of how irreplaceable they are. But, alas, here they are trying to convince the world that they *are* utterly replaceable at home, but irreplaceable at work. No one can possibly replace them at home! It is truly diabolical illogic.

Objection #9: We need women in certain professions.

Okay, so you prefer a female doctor, hairdresser, or babysitter. Fair enough, but your thinking has been distorted by the sexual revolution and its subsequent decades.

Furthermore, in the world after the sexual revolution, single rather than married women ought to occupy these roles. Indeed, many of the natural female virtues—like nurturing, empathy, certain forms of artistic expression—are custom fit for the unmarried women. As a matter of fact, that's why we once had women religious staffing such occupations. And there will always be single and religious women for those kinds of jobs.

To the many who fear a shortage of professionals in certain fields if married women returned home, I answer that their hypothetical would present a win-win: the fewer women who enter the workforce, the easier it is for men (along with single women) to find work. Too, the unemployment rate would plummet, since it only involves those actively seeking jobs.

That's an even more ambitious claim than the one—also defensible—that the so-called "wage gap"[79] between men and women is fictitious. But it is easily defensible. Just think about it: without so many women in the workplace, heads of households would find employment more easily, no longer having to compete with most women. Needless to say, I was not among the majority of people who approvingly read the *Wall Street Journal* headline, "Women Overtake Men as Majority of U.S. Workforce."[80]

---

79 Women who make less than men do so because they take time off for childbirth and maternity leave. Also, they are often more likely to take part-time jobs and call in sick to meet the demands of their families. In short, women's decisions, not discrimination, explain why they often make less than their male counterparts—who don't require as much time off or seek part-time wages.

80 Omeokwe, Amara. "Women Overtake Men as Majority of U.S. Workforce." *The Wall Street Journal*, 10 Jan. 2020, www.wsj.com/articles/women-overtake-men-as-majority-of-u-s-workforce-11578670615.

With great sadness, I note that the rate of American working mothers has risen dramatically since 1976. This upward trend has been most precipitous—and thus especially bothersome—among mothers of children aged zero to three years old. The rise among working mothers was the second most steep among mothers of children aged zero to six. Just take a look at this horrifying chart, published by the US Department of Labor:[81]

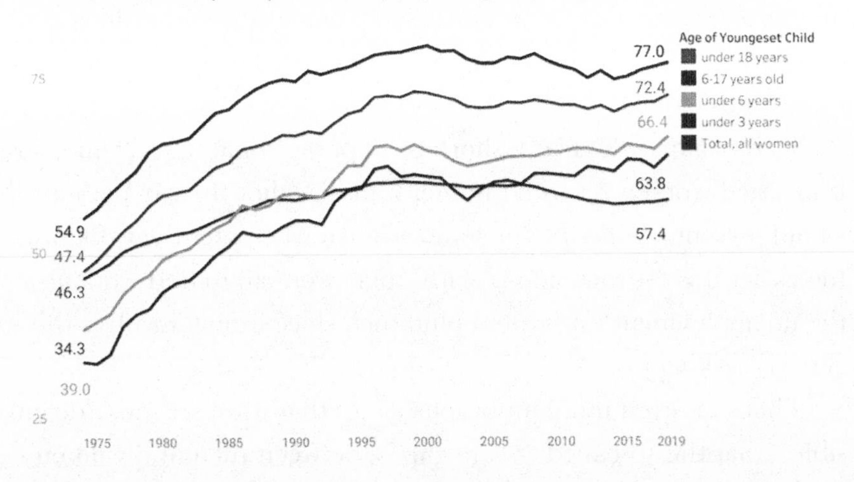

Notwithstanding all the new latch key kids after 1976 (those with moonlighting moms), the sufferers most unrepresented in the above chart are the male heads of households. Remember, male householders compete as part of their very vocation in the workforce; they don't do so at the behest of some whimsical fancy to "fulfill themselves." Men

81 *Mothers and families*. United States Department of Labor. (n.d.). Retrieved 18 Apr. 2022, from https://www.dol.gov/agencies/wb/data/mothers-and-families. (Data, in case printing does not represent color on chart: Total, all women, 1975: 46.3% to 57.4% in 2019; women with children under 3, 1975: 34.3% to 66.4% in 2019; women with children under 6, 1975: 39.0% to 63.8% in 2019; women with children under 6-17, 1975: 54.9% to 77.0% in 2019; women with children under 18, 1975: 47.4% to 72.4% in 2019.)

with families must work. Yet they are now applying for jobs they are statistically less likely to secure than they once were. As such, they now constitute the disadvantaged sex.

Today, "woke" companies prefer to hire less qualified women in place of more qualified men, in the name of "inclusivity" and "diversity." Women, a recent study found, are actually 16% to 18% *more likely* to be hired than men.[82] Worse still, these numbers perpetuate the vicious cycle that married women "need" to work because their husbands can't find jobs as easily as they can.

If married women simply returned home, their corresponding heads of households would be able to land better-paying jobs to provide for their families. And society functions best when the mother is home leaving employment spots open so the father may easily find jobs to provide for his family. In turn, this fact would nullify the next objection on the list.

Objection #10: My husband doesn't make enough money to support us. I must work.

If more women took themselves out of the workforce, then it would be easier for your (and others') heads of households to find jobs that provide competitive wages. Transitioning from a two-wage lifestyle to a one income household is a moderate challenge. But it's eminently doable.

More important than keeping our checkbooks balanced—everyone's situation is different—are the implications for the moral life we are called to live in matrimony. Either way, you might need to reevaluate and rebalance your priorities (if you find yourself pitching Objection #10). It's unreasonable to say that wage and expenditure changes in your household could not actually be accomplished, if your

---

82 "New Report: Women Apply to Fewer Jobs Than Men, But Are More Likely to Get Hired." LinkedIn Talent Blog, business.linkedin.com/talent-solutions/blog/diversity/2019/how-women-find-jobs-gender-report.

life depended upon it.[83] If staying home to tend to your family *was* a top priority, you would certainly quit your job. Truthfully, most people recur to this excuse precisely when the wife's staying home *isn't* a priority because she doesn't want to change her lifestyle.

In addition to pride and habituation, it all comes down to discretionary income.[84] A 2007 study found that after paying for necessities Americans have *a lot* of money to play with:

> About 73 million US households now have discretionary income, up from about 57 million in 2002, according to a report by The Conference Board. The proportion of the US population with discretionary income has increased to nearly 64%, up from 52% in 2002. Households with discretionary income, as defined by the study, are those whose spendable income exceeds that held by households with similar demographic features. Total discretionary income in the US topped $1.7 trillion in 2006, with the household average at $24,335. Per capita income stood at $9,148.[85]

Even the 36% of Americans whose discretionary income didn't rise during this period of study aren't off the hook. I've met plenty of low-middle-class couples who, upon learning the Catholic teaching at issue, took a year and in that time, restored the wife to the home. They accomplished "impossible" feats such as: moving to a more affordable location, finding a smaller home, selling needless possessions, cutting

---

83 Imagine finding yourself in the plot of a film wherein you would lose your very life—and your family would lose theirs—if you didn't make this single change. Under those drastic circumstances, one comes to see how very easy it is to re-prioritize one's income-outcome situation (as a matter of fact, the punishment for failing to re-prioritize by staying home may actually be much worse than losing one's life—i.e. it could well be losing one's salvation. More on this in the following chapter.).

84 Discretionary income is different than disposable income. Discretionary income is income left over after paying for personal necessities like food, shelter, etc. Disposable income is the income left over after paying your federal, state, and local taxes.

85 "64% Of Americans Have Discretionary Income." *Marketing Charts,* 13 Nov. 2007, www.marketingcharts.com/industries/financial-services-2340.

creature comforts such as cable TV, economizing meal-preparation, and simplifying family vacations. When my husband was in law school, we lived in a two-bedroom apartment, drove one car, and ate frozen pot pies multiple nights of the week so that I could remain at home with our growing family. In other words, we lived simply in order for me to remain at home and tend to my vocation as the Church requires. Although this was a sacrifice, this did not require a supernatural miracle as many incorrectly believe to be the case.

Not coincidentally, the frugal days from our early marriage represent some of our fondest memories. Being poor helped us to focus on our priorities and our affections. As Cardinal Robert Sarah points out, our moderate but joyful poverty made us thankful for each and every little boon. It made us cherish the things (and maximize the use of those things) we already possessed, rather than chasing after the latest fads.

> The Gospel is not a slogan. The same goes for our activity to relieve people's suffering … [which turns out to be a proposition consisting] of working humbly and having a deep respect for the poor. For example, I remember being disgusted when I heard the advertising slogan of a Catholic charitable organization, which was almost insulting to the poor: "Let us fight for zero poverty" … Not one saint … ever dared to speak that way about poverty and poor people.
>
> Jesus himself had no pretention of this sort. This slogan respects neither the Gospel nor Christ. Ever since the Old Testament, God has been with the poor; and Sacred Scripture unceasingly acclaims "the poor of Yahweh." …
>
> Poverty is a biblical value confirmed by Christ, who emphatically exclaims, "Blessed are the poor in spirit, for theirs is the Kingdom of heaven" (Mt 5:3). … The poor person is someone who knows that, by himself, he cannot live. He needs God and other people in order to be, flourish and grow. On the contrary,

rich people expect nothing of anyone. They can provide for their needs without calling either on their neighbors or on God. In this sense wealth can lead to great sadness and true human loneliness or to terrible spiritual poverty. If in order to eat and care for himself, a man must turn to someone else, this necessarily results in a great enlargement of his heart. This is why the poor are closest to God and live in great solidarity with one another; they draw from this divine source the ability to be attentive to others.

The Church must not fight against poverty but, rather, wage a battle against destitution, especially material and spiritual destitution. … [to the extent that everyone] might have the minimum they require in order to live. …But we do not have the right to confuse destitution and poverty, because in so doing we would seriously be going against the Gospel. Recall what Christ told us: "The poor you will have always with you …" (Jn 12:8). Those who want to eradicate poverty make the Son of God a liar.

[In a 2014 sermon on the matter, Pope Francis] espoused what St. Francis called "Lady Poverty." … St. Francis of Assisi wanted to be poor because Christ chose poverty. If he calls poverty a royal virtue, it is because it shone brilliantly in the life of Jesus … and in the life of his mother, Mary of Nazareth. Similarly, I often think about the vow of poverty taken by religious … [the religious] do so in order to be as close as possible to Christ. The Son [viz. the Second Person of the Trinity] wanted us to be poor in order to show us the best path by which we can return to God.

The Son of God loves the poor; others intend to eradicate them. What a lying, unrealistic, almost tyrannical utopia! I always marvel when *Gaudium et Spes* declares, "The spirit of poverty and charity is the glory and witness of the Church of

> Christ" (GS 88). We must be precise in our choice of words. The language of the UN and its agencies, who want to suppress poverty, which they confuse with destitution, is not that of the Church of Christ. The Son of God did not come to speak to the poor in ideological slogans! The Church must banish these slogans from her language. For they have stupefied and destroyed peoples who were trying to remain free in conscience.[86]

Cardinal Sarah warns against confusing poverty with destitution. Still, even those families who are poor may improve their situation. For instance, many husbands switch careers if making major spending cutbacks won't solve their financial quandary. In our case, my husband changed careers multiple times throughout our marriage. As noted above, he did so to meet the growing financial demands of our family. In each instance, it took both preparatory time (beforehand) and adjustment time (afterward) for him do so, but it was always worth the effort. Not once did we regret the change. Frankly, changing careers actually *grew* my husband's skill set; accordingly, he is now capable of wearing as many hats as he needs to, if we need extra monthly income. During our marriage, he has taught, attended school, worked in law, and wrote political commentary—just to bring enough money to provide for our family's necessities.

If conditions in the home are such that poverty begins to approach destitution, and one parent needs to work a second job outside the home, it *must* be the father. This is a common dilemma among large families. I've heard some argue that the husband shouldn't take on a second job because it takes *him* out of the house too much. Even if I agree that this situation is less than comfortable, the Church has perennially taught that having the stabilizing force of the wife and/or mother at home is morally mandatory. It's impossible to argue that *some* combination of these suggestions wouldn't work if you're honestly

86 Sarah, Cardinal Robert. *God or Nothing: A Conversation in Faith with Nicholas Diat.* Ignatius Press, 2015, pp. 140-142.

interested in fulfilling the Christian practice of staying at home as a wife—and if you're honestly not laboring merely to defend the lifestyle, you're presently comfortable with. After all, is the meager sum left over after paying exorbitant childcare costs worth the abject failure to discharge your home duties? Shockingly, "A new research paper from the Economic Policy Institute (EPI), a worker advocacy group, finds that caretaking costs have become so exorbitant that in most parts of the U.S., families spend more on childcare than they do on rent (included in that number: babysitting, nannies, and out-of-home day care centers)."[87] To further this point, "in 2014, a low-income family earning less than $50,000 per year that made childcare payments spent one-third of this income on child care alone."[88] Clearly, the cheaper option is to find a way for the wife to remain at home rather than paying exorbitant prices for a stranger to do her *real* job. Or in the words of American humorist Sam Levenson, "A woman's place is in the home. Why should she go out and take away a workingman's pay instead of staying home and stealing out of his jacket like a good wife?"[89]

Objection #11: I don't like being at home and prefer to work.

Short answer is suck it up, buttercup. Long answer is God called you to the married vocation and you chose it. Take it up with Him. But I'm confident there's plenty of things about your nine-to-five job that you hate, yet you remain. All in all, you're placing your preferences over the good of your family. This was formerly called "selfishness" in higher-functioning epochs of human history, long since passed. This may come as a shock to the women who make or share this objection,

---

87 Gould, Elise and Cooke, Tanyell. "High Quality Child Care Is out of Reach for Working Families." *Economic Policy Institute*, 6 October, www.epi.org/publication/child-ca re-affordability/.

88 Malik, Rasheed. "Working Families Are Spending Big Money on Child Care." *Washington: Center for American Progress*, 2019, available at https://www.americanprogress .org/issues/early-childhood/reports/2019/06/20/471141/working-families-spending-big-mo ney-child-care/.

89 Quote attributed to humorist Sam Levenson.

but no housewife I've ever met gets really "psyched" to scrub a toilet. Neither working mothers nor non-working mothers find themselves bursting with excitement at every moment of their daily grind, but at least the latter can say they are serving the Lord as they press on.

Knowing that I'm serving the Lord and helping Him carry His Cross helps me to persevere through the tough days. To joyfully embrace our crosses until death is the most important lesson we can learn and the secret to a peaceful home. Three of my seven children once simultaneously had the stomach flu and none of them knew how to vomit into a toilet. I did the Lord's work that day. It was unglamorous but holy. If you are a woman who vehemently hates the domestic life, it's a great opportunity for you to sacrifice your preferences for Our Lord's, Who sacrificed far more than that for your ultimate good. In short, "offer up" your suffering to Him Who will strengthen you.

Objection #12: Children in daycare are at no statistical disadvantage compared to children who remain at home with their mothers.

No, seriously, who actually believes this nonsense? For those who do, let's explore the findings.

On the laundry list of unwanted items that children in daycare acquire, let's begin with the behavioral issues. Well, consider this: "Children who are in day care for a year or more have been shown to be more disruptive in class as long as into the sixth grade, according to a *New York Times* report on the 'Study of Early Child Care and Youth Development.' Even children in high-quality centers were shown to exhibit disruptive behavior."[90] (As a homeschooling mother, I'm always reminded by complete strangers that my kids are at a disadvantage because they aren't getting "socialized" outside of the home.)

Disruptive behavior is just the beginning for children in daycare.

90 Miller, Christa. "Psychological Effects of Sending Children to Day Care." *Hello Motherhood*, 6 Dec. 2019, www.hellomotherhood.com/psychological-effects-of-sending-children-to-day-care-4102639.html.

The longer young children are in daycare the more prominent their presentation of anxiety, detachment, and depression becomes.

According to the *CBS News* article, "The Negative Effects of Childcare," two new studies in the journal, *Child Development*, have rekindled the debate over the effects of non-maternal childcare on children's behavior. Both studies found evidence that suggests the longer a child spends in childcare, the more stress they may experience, and that could lead to the young to become aggressive and disobedient.[91]

The same article notes the higher occurrences of stress and aggression found in young children who spend "long hours" in daycare:

> The first study, conducted again by the National Institute of Child Health and Human Development, found that those who spend long hours in childcare may experience more stress and are at increased risk of becoming overly aggressive (17 percent) and developing other behavior problems.[92]

So much for "socialization" and supposedly salubrious effects stemming from day care. Moreover, consider another study:

> The second study was smaller and was conducted by the Institute of Child Development of the University of Minnesota. It dealt only with children in daycare and found that in kids younger than three, levels of cortisol, a hormone associated with stress, rose in the afternoon during full days they spent in day care, but fell when they got home.[93]

Why on earth would their cortisol levels "fall" at home if daycare is undistinguishably accommodating to the young child's temperament?

Even minor health issues appear in the catalogue of unwanted ramifications of day care: "children in more hours of childcare each week

---

91 Neal, Rome. "The Negative Effects of Childcare?" *CBS Interactive*, 17 July 2003, www.cbsnews.com/news/the-negative-effects-of-childcare/.

92 Ibid.

93 Ibid.

during their first year of life were 8 percent more likely to have an ear infection."[94] The study goes on to report that "children in more hours of care each week during their first year of life were 4 percent more likely to have stomach illness (such as an upset stomach or brief stomach "flu")." Respiratory illnesses are also evidently more common for children in daycare: "children in large group care were more likely to have an upper respiratory illness than were children who were reared at home or in small group settings."[95]

However, children in daycare average slightly higher on language tests,[96] so by all means ignore everything referenced above and keep rationalizing the damage done to its unfortunate wards.

Objection #13: Pope St. John Paul II encouraged women to work! Isn't a single pope's permission all I need?

As a preliminary reminder, I will discuss the controversial teaching (in this domain) by Pope St. John Paul II in the next chapter. For now, it should suffice to say: God alone makes the rules and popes are supposed to follow and protect those rules. Further, popes are emplaced such as to make sure God's rules are enforced, and yet they do so imperfectly. Catholics ought to be warned against turning everything a pope says into infallible truth. This is not the Catholic way. In the ordinary course of events, only Scripture and Tradition infallibly teach inerrant truths. History is rife with popes saying and/or doing things that aren't in line with Catholic teaching. When a pope teaches,

---

94 Alexander, Duane T. United States of America. U.S. Department of Health and Human Services. National Institute of Child Health and Human Development. *The NICHD Study of Early Child Care and Youth Development.* Rockville: U.S. Department of Health and Human Services, 2006. Online. https://www.nichd.nih.gov/sites/default/files/publications/pubs/documents/seccyd_06.pdf=

95 Ibid.

96 "The higher the quality of childcare (more positive language stimulation and interaction between the child and provider), the greater the child's language abilities at 15, 24, and 36 months, the better the child's cognitive development at age two, and the more school readiness the child showed at age three." https://www.purdue.edu/hhs/hdfs/fii/wp-content/uploads/2015/07/s_mifis01c03.pdf.

writes, or speaks we ought to be asking ourselves if he is in line with Catholic teaching. Sometimes, this requires a whole lot of research. I will dedicate the next chapter to that very research in the realm of the Catholic teaching on women in the workplace.

You've probably heard by now: popes are only infallible (speaking without error) when they deliberately offset their teaching with a disclaimer, teaching in accordance with Holy Scripture and Tradition. It has only happened—get this—twice in two thousand years. This doesn't mean a pope is barred from publicly expressing his private opinions. He may do so. But publicly expressed private papal opinions are not Catholic teaching. As Catholics, we must understand when the pope is speaking infallibly—statistically, popes do so once per millennium—and when he is merely giving his opinion.

Catholic Answers summarizes this topic quite nicely:

> The Catholic Church's teaching on papal infallibility is one that is generally misunderstood by those outside the Church. In particular, Fundamentalists and other "Bible Christians" often confuse the charism of papal "infallibility" with "impeccability." They imagine Catholics believe the pope cannot sin. Others, who avoid this elementary blunder, think the pope relies on some sort of amulet or magical incantation when an infallible definition is due.
>
> Given these common misapprehensions regarding the basic tenets of papal infallibility, it is necessary to explain exactly what infallibility is not. Infallibility is not the absence of sin. Nor is it a charism that belongs only to the pope. Indeed, infallibility also belongs to the body of bishops as a whole, when, in doctrinal unity with the pope, they solemnly teach a doctrine as true. We have this from Jesus himself, who promised the apostles and their successors the bishops, the magisterium of the Church: "He who hears you hears me" (Lk 10:16).[97]

97 Catholic Answers. "Papal Infallibility." *Catholic Answers, Catholic Answers*, 23 May 2019, www.catholic.com/tract/papal-infallibility.

There have been so very few times in which a pope has declared something "from the chair," or *ex cathedra*, that a Catholic need not expect it to happen in his own lifetime. It might as well mean, "an over sourced phenomenon that need not be discussed so much," but doesn't:

> *Ex cathedra* is a Latin phrase which means "from the chair." It refers to binding and infallible papal teachings which are promulgated by the pope when he officially teaches in his capacity of the universal shepherd of the Church a doctrine on a matter of faith or morals and addresses it to the entire world. The concept derives from Jesus.[98]

In neither instance of *ex cathedra* were working mothers discussed. Actually, both statements concerned teaching regarding the Virgin Mother:

> There is no set list of *ex cathedra* teachings, but that's because there are only two, and both are about Mary: her Immaculate Conception (declared by Pope Pius IX in 1854 and grandfathered in after the First Vatican Council's declaration of papal infallibility in 1870) and her bodily Assumption into heaven (declared by Pope Pius XII in 1950).[99]

Now that we have prefaced—more to come on this topic in the next chapter—how to properly understand what weight is attached to a pope's *statements*, let's tackle how to properly weigh a saint's *actions*.

---

98 Staff, Catholic Answers. "What Does the Term Ex Cathedra Mean, and Where Did the Catholic Church Come up with It?" *Catholic Answers. Catholic Answers*, 23 Feb. 2019. Web. 19 Apr. 2021.

99 Considine, Kevin P., et al. "Is There a List of Infallible Teachings?" *U.S. Catholic Magazine - Faith in Real Life*, 3 Feb. 2021, uscatholic.org/articles/201105/is-there-a-list-of-infallible-teachings/.

The St. Gianna Molla "Gotcha"

Here we come to it: the most highly preferred "gotcha" question of the Catholic feminist. It usually goes something like, "What about St. Gianna?! She was a working mother, and she became a saint!"

If anyone is unfamiliar with the story of St. Gianna, she is a much beloved saint for her commitment to the pro-life cause. Indeed, she even gave up her life for it. Many Catholic couples (including my husband and I) have named their daughters after her. Here is a brief account of why she is, rightly, venerated as a great Catholic saint:

> Early in the pregnancy it was discovered that Gianna had a fibroma, a benign tumor, on her uterine wall. Surgery that would involve aborting the baby was suggested, but the Mollas instantly and firmly rejected this idea, and chose surgery that would remove only the tumor. Because of her medical knowledge, Gianna understood more fully than most the risks involved in this delicate surgery-both to her and to her unborn child. She insisted that the baby be protected at all costs. The surgery successfully removed the fibroma, and the pregnancy continued, apparently normally, and the family made plans for the future in joy and hope. But all was not well, and a few days before the baby was born, Gianna realized it would be a difficult—possibly life-threatening— delivery.
>
> She asked her husband to promise that if it were necessary to choose between saving her and saving the baby, he should choose the baby. "I insist", she said. On Good Friday, Gianna entered the hospital. And a lovely, healthy baby daughter, Gianna Emanuela, was born the next day, April 21, 1962. But the mother had developed a fatal infection-septic peritonitis. (Modern antibiotics most likely would have saved her.) The inflammation caused immense suffering during her final week on earth. In the midst of her terrible pain, Gianna called to her

> own mother, Maria, who had died in 1942—and she prayed. As she lay dying, she repeated, "Jesus, I love you", over and over. Her agony ended on April 28 at home.[100]

It should be obvious that St. Gianna became a saint because she sacrificed her life for that of her unborn child and subsequently, certain miracles were attributed to her intercession after she had died. She *did not* become a saint because she was a working mother.

Every action or decision a saint makes in his lifetime isn't guaranteed to be saintly.

Every saint—aside from the Virgin Mary—made unfortunate decisions in his lifetime. Aside from his mother, Christ was the only one who had the honor of "doing everything right." St. Paul killed Christians before he came into the fullness of the faith. St. Augustine lived a hedonistic lifestyle and fled from his holy mother all across the Mediterranean. Certainly, St. Gianna was not without her flaws, even if only minor, because only the Holy Family perfectly fulfilled the Gospels.

Perhaps you may be thinking. "St. Gianna's service as a compassionate doctor and St. Paul's mass-murder of innocents prove to be unfair analogates, don't they?" Only as a distinction of degree, not kind: one is bad; the other is worse. The point is that extreme, obvious, repeated acts of grave evil can and do *still* haunt the biographies of great saints, just as such acts haunt the private lives of unrepentant sinners. The only difference lies in the *reaction* of the given sinner: either root deeper into the sin and rationalize it—thereby normalizing it—or honestly appraise the sin as a path to certain death and begin to root it out. (Obviously, killing innocent people is far worse than willingly being a working wife, but the point remains: no sin is advisable.) The

100 Hitchcock, Helen. "Saint Gianna: A Model for Mothers." Foreword to '*Saint Gianna Molla: Wife, Mother, Doctor,*'" Ignatius Insight, 2004. www.ignatiusinsight.com/features2005/hhitchcock_stgianna_feb05.asp.

greatest saints overcame their vices, replacing their wayward habits with virtue.

During my "St. Gianna dialogue" with Catholic feminists, I often hear the objection that St. Gianna worked almost until her death. Accordingly, I will be asked, wouldn't it follow that being a working mother was *somewhat* tied to her canonization? I don't think so.

It appears that St. Gianna *did* experience a St. Paul "being knocked off the horse" moment, occurring shortly before her death and in specific regard to being a working mother. St. Gianna and her husband reached an agreement that she would *stop* working!

That's huge, so I'll restate it: *Gianna and her husband agreed that she would not continue to work after she gave birth to her fourth child.* Catholic feminists typically deny this truth, but her biography is clear:

> In his own account of these years, Pietro Molla says that he did not object to Gianna's continuing her medical practice, because she was so deeply attached to her patients, though after she became pregnant with their fourth child, Pietro and Gianna had agreed that she would stop working outside the home after the baby was born.[101]

Here is Pietro Molla (St. Gianna's husband), himself, on the subject:

> Already during our engagement, Gianna had asked me about continuing her profession at least as long as her obligations as wife and above all as mother allowed it. I did not oppose that because I knew well how enthusiastically she practiced medicine, how attached she was to her patients. Later, by mutual agreement, we made the decision that she would stop at the birth of our fourth child. In this understanding, she continued her profession until her last confinement.[102]

---

101 Ibid.

102 Molla, Pietro, Elio Guerriero, and James G. Colbert. *Saint Gianna Molla: Wife, Mother, Doctor*. San Francisco, Ignatius, 2004.

Another account of St. Gianna's decision to quit working gives a bit more gloss to this account. In *St. Gianna Beretta Molla: A Woman's Life*, author Giuliana Pelucchi details this story from Pietro Molla, himself. Although hesitant to quit her medical practice, Gianna began to lovingly heed her husband's wishes to serve her own family first—her true vocational calling:

> After returning to Ponte Nuovo, Gianna tried to reorganize her life, wanting to find time for everything: Pietro and her children, the management of her household, and her medical practice. Pietro saw how busy she always was and asked if she would consider giving up her practice. The look Gianna gave him in response, however, discouraged Pietro from asking again. "I promise you," she told him one day, "that when we have one more child, I will stop my medical work and will be a full-time mother, even though that will be difficult for me."[103]

When I encountered the above passage, I felt like finally someone understands my point of view, at least in some ways. The Mollas' dialogue seems to confirm the notion that it's physically impossible for anyone to perform two jobs brilliantly at the same time. Better late than never. It also appears that St. Gianna's "passion" for her profession *was* affecting her family life, so she eventually chose the latter. And why wouldn't she have, "she's a saint," after all?

It is also apparent that even during their engagement the couple acknowledged the obvious fact that Gianna's medical career would adversely affect her domestic duties. The couple even had a provision for her to stop working when that eventuated. If anything, Gianna's culpability was lessened to the extent that her husband appears, in retrospect, a bit reluctant: he should have given his wife a more direct order sooner.

Nevertheless, this early acknowledgement in their marriage confirms

---

103 Pelucchi, Giuliana. *Blessed Gianna Beretta Molla: A Woman's Life, 1922-1962*. Boston: Pauline Books & Media, 2002.

the article of common sense that wives lack the physical capability (and the time) to serve their homes and their workplaces equally. It's a basic point: one cannot serve two masters (See Mt 6:24). Frequently, women like St. Gianna will admit this truth in small ways before they are willing to acknowledge it more prominently. In Gianna's case, it took time for her will to concede fully to the demands of her intellect. Until it did, her husband waited patiently—too patiently (whereas a direct order would have remedied this)—until Gianna's will finally gave way during her fourth pregnancy.

Let's circle back to the errant popular logic of the hapless "canonization" of every last act made by a saint in his lifetime. By this faulty and relativistic logic, must not we then "canonize" simultaneous opposites—up and down, getting a job and quitting the job, vice and virtue—without troubling to stipulate a saint's particular strengths? It's far more honest—and accurate—to speak of patron and patroness saints, whom we do not characterize as perfect in the all-encompassing ways in which Jesus and Mary uniquely were perfect.

Further, since St. Gianna and her *very* permissive husband eventually came to the proper way of running a Christian household, perhaps she could *secondarily* be hailed as the patron saint of "no-longer-working" mothers: a.k.a. the patroness of "better late than never." She is acknowledged for as much, in the Gordon household, at any rate. (St. Gianna could also be the patron saint of "admitting wrong and changing course," which is precisely why I pray to her that my Catholic feminist friends follow her example and quit their jobs.)

After all, if St. Gianna was required by the dictates of the faith to walk away from one of the most esteemed careers—that of a medical doctor—in order to focus on her family, Catholic feminists out there can quit your jobs, too, whatever they may be.

The last remaining difficulty—our chapter closer—involves situations like St. Gianna's in which the husband either permits the wife to work, or balks at her career yet dithers under wifely pressure. Wouldn't the husband's approval challenge Catholic teaching that the wife is to do what her husband instructs (or allows) her to do? After all, does it not say in the *Catechism of Trent* that "the wife should love to remain at home, unless compelled by necessity to go out; and she should never presume to leave home without her husband's consent?"[104]

This presents a slightly trickier scenario since it will depend on which part of the sentence above one chooses to emphasize. Should we emphasize the words, "the wife should love to remain at home, unless compelled by necessity to go out"? On the other hand, should we adhere to the words, "she should never presume to leave home without her husband's consent"? In most cases throughout history, a Catholic husband would insist on the former, thus clarifying and simplifying the latter, but today most Catholic husbands whisper or suggest hesitantly as in the case of Gianna and Pietro. In doing so, these husbands allow their wives to work at the behest of wifely and social pressure; in these cases, the second condition is technically fulfilled, even if pressure was applied to the husband in order to secure permission for the wife to work. If a wife, as in the case of St. Gianna, has her husband's permission to "go out," can't she still honor her husband by working?

Not so fast. The *Catechism* goes on to clarify,

> Again, and in this the conjugal union chiefly consists, let wives never forget that next to God they are to love their husbands, to esteem them above all others, yielding to them in all things not inconsistent with Christian piety, a willing and ready obedience.[105]

The husband is the wife's boss. On the contrary, the husband's only boss is the Lord. Accordingly, a wife should not seize upon opportune social pressure, which she may implement against her husband's hesitation to demand that she stay in the home. This modern two-step is something like *disobedience by proxy*. For his part, if he experiences

---

104 *Catechism of the Council of Trent*. 1st ed., Baronius Press, 2018.

105 Ibid.

any doubts on this score at all, the husband is *not* free to give his wife permission for anything that is "inconsistent with Christian piety, a willing and ready obedience." Even the husband cannot, to satisfy his own preferences or to avoid his wife's inconvenient wrath, allow her to perform acts that go against the teachings of the Church.

Modern society is attempting to amend Holy Scripture to meet the cultural preferences of the day, which at the same time undermines the longstanding Catholic teaching on working wives. The thirteen objections above provide ample evidence of this.

So, let's explore what the Catholic Church actually teaches about working wives. As we do so, we will keep in mind the above segment of the Council of Trent that we are *not permitted* to distort Holy Scripture and the unanimous teaching of the Church Fathers in order to accommodate our own modern biases and predilections. Indeed, the Church is here to instruct us away from personal prejudice.

5

Inerrant Catholic Teaching versus Working Wives

When we speak of inerrant teaching, Catholics separate what we are taught into two categories: Scripture and Tradition. If we expand our parameters to include teaching which is not *necessarily* infallible, then we might also speak of a third Catholic teaching mechanism: the Magisterium. Accordingly, let's divide the Church's timeless teaching on the duties of a wife and mother into those same categories.

When I argue below that Scripture forbids feminism's centerpiece—ordinary wifely work outside the home—my meaning should be apparent: the Bible contains several passages disallowing modern wifely careerism. No one denies this reality, although many will stomp their feet in defiance when books such as this one raise the issue.

All non-Catholics (and even many Catholics) frequently wonder what sacred Tradition is, and why it is so important to Catholics. The significance of Tradition can be explained as such:

> Protestants claim the Bible is the only rule of faith, meaning that it contains all of the material one needs for theology and that this material is sufficiently clear that one does not need Apostolic Tradition or the Church's Magisterium (teaching authority) to help one understand it. In the Protestant view, the whole of Christian truth is found within the Bible's pages. Anything extraneous to the Bible is simply non-authoritative, unnecessary, or wrong.

> Catholics, on the other hand, recognize that the true "rule of faith"—as expressed in the Bible itself—is Scripture plus Apostolic Tradition, as manifested in the living teaching authority of the Catholic Church, to which were entrusted the oral teachings of Jesus and the apostles, along with the authority to interpret Scripture correctly.[106]

Now, Sacred Tradition and the Holy Magisterium are distinguishable. The former teaching voice of the Church informed the canon selection process, by which the books of the New Testament were determined, and must thus be inerrant (lest Scripture itself be errant). Strictly speaking, Sacred Tradition ended when the last surviving apostle died.

But in another sense—a looser sense of "Tradition" which does not necessarily bear the charism of inerrancy—the non-Scriptural teaching voice of the Church continues generationally, such that those successors of the apostles, the bishops, inform what we call the Magisterium. Now, it requires a lifetime of study to understand exactly how the Magisterium works, but it suffices for our purposes to stipulate that the teachings of the Magisterium can *sometimes*, when habitually repeated intergenerationally, be labelled "inerrant."

There exist inerrant teachings of the Magisterium on the subject matter at hand. In this conjoined sense, we will treat of the Catholic teachings of Tradition and Magisterium in a combined section later in this chapter.

Round One: Scripture vs. Working Wives

What does Sacred Scripture express in regard to the duties of a married woman? Immediately, we run into a minor challenge. Because wives didn't ordinarily work outside the home in Biblical times, there's far fewer explicit admonitions in Sacred Scripture than in the modern

106 Catholic Answers. "Scripture and Tradition." *Catholic Answers*, 23 May 2019, www.catholic.com/tract/scripture-and-tradition.

Magisterium.[107] (This proves to be an article of common sense: the Church, for example, didn't begin admonishing against lay investiture[108] until it became a major problem in the Middle Ages—which does *not* signify that before the Middle Ages the Church accepted lay investiture. Rather, it means that the Church does not trouble to proscribe vices before they become common practice.). Nonetheless, a satisfactory amount of evidence against wifely careerism is offered in Scripture which presupposes and reinforces that wives should ordinarily remain at home.[109]

This configuration of historical facts helps to show why Catholics must rely upon the Magisterium in addition to Scripture: namely, human history abundantly shows that, through sin, each new generation creates new problems rather creatively. That is, feminists came along in full force well after the canonization of Scripture. As such, we need an ever-present Magisterium to apply the "law" (Scripture and Tradition) to the "facts" of our own day.

Like an illegal immigrant hostile to his new country's culture, feminists have flooded Christianity since the latter half of the nineteenth-century, and thereby "softened the ground" such that many Christians now errantly believe our teachings may be able to avail the feminists. They wait in vain.

---

107 "It is important to note that, when the Bible was penned, women had few employment options outside the home. It was assumed that, when a woman married, her sole focus would be on keeping house, bearing children, and helping her husband (Genesis 2:18; Titus 2:4–5). Life was more difficult before modern conveniences, and simply running a household was more than a full-time job. Many women whose husbands could afford it had maidservants (Genesis 16:3; 29:24, 29; 2 Kings 5:2). Others trained daughters to help as soon as they were old enough, just as sons were apprenticed by their fathers and grandfathers in the family business." GotQuestions.org. "Home." GotQuestions.org, 5 Apr. 2018, www.gotquestions.org/biblical-homemaking.html.

108 Lay investiture was the harmful medieval practice of investiture of clerics by monarchs.

109 In Paul's day, women served society primarily by caring for a husband and family, and women had few options for working outside the home. "Mothers Working Outside the Home?" *Verse by Verse Ministry International*, www.versebyverseministry.org/bible-answers/should-christian-mothers-work.

Married Women Working in Scripture?

Much needless confusion regarding working wives seems to emanate from the fact that Scripture sometimes references "working" women.

> The Bible mentions women who worked in commercial trade (Prov. 31:16a, 24; Acts 16:14), in agriculture (Josh. 15:17-19; Ruth 2:8; Prov. 31:16b), as millers (Exod. 11:5; Matt. 24:41), as shepherds (Gen. 29:9; Exod. 2:16), as artisans, especially in textiles (Exod. 26:1 NIV; Tobit 2:11ff NRSV; Acts 18:3), as perfumers and cooks (1 Sam. 8:13), as midwives (Exod. 1:15ff), as nurses (Gen. 35:8; Exod. 2:7; 2 Sam. 4:4; 1 Kings 1:4), as domestic servants (Acts 12:13, etc.), and as professional mourners (Jer. 9:17). Women could also be patrons (Acts 16:40; Rom. 16:1-2), leaders (Judg. ch 4-5; 2 Sam. 20:16) and ruling queens (1 Kings 10:1ff; Acts 8:27). One Bible woman even built towns (1 Chron. 7:24).[110]

Desperate promoters of working wives regularly provide such lists as "proof" that women have always worked, and that both the Old and the New Testaments long supported the practice.

What they conveniently fail to mention is that virtually all of this outside-the-home work was being accomplished by *single women*, who were and are of course permitted to work. In a minority of cases, any of the above work accomplished by married women is referred to as "women's work," which is to say *chores being done in or around the home* (crafting, farming, shepherding, milling, sewing, etc.). Take, for instance, the wife Anna who is making a wage selling her wares:

> Then my wife Anna earned money at women's work. She used to send the product to the owners. Once when they paid her wages, they also gave her a kid; and when she returned to me it began to bleat. So I said to her, "Where did you get the kid?

---

110 Mowczko, Marg. "Working Women in the New Testament: Priscilla, Lydia & Phoebe." 25 Sept. 2020, margmowczko.com/new-testament-working-women/.

> It is not stolen, is it? Return it to the owners; for it is not right to eat what is stolen." And she said, "It was given to me as a gift in addition to my wages." But I did not believe her, and told her to return it to the owners; and I blushed for her. Then she replied to me, "Where are your charities and your righteous deeds? You seem to know everything!"[111]

Anna's work was permissible not because wifely careers are licit but rather because she worked from home.

Anna presents a Biblical instance of a known working wife (permissible, again, since she worked from home). But in many cases, the everyday Greek and Hebrew word "woman" was the same as that for "wife." So, we simply don't know whether the working women mentioned in the Bible *were actually married* unless their husbands or children are specifically mentioned.[112] However, in virtually all of the cases where it can be confirmed that a Biblical, laboring woman was married, she is most always doing "woman's work" inside her own home or its immediate vicinity (like farming, tending to animals, etc.).

Even "gender archeologists"[113] concur that women in Biblical ancient Israel "worked" inside their homes or in its vicinity:

> The tasks of women and men overlapped in certain circumstances but were not the same. Women were responsible for what some gender archaeologists call "maintenance activities," a term for the set of "practices and experiences concerning the sustenance, welfare, and long- term reproduction" of the household. (González-Marcén, 3-8) These practices are the basic tasks of daily life; many required specialized knowledge and were essential to regulate and stabilize both household and community life. (González-Marcén, 3) They include

111 Tobit 2:11–14.tt

112 The everyday word for "wife" also means "woman" in Greek (γυνή) and in Hebrew (אִשָּׁה).

113 Whatever that is, I do not know.

> economic, social, political, and religious activities—far too many to be considered in this paper. (Rediscovering Eve, 125–70) Here I describe briefly women's economic activities, many of which leave traces in the archaeological record and can thus be interpreted with respect to gender roles and relationships. Economic activities were an integral part of household life in ancient Israel as in all traditional agrarian societies. It can be shown that women were largely responsible for food processing, textile production, and the fashioning of various household implements and containers (grinding tools, stone and ceramic vessels, baskets, weaving implements, and sewing tools). (Rediscovering Eve, 125–70) Many of these tasks were not only time-consuming and physically demanding but also technologically sophisticated. In the aggregate, they likely required more technological skill than did men's. As anthropologist Jack Goody noted, because women could transform the raw into the cooked and produce other essential commodities, they were seen as having the ability to "work ... wonders." (Goody, 70)[114]

In other words, they did women's work in a modified context. Most working wives today work away from the vicinity of the home for the majority of the day—leaving their main duties, the truest "woman's work," to be completed by others. Admittedly, most stay-at-home mothers today aren't tending to sheep like they were in Biblical times, though most of the essential tasks remain the same. So, merely cataloguing Scriptural women as "working" does little or nothing to signify that modern married women can licitly work outside of their homes.

What such instances do demonstrate amply is a proposition about which *no one is arguing*: that it has never been illicit for wives to complete chores—or sell the wares they make—from *inside* the home.

---

114 Meyers, Carol L. "Was Ancient Israel a Patriarchal Society?" *Journal of Biblical Literature*, Spring 133.1, 2014, pp. 8-24.

No, Wives Don't Have to Be Shut-ins

In Proverbs, we see a married woman, "more precious than rubies" to her husband, because she works all day at her domestic work. By inference, the careful reader notes from her description (by Solomon) that this virtuous woman exhausts her time and effort on her domestic chores as opposed to working outside the home. She is described as a "hard worker" because of her faithfulness in completing her many domestic chores: cooking, cleaning, farming, sewing, crafting, etc.

> A good wife who can find? She is far more precious than jewels. The heart of her husband trusts in her, and he will have no lack of gain. She does him good, and not harm, all the days of her life. She seeks wool and flax, and works with willing hands. She is like the ships of the merchant, she brings her food from afar. She rises while it is yet night and provides food for her household and tasks for her maidens. She considers a field and buys it; with the fruit of her hands she plants a vineyard. She girds her loins with strength and makes her arms strong. She perceives that her merchandise is profitable. Her lamp does not go out at night. She puts her hands to the distaff, and her hands hold the spindle. She opens her hand to the poor, and reaches out her hands to the needy. She is not afraid of snow for her household, for all her household are clothed in scarlet. She makes herself coverings; her clothing is fine linen and purple. Her husband is known in the gates, when he sits among the elders of the land. She makes linen garments and sells them; she delivers girdles to the merchant. Strength and dignity are her clothing, and she laughs at the time to come. She opens her mouth with wisdom, and the teaching of kindness is on her tongue. She looks well to the ways of her household, and does not eat the bread of idleness. Her children rise up and call her blessed; her husband also, and he praises her: "Many women have done excellently, but you surpass them all." Charm is

> deceitful, and beauty is vain, but a woman who fears the Lord is to be praised. Give her of the fruit of her hands, and let her works praise her in the gates.[115]

Today's feminist advocates for outside-the-home wifely labor get particularly excited at Scriptural mentions of wives earning wages for their handicrafts. In reality, their argument backfires. Even today, stay-at-home mothers continue the Old Testament practice of selling hand-made goods in person at tradeshows or online. Obviously, the latter case proves optimal since such mothers can make money to augment household incomes in small unobtrusive ways, without leaving their homes.

As I have discussed in previous chapters, after a woman has tended to her domestic responsibilities, she is *then* free to pursue private hobbies and interests. Naturally, she may even earn a wage from them, in certain cases. The relevant moral distinction involves candid self-reflection: even if *geographically proximate* to the home, how much *time* does such a home-hobby or business divert away from one's wifely obligations in her primary endeavors. Even if she never exits her front door, if she relies on surrogates to complete her obligations to her home, then she rejects her wifely vocation.

Occasionally leaving home for little errands, such as selling wares, was not then as uncommon as many women today assume. The "take-away" point is this: regularly leaving one's children in the care of others to pursue commercial jobs or errands would have been entirely foreign (and morally offensive) to the women in Jesus' day.

On the other hand, being a stay-at-home-wife doesn't require *never leaving the house*. More realistically, it involves seldom or infrequently going about town, and in the case of wives with children, bringing those children along when one goes. Wives need not be chained to their stoves all day, as the feminists and Marxists exaggerate. "Woman's work" sometimes requires housewives to accomplish errands outside of, but not far from, the home.

---

115 Proverbs 31:10-31.

All this goes to say that when a woman leaves her home, she leaves the house *rarely* and with her husband's permission. The *Catechism of Trent* clearly states as much: "the wife should love to remain at home, unless compelled by necessity to go out; and she should never presume to leave home without her husband's consent."[116] Well-ordered marriages presumably already follow the custom of men knowing where their wives are throughout the day. Accordingly, asking your "husband's consent" isn't nearly as foreign a practice as the feminists will attempt to make it sound.

Let's now investigate the multiple Scriptural instances whereupon married women are clearly instructed to complete their duties *inside* the home.

In Titus, for example, wifely grace is explicitly connected to domesticity:

> Bid the older women likewise to be reverent in behavior, not to be slanderers or slaves to drink; they are to teach what is good, and so train the young women to love their husbands and children, to be sensible, chaste, domestic, kind, and submissive to their husbands, that the word of God may not be discredited.[117]

The notion that a woman's chief role inheres in homemaking is further established when young widows are instructed to re-marry, in Timothy: "So I would have younger widows marry, bear children, rule their households, and give the enemy no occasion to revile us."[118]

Even Protestants and anti-traditional Catholics like those at the Jesuit magazine, *America*, admit that women's submissive role in Biblical times was expected. These anti-tradition groups (big "T" and little "t") seem to agree that women back then *rarely* took leadership roles, and that extenuating circumstances merited whatever scarce exceptions arose in their favor:

---

116 *Catechism of the Council of Trent.* 1st ed., Baronius Press, 2018.

117 Titus 2:4-5.

118 1 Timothy 5:14.

> Normally, women in the Bible appear in subsidiary roles, for the action most often takes place in the public square, the exclusive domain of men in the ancient world. But "normally" does not mean "always." There is an important and often overlooked side to biblical history: It does not move forward in an unbroken stream but rather bumps along and in critical moments turns in new directions. In those turning points, women, surprisingly, take on leadership roles. Consider three such turning points in biblical history. In each one, male leadership fails or is absent and women take up the slack, employing wit and courage rather than recognized authority and power to lead the community. The three turning points are the transition from one elect family (Abraham's) to one elect nation (Israel); the transition from the failed rule of tribal chieftains (the Book of Judges) to Davidic kingship; and the climactic biblical moment—the transition from Jesus' crucifixion to his resurrection as risen Lord.[119]

To the chagrin of many liberals and radicals today, societies in Biblical times had a proper view of the true feminine virtues. As a whole, those women were not trying to step out of their homes—thereby abandoning their primary duties to their own families—in order to usurp the roles of men, like wives are doing almost ubiquitously today.

Even though our Protestant brethren have departed from the One True Faith, many still preach the proper role of Christian women. Such intuitive Protestants seem to have a "feel" for how women were once celebrated for their true, faithful femininity in Scripture:

> Scripture never discounts the female intellect, downplays the talents and abilities of women, or discourages the right use of women's spiritual gifts. But whenever the Bible expressly talks

---

119 Clifford, Richard J., et al. "Women Have Been Leading since Biblical Times-They Can Lead Again Today." *America Magazine*, 30 Nov. 2018, www.americama gazine.org/fa ith/2018/11/08/women-have-been-leading-biblical-times-they-can-lead-again-today.

> about the marks of an excellent woman, the stress is always on feminine *virtue*. The most significant women in Scripture were influential not because of their careers, but because of their *character*. The message these women collectively give is not about "gender equality"; it's about true feminine excellence. And that is always exemplified in moral and spiritual qualities rather than by social standing, wealth, or physical appearance.[120]

The Protestant author above further notes the distinct ways in which the secular, modern worldview distorts the idea of traditional femininity:

> Even when secular movements have arisen claiming to be concerned with women's rights, their efforts have generally been detrimental to the status of women. The feminist movement of our generation, for example, is a case in point. Feminism has devalued and defamed *femininity*. Natural gender distinctions are usually downplayed, dismissed, despised, or denied. As a result, women are now being sent into combat situations, subjected to grueling physical labor once reserved for men, exposed to all kinds of indignities in the workplace, and otherwise encouraged to act and talk like men. Meanwhile, modern feminists heap scorn on women who want family and household to be their first priorities; in so doing they disparage the role of motherhood, the one calling that is most uniquely and exclusively feminine. The whole message of feminist egalitarianism is that there is really nothing extraordinary about women. That is certainly not the message of Scripture. Scripture honors women *as women,* and it encourages them to seek honor in a uniquely feminine way (Proverbs 31:10-30).[121]

---

120 MacArthur, John. "The Biblical Portrait of Women: Setting the Record Straight." *Grace to You*, 18 Aug. 2016, www.gty.org/library/articles/A265/the-biblical-portrait-of-women-setting-the-record-straight.

121 Ibid.

Ben Witherington III, a Protestant New Testament scholar, notes that Scripture "limited women's roles and functions to the home, and severely restricted: (1) their rights of inheritance, (2) their choice of relationship, (3) their ability to pursue a religious education or fully participate in synagogue, and (4) limited their freedom of movement."[122]

Scriptural verses condemning wifely work do not prove as plentiful as those instructing wives to submit to their husbands. It is worth noting a second time that this is due to the fact that wives typically didn't work outside their homes in Biblical times. It wasn't a problem or even an imaginative new fabrication that people entertained 'back then.' It was simply unheard of.

However, on the topic of wifely submission, the Bible is *abundantly* clear in numerous passages throughout the Old and New Testaments.

How Is Submission to One's Husband Related to Careerism?

Submission to one's husband and working only within the home may appear to be unrelated, but a closer analysis reveals their interconnectivity. In order to run a home economy, the wife must be present. In addition to mere geographical presence or proximity (in the case of farming gals), she cannot properly serve in her home if she does not enthusiastically embrace that her husband holds dominion over her. Conversely, a married woman who understands and even enjoys that her husband is the rightful head of the family will energetically serve her household as his right hand "woman." Within this model, she will unlikely challenge her husband's authority. Outside this model, she will be tempted to challenge it, causing frequent and bitter power struggles. (Anecdotally, those wives I've met who accept their place as helpers within the confines of the household Christian Patriarchy enjoy far happier marriages than those who do not.)

To put it simply, women *must submit* to their husbands and govern

---

122 Mcknight, Scot. *1 Peter: The NIV Application Commentary*. Grand Rapids, Michigan: Zondervan, 1996.

their homes and children by day. To do so, they simply must be in the home.

In 1 Peter 3:1-6, Christian wives are rather clearly exhorted as follows:

> Wives, be submissive to your husbands, so that some, though they do not obey the word, may be won without a word by the behavior of their wives, when they see your reverent and chaste behavior. Let not yours be the outward adorning with braiding of hair, decoration of gold, and wearing of fine clothing, but let it be the hidden person of the heart with the imperishable jewel of a gentle and quiet spirit, which in God's sight is very precious. So once the holy women who hoped in God used to adorn themselves and were submissive to their husbands, as Sarah obeyed Abraham, calling him lord. And you are now her children if you do right and let nothing terrify you.[123]

More than any of the other New Testament authors, St. Paul composed the most specific verses concerning how Christian women, in general, ought to conduct themselves. Women, he writes, must keenly recognize and happily accept their secondary rank within nature and within the Christian household hierarchy. Among St. Paul's writings, the verses particularly decried by feminists are those comprising his teachings against female teaching. Bear in mind, dear reader, that the following verses of Scripture are all part of inerrant Christian teaching. If you have a problem with these, *then take it up with Jesus*:

> Let a woman learn in silence with all submissiveness. I permit no woman to teach or to have authority over men; she is to keep silent. For Adam was formed first, then Eve; and Adam was not deceived, but the woman was deceived and became a transgressor. Yet woman will be saved through bearing children, if she continues in faith and love and holiness, with modesty.[124]

---

123 1 Peter 3: 1-6.

124 1 Timothy 2: 11–15.

In 1 Corinthians 14: 34-35, St. Paul goes even further:

> The women should keep silence in the churches. For they are not permitted to speak, but should be subordinate, as even the law says. If there is anything they desire to know, let them ask their husbands at home. For it is shameful for a woman to speak in church.[125]

Note the domestic emplacement St. Paul presupposes of Christian women: *at home*. Not to put too fine a point on it, but also note St. Paul's clever prefigurement of the title of this book: *let them ask their husbands at home*!

Wifely subjugation to the husband's headship is another recurring theme with St. Paul. Pay special attention to the final sentence of the following passage. Specifically, woman is the glory of man, while man is the glory of God—which reconfigures our point in bold color:

> I want you to understand that the head of every man is Christ, the head of a woman is her husband, and the head of Christ is God. Any man who prays or prophesies with his head covered dishonors his head, but any woman who prays or prophesies with her head unveiled dishonors her head—it is the same as if her head were shaven. For if a woman will not veil herself, then she should cut off her hair; but if it is disgraceful for a woman to be shorn or shaven, let her wear a veil. For a man ought not to cover his head, since he is the image and glory of God; but woman is the glory of man.[126]

A lineage of properly arranged authority can be detected above: God is man's "boss," indeed—and man his steward—but man is woman's boss. It involves no stretch of the imagination to see how and why man needs his helper at home, keeping it orderly and lovely while he is away by day. This familial hierarchy, which turns out to be called

125 1 Corinthians 14: 34-35.

126 1 Corinthians 11:3–7.

headship (no pun intended) explains the Christian practice of veiling, which is far more theologically relevant than one might assume. While affirming that wives are under the headship of their husbands, St. Paul also notes that husbands have undeniable duties to their wives:

> Wives, be subject to your husbands, as to the Lord. For the husband is the head of the wife as Christ is the head of the church, his body, and is himself its Savior. As the church is subject to Christ, so let wives also be subject in everything to their husbands. Husbands, love your wives, as Christ loved the church and gave himself up for her, that he might sanctify her, having cleansed her by the washing of water with the word, that he might present the church to himself in splendor, without spot or wrinkle or any such thing, that she might be holy and without blemish. Even so husbands should love their wives as their own bodies. He who loves his wife loves himself. For no man ever hates his own flesh, but nourishes and cherishes it, as Christ does the church, because we are members of his body.[127]

As above, the references in Scripture to wifely submission are comprehensive and manifold: *comprehensive* because such references summarize more or less everything wives must do (namely, obey husbands); *manifold* because in most of these passages, the admonition is repeated at least twice.

It's surprising that such clear, repeated, robust, and undeniable biblical instruction on wifely submission is not only bitterly opposed, but also dishonestly vilified, in the world today. Even in Scriptural passages we'd likely deem *unpleasant*, wifely submission makes an undeniable appearance. For instance, in Genesis's famous catalogue of curses: "To the woman he said, 'I will greatly multiply your pain in childbearing; in pain you shall bring forth children, yet your desire shall be for your husband, and he shall rule over you'."[128] In more upbeat New

127 Ephesians 5:22-30.

128 Genesis 3:16.

Testament passages, such as Colossians 3: 18, we read the exact same substantive message: "Wives, be subject to your husbands, as is fitting in the Lord."[129] Again, in more passing references within discourses on other topics, such as 1 Peter 3: 5, holy writ states: "So once the holy women who hoped in God used to adorn themselves and were submissive to their husbands."[130] And lastly in juridical passages, such as Romans 7:2: "Thus a married woman is bound by law to her husband as long as he lives; but if her husband dies she is discharged from the law concerning the husband."[131]

Are you keeping track? I certainly hope so. So far, I have referenced at least nine verses strongly admonishing wives to submit to their husbands: 1 Tim 2: 11–15; 1 Corinthians 14: 34-35; 1 Corinthians 11:3–7; Ephesians 5:22-30; 1 Peter 3: 1-6; Genesis 3:16; Colossians 3:18; 1 Peter 3:5; and Romans 7:2. We've only just begun. Clearly, many modern women are shamelessly reading a different Bible (or more accurately, not reading a Bible at all!).

Dignity Is Accepting What God Created You For

So-called "Christian feminists" and Catholic working wives have long attempted, in vain, to employ the following words of St. Paul against his own vastly anti-feminist teachings: "There is neither Jew nor Greek, there is neither slave nor free, there is neither male nor female; for you are all one in Christ Jesus."[132] It should be readily apparent to all that St. Paul is here advocating his own position from the Council of Jerusalem: namely, Christian dignity is afforded to each person regardless of his previous societal status. He's not stating that there *are no* societal statuses; he's asserting that baptized Gentiles need not keep kosher or circumcision, since under the New Covenant, God loves us

129 Colossians 3:18.

130 1 Peter 3:5.

131 Romans 7:2.

132 Galatians 3:28.

all equally and asks only that we keep faithful under the sacraments. We are equal, but only in dignity.[133] In fact, our dignity enjoins us to fill specific roles preordained for us. Dignity by its very nature calls us to hierarchy.

Married women, there is great dignity in accepting that which God has created you for: serving a husband (with or without eventual children) at home. Stop contesting this basic moral fact of nature. It constitutes a rebellion against God.[134]

There are many Scriptural verses which the "Christian feminists" may recur to for inspiration as they seek to conform their own wills in rectitude to God's will. Be heartened: repudiating virtually everything the popular culture of the world urges you to do is no small task. We are warmly encouraged when we read Galatians 6: 3-5: "For if anyone thinks he is something, when he is nothing, he deceives himself. But let each one test his own work, and then his reason to boast will be in himself alone and not in his neighbor. For each man will have to bear his own load."[135] And again in Romans 12:2: "Do not be conformed to this world but be transformed by the renewal of your mind, that you may prove what is the will of God, what is good and acceptable and perfect."[136] Also, the book of James 1: 5 states, "If any of you lacks wisdom, let him ask God, who gives to all men generously and without reproaching, and it will be given him."[137]

---

133 The Catholic definition of human dignity affirms that: "The dignity of the human person is rooted in his creation in the image and likeness of God (article 1); it is fulfilled in his vocation to divine beatitude (article 2). It is essential to a human being freely to direct himself to this fulfillment (article 3). By his deliberate actions (article 4), the human person does, or does not, conform to the good promised by God and attested by moral conscience (article 5). Human beings make their own contribution to their interior growth; they make their whole sentient and spiritual lives into means of this growth (article 6). With the help of grace they grow in virtue (article 7), avoid sin, and if they sin they entrust themselves, as did the prodigal son, to the mercy of our Father in heaven (article 8). In this way they attain to the perfection of charity." (*Catechism of the Catholic Church*. #1700).

134 Gordon, Timothy. *The Case for Patriarchy*. Crisis Publications, 2021, pp. 115.

135 Galatians 6:3-5.

136 Romans 12:2.

137 James 1:5.

Women must accept that it is husbands who are charged with providing for their families.[138] Remember, *manual* labor was Adam's curse; *birthing* labor was Eve's curse:

> And to Adam he said, "Because you have listened to the voice of your wife, and have eaten of the tree of which I commanded you, 'You shall not eat of it,' cursed is the ground because of you; in toil you shall eat of it all the days of your life; thorns and thistles it shall bring forth to you; and you shall eat the plants of the field. In the sweat of your face you shall eat bread till you return to the ground, for out of it you were taken; you are dust, and to dust you shall return."[139]

As it says in 1 Timothy 5: 8: "If any one does not provide for his relatives, and especially for his own family, he has disowned the faith and is worse than an unbeliever."[140]

Concluding Words on Scripture

To conclude this section on Scripture, we have confronted a few basics. Firstly: there are indeed instances in Scripture in which married women worked. Secondly: the work being referenced in such places as "woman's work" equated to domestic chores or agricultural labor in the vicinity of the home. Thirdly: Scripture emphasizes with special zeal that wives and husbands have different responsibilities and duties.

Moreover, there exist ample Scriptural passages which speak more *directly* to universal questions of matrimony such as wifely obedience—and *anachronistically* to modern questions such as feminist careerism. Under this heading, married women are instructed by the inerrant words of St. Paul to: submit themselves to their husbands' leadership

---

138 Gordon, Timothy. *The Case for Patriarchy*. Crisis Publications, 2021, Footnote 108, citing Katie Scot-Marshall, "The Enduring Legacy of the Original Dangerous Woman," *Dangerous Woman Project*, 9 Oct. 2016.

139 Genesis 3:17-19.

140 1 Timothy 5:8.

(1 Cor 11:3–7), have children (Tim 2:15), and to raise children in the home (Titus 2:4-5). Note how impossible these categorical imperatives would prove to be for a woman employed outside of the home by a boss besides her husband. A married woman can have only one earthly master.

It is painstakingly evident that the manner in which households are typically conducted today *severely* violates Holy Scripture. In order to achieve material gain, husbands and wives now regularly borrow from one another's pool of responsibilities—or farm them out for others to complete. This, in turn, created a "gender-fluid" society implicitly run by females, wherein neither sex is recognized as superior to the other at anything. And this has destroyed Christian complementarity and rendered both sexes miserable.

After all, to live outside of the light and the wisdom of Scripture is to willingly invite misery into one's vocation. For instance, consider the repercussions of the bad tempered, non-domestic wife who wins bread for her husband. According to the book of Sirach, her misbehavior and role-perversion subverts the natural order of the Christian household:

> I would sooner keep house with a lion or a dragon than keep house with a spiteful wife. A woman's spite changes her appearance and makes her face as grim as a bear's. When her husband goes out to dinner with his neighbours, he cannot help heaving bitter sighs. No spite can approach the spite of a woman, may a sinner's lot be hers! Like the climbing of a sandhill for elderly feet, such is a garrulous wife for a quiet husband. Do not be taken in by a woman's beauty, never lose your head over a woman. Bad temper, insolence and shame hold sway where the wife supports the husband. Low spirits, gloomy face, stricken heart: such is a spiteful wife. Slack hands and sagging knees: such is the wife who does not make her husband happy. Sin began with a woman, and thanks to her we must all die. Do

> not let water find a leak, nor a spiteful woman give free rein to her tongue.[141]

Sadly too many modern Christian households will find themselves all too familiar with the kind of dysfunction described above—unsurprisingly, it is *women* who prove to be most miserable. A study from the U.K.'s *National Health Service* (NHS) concludes that women are unhappier than men *for most of their lives*, until they enter their old age, specifically their eighties.[142] What we see, en masse, is the spectacle of married women abandoning their God-given duties in exchange for those which prove unnatural to their sex, depressing their spirits and altering their nature.

As we move on, we will see that the *Magisterial Tradition* of the Catholic Church has quite recently applied the moral requirements of Scripture to historical developments subsequent to the apostolic era. In other words, the Magisterium blesses us by elucidating the timeless truths of Holy Mother Church in light of the recent anti-Christian and anti-family ideologies like Marxism and feminism. Accordingly, the Magisterium has more specific things to say to would-be "Christian feminists" about wifely labor.

Round Two: Catholic Magisterium and Sacred Tradition vs. Working Wives

With the remainder of this chapter, I will methodically examine the Church's view on the role of women. For ease, I will do so in chronological order; first focusing on the opinions of the Church's Patristic fathers, then moving onto the generally more recent views of the Holy Fathers.[143]

---

141 Sirach 25: 16-25.

142 Aggeler, Madeleine. "Women Are Unhappier Than Men, But Only Until We're 85!" *The Cut*, 14 Dec. 2017, www.thecut.com/2017/12/study-women-are-unhappier-than-men-but-only-until-were-85.html.

143 I will cover two special sections on the opposing views of the feminist leanings of Pope John Paul II and the anti-feminist leanings of Pope Pius XI.

Non-Catholics often ask Catholics why Sacred Scripture isn't the only authority required to interpret faith and morals. A common objection to the Catholic reliance upon Tradition in addition to Scripture is: "Christians only have to rely on Scripture, alone, to find the answers to life's mysteries. I don't need a third party to tell me what Christ expects. It's all there in the Bible."

The above Protestant notion of learning "by Scripture alone" is also commonly known as *sola scriptura*, and ironically, no Biblical passage exists which supports it. For over five hundred years, the Catholic reply to *sola scriptura* has been: "Dear Protestant brothers and sisters, how, pray-tell, did Christians born *after* Christ's Passion and *before* the canonization of the Bible know what Christ expected of them?"

Many of our brothers and sisters in Christ simply don't realize that for almost *four hundred years* after the death of Christ there was no Bible to be read. So, what enabled Christians in those textually desolate (yet spiritually rich) centuries—centuries where brave souls freely shed their blood for Christ— to access the immutable truths that would eventually be assembled by the Catholic Church into the Holy Bible?

The answer is twofold: firstly, the Magisterium, which interprets the Bible definitively; and secondly, bimillennial Tradition, which informed the canon-selection process in the days prior to the existence of the Bible. After all, *some* infallible authority had to be in place for those several centuries leading to the canonization of the Bible. It was Tradition that kept the Christian faith alive until sacred Scripture could be assembled, constitutive of the many books we recognize today as the Holy Bible. And it is the living Magisterium—all of the living bishops together, acting in accordance with past bishops—which alone authoritatively interprets the Bible.

Tradition (along with Scripture) is infallible; the Magisterium is not in every case infallible. For our purposes at present, we will consider the Magisterium and the Tradition (hereinafter: "Magisterial Tradition") as one, although technically these comprise two distinct voices of the three[144] within the Catholic Church.

Protestants are even more astounded to learn that, for Catholics, Tradition is not only important, but it is *as important* as Scripture, because Tradition was largely the basis by which the Catholic Church canonized the books of the New Testament.[145] What follows is a Trinitarian analogy for and explanation of why Scripture and Tradition are equal to each other:

> Sacred Tradition faithfully preserves and transmits the entirety of the Gospel or Deposit of Faith in a living way in the Church, through the Apostles and their successors (the Bishops), all accomplished in the Holy Spirit, and it is every bit as authoritative as Sacred Scripture (see CCC 76-78 and 81-82). And unquestionably, the Church in the first 400 years of Christianity was very much a church of Oral (Sacred) Tradition. The New Testament writings were not even finished or available in the first 40 to 60 years of the Church, and the books of the Bible would not be finally discerned by the Catholic Church until the late 300's AD. So there was no actual finalized Bible to follow until then, and many different writings were being proposed as "inspired" before the Canon was finally closed. And even after all the books of the Bible were finally discerned, there were no printing presses to get it into the hands of individuals until the 1500's, and most couldn't read anyways. Additionally, many Christian teachings are just not clear from the Bible alone – there must be an authoritative means to interpret it, or we end up with exactly what we have today: 35,000 plus Christian denominations and growing, all with their own contradictory twists to interpreting Scripture, and some of them involving

144 Scripture, Tradition, and the Magisterium comprise the three teaching pillars of the Church.

145 Check out Catholic Answer's online article *Who Compiled the Bible and When*, https://www.catholic.com/qa/who-compiled-the-bible-and-when, for more information.

> very important issues! The idea of following the Bible alone as the sole authority for Christian doctrine was not only unheard of in the first 1500 years of the Church, but it was also completely impractical. And ultimately, it just didn't work! The Fruit of following the Bible Alone apart from Sacred Tradition and the teaching authority of the Church has been massive disunity –in complete opposition to the unity that Jesus prayed for [sic] In John 17:17-23. No, the Early Church was very much an oral church. "Faith comes from what is heard", St Paul would write in Romans 10:17.[146]

Ask Your Church Father(s)

Like Sacred Scripture, Magisterial Tradition strongly and clearly admonishes against wifely work outside the home. It does so on even more specifically articulated grounds than we saw Scripture do above.

Fortunately, that is, the Church has been providing intellectually satisfying commentaries on the proper roles of women for millennia. We find such commentaries in the form of papal rescripts, encyclicals,[147] apostolic exhortations,[148] homilies, and speeches. In fact, the

---

146 Osborne, Graham. "Why Do Catholics Believe in Sacred Tradition?" *The B.C. Catholic*, 15 July 2016, bccatholic.ca/voices/graham-osborne/why-do-catholics-believe-in-sacred-tradition.

147 "According to its etymology, an encyclical (from the Greek enkuklios, kuklos meaning a circle) is nothing more than a circular letter. In modern times, usage has confined the term almost exclusively to certain papal documents which differ in their technical form from the ordinary style of either Bulls or Briefs, and which in their superscription are explicitly addressed to the patriarchs, primates, archbishops, and bishops of the Universal Church in communion with the Apostolic See. By exception, encyclicals are also sometimes addressed to the archbishops and bishops of a particular country." Cited from Catholic Answers. "Encyclical." *Catholic Answers*, 21 Feb. 2019. Web. 23 Apr. 2021.

148 Apostolic exhortations are magisterial documents authored by the pope. They are considered third in importance, after apostolic constitutions and encyclicals. "Exhortations generally encourage a particular virtue or activity. Apostolic exhortations are frequently issued following a Synod of Bishops, in which case they are known as

Patristic Church Fathers,[149] those holy men who lived mostly between the first and the fourth Christian centuries, commented clearly on the proper roles of women. More to the point still, the Church Fathers further agreed on the specific role of *wives*.

Catholic News Herald explains the role of the Church Fathers:

> The Church Fathers were influential theologians, bishops or scholars whose writings explained key Scriptural principles in the early Church. They were not all ordained, not all of them became saints, and they were not infallible. But they had powerful communication skills, personal holiness and doctrinal orthodoxy, so we honor them unofficially as "fathers" for their proximity to the Apostles, their explanations of how to understand and apply Scripture, and their ability to teach the Catholic faith.[150]

I will lay before you the many instances where Magisterial Tradition expresses—in terms of both natural and supernatural law—the manner in which rightly ordered wives ought to comport themselves in a Christian society. I will conclude with a cautionary statement on Saint Pope John Paul II, whom modern-day Catholic feminists credit for their "liberation" from thousands of years of Tradition-imposed bondage.

Some of the earliest writings on the proper roles of women emerge from the Church Fathers. Men like St. Polycarp (AD 65-155), St. John Chrysostom (AD 347-407), St. Jerome (AD 347-420), and St. Augustine of Hippo (AD 354-480) all helped to formulate and codify Church doctrine on the duties of wives.

Certain special souls such as Sts. Ambrose and Augustine are both Doctors of the Church and Church Fathers. These holy men and

---

post-synodal apostolic exhortations. They do not define Church doctrine and are not considered legislative." "Apostolic Exhortation." Wikipedia. Wikimedia Foundation, 07 Apr. 2021. Web. 23 Apr. 2021.

149 Patristics involves the study of the Church Fathers' lives and orthodox teachings.

150 "Catholicnewsherald.com." Catholicnewsherald.com. Web. 19 Apr. 2021. Catholicnewsherald.com/faith/198-news/faith/faith-facts/497-the-fathers-of-the-church.

powerhouses of theological wisdom would be thoroughly scandalized by what has become, by our own day, a commonplace fact of life: married women abandoning their household duties in pursuit of their own wealth and professional accolades. For starters, Apostolic Father and martyr Polycarp's frequently cited *Epistle to the Philippians* (ca. roughly a century after Christ's death) brilliantly warns against the seeking of riches as the "root of all evils." Modern men and women alike do themselves great disservice if they reject his warnings as being too broad or too old fashioned. The fact that this exhortation applies also to men does not mitigate its force in the context of feminist careerism among Christian wives of the twenty first century.

But wait, there's more! St. Polycarp prefigures an attack on what would only be termed, in his day, the anachronism of feminism:

> "But the love of money is the root of all evils." Knowing, therefore, that "as we brought nothing into the world, so we can carry nothing out," let us arm ourselves with the armour of righteousness; and let us teach, first of all, ourselves to walk in the commandments of the Lord. Next, [guide] your wives in the faith given to them, and in love and purity tenderly loving their own husbands in all truth and loving all equally in all chastity; and to train up their children in the knowledge and fear of God. Teach the widows to be discreet as respects the faith of the Lord, praying continually for all, being far from all slandering, evil-speaking, false-witnessing, love of money, and every kind of evil; knowing that they are the altar of God, that He clearly perceives all things, and that nothing is hid from Him, neither reasonings, nor reflections, nor any one of the secret things of the heart.[151]

Today, Polycarp would find the aberration of women fashioning themselves into weak-armed "mini-men," according to the systematic

151 Palmer, Robert Palmer. "The Epistle of Polycarp to the Philippians." *Bible Translation*. Trans, May 2015, Web, 18 Apr. 2021.

eradication of the feminine virtues typically offset by docility, silence and listening, and fealty. As such, these are often esteemed less in our society than their male counterparts. Indeed, the female virtues certainly aren't as "flashy." But they are just as important.

Accordingly, feminists loathe true femininity, mostly due to the fact that they strive to be "noteworthy" in the modern sense—which means notable for their skills in the workplace and outside of the home. Feminine virtues are narrowly tailored, by nature, for homemaking, mothering, privacy, and being a helpmate. Naturally, feminists wish to "swap out" their natural strengths for those of men. (Any woman shares with any man the intelligible goal of Heaven—but in the domestic context, she achieves it through perfectly opposite means, differing formal (*ergon*) and final (*telos*) causes. Hence, in a rightly ordered family, the wife will be good at following whereas the husband will be proficient at leading. In a disordered family, she will seek to supplant him.)[152] In order to survive in the cutthroat workforce of the twenty-first century, feminists have "culturally appropriated"[153] the manly virtues such as breadwinning, audacity, and leadership. Women can never be good at being men, but that won't stop them from trying (and repeatedly failing).

Today, of course, married women seek leadership roles in the workforce, instead of submitting to the rightful leadership of their husbands. While these wives fruitlessly seek manly honor at a job, they too often fail to count the opportunity cost: flourishing with their feminine virtues in the home. That is, nature built them for the homeplace, where they would thrive easily, and yet they remain oblivious to this reality.

The Church Fathers were fully aware of a women's natural fit in

---

152 As my husband, Timothy Gordon, puts it, "Patriarchy is mandatory." (*The Case for Patriarchy*. Crisis Publications, 2021.)

153 Many members of the ideological left accuse anyone of "appropriation" if they assume any characteristic of a race they do not belong to. They, however, miss the fact that "transgender males" appropriate the culture of women, or that women who forgo their feminine natures in pursuit of well-established manly virtues are "appropriating" male virtues.

her home. Hence they believed that the woman is far better suited at home because her unique feminine attributes accommodate the functions and tasks of the home, rather than those of the public sphere. St. John Chrysostom delivers a devastating blow to feminism's insistence on publicizing female life by stating:

> Our life is customarily organized into two spheres: public affairs and private matters, both of which were determined by God. To woman is assigned the presidency of the household; to man, all the business of state, the marketplace, the administration of justice, government, the military, and all other such enterprises. A woman is not able to hurl a spear or shoot an arrow, but she can grasp the distaff, weave at the loom; she correctly disposes of all such tasks that pertain to the household. She cannot express her opinion in a legislative assembly, but she can express it at home, and often she is more shrewd about household matters than her husband. She cannot handle state business well, but she can raise children correctly, and children are our principal wealth. At a glance she can detect the bad behavior of the servants and can manage them carefully. She provides complete security for her husband and frees him from all such household concerns, concerns about money, woolworking, the preparation of food and decent clothing.[154]

Also, St. John Chrysostom tenders a convincing answer to a question no one in his own day asked: *why women are not to be in positions of power over men.* Woman, he argues, was deceived by a "lesser creature" (viz. the serpent in the Garden) unlike Adam, who was deceived by creature of equal dignity (viz. Eve):

> Now it is not the same thing to be deceived by a fellow creature, one of the same kind, as by an inferior and subordinate

154 Chrysostom, St. John. "From the Archives: The Wife's Domain: Christian History Magazine." *Christian History Institute*, no. 17, christianhistoryinstitute.org/magazine/article/women-archives-wifes-domain/.

> animal. This is truly to be deceived. Compared therefore with the woman, he is spoken of as "not deceived." For she was beguiled by an inferior and subject, he by an equal. Again, it is not said of the man, that he "saw the tree was good for food," but of the woman, and that she "did eat, and gave it to her husband": so that he transgressed, not captivated by appetite, but merely from the persuasion of his wife. The woman taught once, and ruined all. On this account therefore he saith, let her not teach.[155]

St. Augustine of Hippo insisted rather strongly that women must assist their husbands in the ways altogether unique to their sex—that is, not as equals to men, but as *complements* to them:

> I don't see what sort of help woman was created to provide man with, if one excludes procreation. If woman is not given to man for help in bearing children, for what help could she be? To till the earth together? If help were needed for that, man would have been a better help for man. The same goes for comfort in solitude. How much more pleasure is it for life and conversation when two friends live together than when a man and a woman cohabitate?[156]

One may reasonably beg to differ with St. Augustine as to the last part of his statement above, but not as to the first part of it: some married couples lack the art of recreational conversation and some do not; no wives, however, lend their husbands as effective a hand in strenuous labor as husbands' friends can. The above Church Fathers are just providing us with what we know to be true already.

In short, a husband does not need a wife to plow a field or to provide him with protection. He does, however, need a wife to provide him with children and a comfortable, welcoming home when he returns

---

155 Chrysostom, St. John. *Compete Works of St. John Chrysostom*, loc. 132419.132433.

156 St. Augustine. *De genesi ad litteram*. 9, 5-9.

from a day's labor. He does need a wife who guards his heart just as he guards her mind and her soul. But the reader should not need anyone to remind him of this. So much of Christian teaching is based on common experience. On the other hand, it is modernity that seeks to complicate and obscure obvious things.

In *The City of God* St. Augustine observes:

> 'And thy turning shall be to thy husband, and he shall rule over thee.' What is said to Cain about his sin, or about the vicious concupiscence of his flesh, is here said of the woman who had sinned; and we are to understand that the husband is to rule his wife as the soul rules the flesh.[157]

Augustine denotes man's natural headship over woman when he writes, "Nor can it be doubted, that it is more consonant with the order of nature that men should bear rule over women, than women over men."[158]

Consonantly, Jerome says, in for *Commentary on Ephesians*: "As long as a woman is for birth and children, she is different from man as body is from soul."[159] The commonsense distinction being made hardly stretches the imagination.

The Angelic Doctor:[160] Men and Women Are Different

St. Thomas Aquinas strengthens what each of the first millennium Fathers taught above: as Christians, we believe that men and women differ in more ways than just our biological makeup. We complement one another in our very differences: "to complement" is a verb meaning that one man and one woman combine in such a way as to maximize

---

157 St. Augustine. *The City of God*, 1993, pp. 487.

158 St. Augustine. *On Marriage and Concupiscence. pp.* 10.

159 St. Jerome. *Commentary on Ephesians.* III ch.5.

160 Saint Thomas Aquinas is often called the "Angelic Doctor."

the strengths of each in the family, such that the whole is greater than the sum of its parts.

St. Thomas will show that it should follow rather closely, then, that men are better suited for some things and women are better suited for others. The family economy maximizes these functional superiorities when Christians submit to the order of nature. Yet our modern minds have been diabolically conditioned to recoil at the mere mention of the natural differences between men and women—and we get *especially* uncomfortable when it is mentioned that men are superior to women at certain things (since feminism has trained us to want to excel at precisely those things we are bad at).

In order to return to a beautiful, natural family life we must unlearn this anti-complementarist propaganda and re-train our minds to accept truths as simple as "only women can have babies and menstrual cycles" and "the average man's muscles and brain are anatomically purposed to different ends than the average woman's." All the biology points us to a clear truth: a woman's place is that of partner and helper to man. Accordingly, man's authority over his wife has been established.

Consider the words of St. Thomas Aquinas on the topic:

> I answer that, it was right for the woman to be made from a rib of man. First, to signify the social union of man and woman, for the woman should neither use authority over man,' and so she was not made from his head; nor was it right for her to be subject to man's contempt as his slave, and so she was not made from his feet.[161]

Women, St. Thomas Aquinas suggests, are not equal with men insofar as they are unfit to hold authority over men; but they aren't slaves, either. Woman's place is at man's side helping him to discharge daily tasks which bring the family closer to God. When a woman

161 Aquinas, Thomas. "Question 92. The Production of the Woman." *Summa Theologiae: The Production of the Woman* (Prima Pars, Q. 92), www.newadvent.org/summa/1092.htm. ST, q. 92, a.3.

ventures away from his side—as our first parents Adam and Eve show us—catastrophe ensues. Mainly, the tasks women are to help men with are procreation and the completion of household duties:

> The two theologians who most profoundly influenced the Catholic concept of woman were Ss. Augustine and Thomas Aquinas. Whereas Augustine largely derived his notions of woman and heterosexual relationships from Plato, Aquinas essentially subscribed to Aristotle's anthropological theories. (Briody, pp. 78-88.) For Augustine and Aquinas, writes Kari Elisabeth Borresen, the sole reason for the creation of woman is the preservation of the human race; the priority of Adam's creation is seen as determining Eve's dependence on him; and the image of God can be found only in man, because woman is a *mas occasionatus*, or a "misbegotten male." (Borresen, p. 158.) Woman's imperfection is not limited to her bodily characteristics but also extends to her rational faculties; as a consequence, man is more perfect in reason and stronger in virtue than woman. (Borresen, p. 172.) After the Fall the special punishments inflicted on Eve that included painful childbirth and domination by Adam rein forced her subordination. (Borresen, p. 214.)[162]

Furthermore, Aquinas remarks that a wife's natural subordination to her husband proves consistent with the teachings of St. Paul:

> First, St. Paul states what should be entrusted to their care; second, how to exercise care; third, the reason behind this advice. In regard to the first he says, "having a care of the house": the wisdom of a woman builds her house, but folly with her own hands tears it down (Prov 14:1). But in exercising care a woman should observe two things, for women are easily

162 Dawes, Helena. "The Catholic Church and the Woman Question: Catholic Feminism in Italy in the Early 1900s." *The Catholic Historical Review,* 2011, pp. 484-526.

> angered: there is no anger above the anger of a woman (Sir 25:23); therefore, he says, "gentle". As if to say: let them govern in meekness. The other thing she must observe is subordination, because when a woman has power she tries to oppose her husband's plans: a woman, if she have superiority, is contrary to her husband (Sir 25:30). Therefore, he says, "obedient to their husbands", hence it is said: your desire shall be for your husband, and he shall rule over you (Gen 3:16). And this, "that the word of God be not blasphemed," i.e., that their disobedience not be an occasion for blasphemy.[163]

And Thomas goes *even further* when he comments on the damage done by a woman's "dominion" over man: "The [Peripatetic] Philosopher says that the dominion of women is the death of a family, as tyrants of a commonwealth."[164]

Although feminism did not exist in his own day, Thomas addresses sexual egalitarianism head on: "Good order would have been wanting in the human family if some were not governed by others wiser than themselves. So, by such a kind of subjection woman is naturally subject to man, because in man the discretion of reason predominates."[165] In his *Shorter Summa,* Thomas continues to attack egalitarianism: "So [the Devil] sought to lead man astray from the straight path of justice by attacking him on his weaker side; that is, he tempted the woman, in whom the gift of light or wisdom shone with a lesser brilliance."[166]

Aquinas develops the theme of male-female difference even further by writing:

---

163 Aquinas, Thomas. *Commentary on the Letters to the Corinthians*, pp. 437.

164 Lacher, Fr. OP. "Saint Thomas Aquinas, Commentary on the Letters of Saint Paul to the Philippians, Colossians, Thessalonians, Timothy, Titus, and Philemon." *Aquinas Institute for the Study of Sacred Doctrine*, Lander, 2012, pp. 272.

165 Aquinas, Thomas. "Summa Theologica." *Summa Theologica*. New York: Benziger Brothers, 1948. q.92 a.1 reply 2.

166 Aquinas, Thomas. *Shorter Summa*. Sophia Institute Press; Manchester, New Hampshire, 1993, Paragraph 189.

> If the aforesaid union were to be dissolved, it would seem to violate justice. For a female needs a male, not only for reproduction, as is the case with other animals, but also for governance, because the male is both more perfect with respect to reason and is stronger in his capacities. It appears to be clearly unsuitable if a wife could send her husband away, since a wife is naturally subject to her husband as her governor, for it is not in the power of the one who is subject to another to depart from his rule. Therefore it would be contrary to the natural order if a wife could desert her husband.[167]

Further, Thomas says in the *Shorter Summa*, "The sin came to the man through the woman's blandishments. He, however, as the Apostle says in 1 Timothy 2: 14, 'was not seduced,' as the woman was."[168]

It proves extremely safe to say that, at the height of the Scholastic period, Thomas Aquinas reinforced the Patristic teachings on sexual difference. Whenever Aquinas and Augustine agree on a matter—alongside the other Patristic powerhouses—a Christian can be very certain that the proposition is safe to believe in.

The Popes down through the centuries have only reinforced—only recently questioning or appearing to question—the longstanding teaching on the proper role of women.

Ask Your Holy Father(s)

Popes have been commenting on the proper role of women since the very beginnings of the Church. One of the very first popes makes the point. And thereafter, very few popes troubled to reinforce the obvious until the first pope of the 20th century. That is, no "feminist" pope challenged the commonsense precepts of sexual differences until it became culturally relevant to do so, well into the 20th century. The

167 Aquinas, Thomas. *Summa Contra Gentiles,* II, pp. 123.

168 Aquinas, Thomas. *Shorter Summa*. Sophia Institute Press, Manchester, New Hampshire, 1993, Paragraph 191.

fourth pope ever, Pope Clement I (AD 88 – 99),[169] advises thus to married Christian women just a few decades after the death of Christ:

> You were submissive to your officials and paid the older men among you the respect due to them. The young you trained to habits of self-restraint and sedateness. The wives you enjoined to discharge all their duties with a conscience pure and undefiled, and to cherish a dutiful affection for their husbands; you taught them also to stay within the established norm of obedience in managing the household with decency and consummate prudence.[170]

"To stay within the established norm of obedience in managing the household" is one way of saying: "married women: you ought to know that your place is *at home, tending to your husbands' needs and comforts.*"

Moving on through the lineage of popes, the 255th pope, Blessed Pius IX (AD 1846 - 1878), reminded us of the wisdom of St. Augustine in regards to a wife's obedience to her husband in his 1849 encyclical, *Nostis Et Nobiscum:*

> For, to use the words of St. Augustine, "the Catholic Church attaches itself not only to God Himself but also to love and charity of one's neighbor, so that it excels in healing all the diseases which men suffer for their sins. It trains and teaches boys in a boyish manner, young men strongly, old men calmly, in accordance with the individual's bodily and spiritual age. It subjects wives to their husbands in chaste and faithful obedience, not for the gratification of lust but for the begetting of progeny and the society of the family; and it places husbands

169 Years in brackets designate the span of a Holy Father's pontificate, not his lifespan.

170 St. Clement. "First Epistle to the Corinthians: EWTN." *EWTN Global Catholic Television Network*, https://www.ewtn.com/catholicism/library/first-epistle-to-the-corinthians-12498.

> over their wives not in scorn of the weaker sex but under the law of pure love."[171]

A married woman's narrow tailoring for birth and children proves, undoubtedly, a *verboten* proposition today. Christian women evidently forgot, sometime between the first Christian century and the twentieth, exactly what God designed us to do. Being made for birth and children means that one forsakes all pursuits which prove to be distractions from those procreative ends. In a reinvigoration of the bimillennial point, during the heyday of first-wave feminism (which had been inaugurated roughly fifty years prior), the 256th pope, Pope Leo XIII (AD 1878 - 1903), reinforces Clement's precept—with no alteration—that women are made for submission to husbands, child-rearing, and domestic chores:

> Women, again, are not suited for certain occupations; a woman is by nature fitted for home-work, and it is that which is best adapted at once to preserve her modesty and to promote the good bringing up of children and the well-being of the family.[172]

The same Pope Leo XIII explicates the distinct duties of each spouse in his encyclical, *Arcanum Divinae*:

> Secondly, the mutual duties of husband and wife have been defined, and their several rights accurately established. They are bound, namely, to have such feelings for one another as to cherish always very great mutual love, to be ever faithful to their marriage vow, and to give one another an unfailing and unselfish help. The husband is the chief of the family and the head of the wife. The woman, because she is flesh of his flesh, and bone of his bone, must be subject to her husband and obey

---

171 Pius IX. *Nostis Et Nobiscum.* Papal Encyclicals, 25 Apr. 2017, https://www.papalencyclicals.net/pius09/p9nostis.htm.

172 Leo XIII. *Rerum Novarum: Encyclical Letter of Pope Leo XIII on the Condition of Labor* (with Discussion Club Outline). New York: Paulist Press, 1940, Section 42.

> him; not, indeed, as a servant, but as a companion, so that her obedience shall be wanting in neither honor nor dignity. Since the husband represents Christ, and since the wife represents the Church, let there always be, both in him who commands and in her who obeys, a heaven-born love guiding both in their respective duties.[173]

Pope Leo XIII makes a brief, yet meaningful plea that husbands are the heads of their families in *Sapientiae Christianae*: "This is a suitable moment for us to exhort especially heads of families to govern their households."[174]

The succeeding pontiff, the 257th, Pope Pius X (AD 1903 - 1914), also strongly derided the newly inaugurated feminist attempt to subvert God's holy order and hierarchy of the Christian household in his *Address to Delegation of the Union of Italian Catholic Ladies*, in 1909:

> After creating man, God created woman and determined her mission, namely, that of being man's companion, helpmate and consolation.[175]

In the same Address, Pius confirms the longstanding Christian view that God's sexually relevant sequence of creation—man before woman—is indeed meaningful. Pius also repudiates the early twentieth century developments of radical egalitarianism he noted within feminism:

> It is a mistake, therefore, to maintain that woman's rights are the same as man's. Women in war or parliament are outside their proper sphere, and their position there would be the desperation and ruin of society. Woman, created as man's

---

173 Leo XIII. *Arcanum Divinae, February 10, 1880,* Web. 22 Apr. 2021, Section 11.

174 Leo XIII. *Sapientiae Christianae*. Papal Encyclicals, 26 Apr. 2017, Web. 23 Apr. 2021, Section 42.

175 Pius X, "*Address to Delegation of the Union of Italian Catholic Ladies,*" 1909.

> companion, must so remain under the power of love and affection, but always under his power.[176]

Thirdly, Pius points up the fundamentally Luciferian ethos of "*non serviam*" endemic to feminism; feminism attempts to "play God":

> How mistaken, therefore, is that misguided feminism which seeks to correct God's work. It is like a mechanic trying to correct the signs and movements of the universe.[177]

Finally, Pius in his Address marks the selfsame distinction that this book has marked in multiple places: viz. indisputably the Bible avers the simultaneity of woman's dependence upon, *but not* slavery before, man:

> Scripture, and especially the three epistles of St. Paul, emphasizes woman's dependence on man, her love and assistance, but not her slavery to him.[178]

Think about it this way: the inchoate stench of feminism wasn't nearly so pungent in the early 1900's as it is today, but it was certainly foul enough that Pope St. Pius X felt the need to address it with an audience full of *women.* (Most modern men would be quaking in the Cotton Dockers they share with their wives.)

One wonders what Pius X would think of Christians today, especially amid the profound feminist stink befouling nearly every single household within Christendom. A more general clue about Pius X's view of modern feminism is to be found in in his *Oath Against Modernism.* In his Oath, Pius X attacks "modernism," which in other places he refers to as the "synthesis of all heresies,"[179] by preempting any heretical attempt to alter Catholic teaching in order to accommodate the biases

---

176 Ibid.

177 Ibid.

178 Ibid.

179 Pius X. *Pascendi Dominici Gregis.* 1907. Pope Pius defines and condemns modernism in both this encyclical and again in his Oath, three years later.

of the modern day. Interrogate how the "Christian feminist" has grown accustomed to the indulgence of their changing view of their own role:

> I firmly embrace and accept each and every definition that has been set forth and declared by the unerring teaching authority of the Church, especially those principal truths which are directly opposed to the errors of this day… I entirely reject the heretical' misrepresentation that dogmas evolve and change from one meaning to another different from the one which the Church held previously… I firmly hold, then, and shall hold to my dying breath the belief of the Fathers in the charism of truth, which certainly is, was, and always will be in the succession of the episcopacy from the apostles. The purpose of this is, then, not that dogma may be tailored according to what seems better and more suited to the culture of each age; rather, that the absolute and immutable truth preached by the apostles from the beginning may never be believed to be different, may never be understood in any other way.[180]

The tailoring of immutable truth to fit the preferences of the day encourages many modern wives to ponder: "Surely, I am made for something greater than just being a lowly housewife…". *Let me stop you right there: you're not.* Mischaracterize and demean the sacred duties of housewife as you wish. But a woman's importance to her family is vital and the importance of her role in society doesn't require her to cross the threshold beyond her own home.

Here we postpone treatment of the Magisterium of the next anti-feminist pontiff, the 259th—namely Pius XI's (AD 1922 - 1939)—on account of its standalone profundity. Accordingly, it deserves its own section (which comprises this chapter's next section).

The 260th in the Petrine succession, Pope Pius XII (AD 1939 - 1958)—according to liberal *The Catholic Historical Review*—harbored the following view of married women who stayed at home:

180 Pius X. *The Oath Against Modernism.* 1 Sept. 1910.

> And what of married women who did stay home? Initially, Pius XII's attitude toward them seemed as conservative as any of his predecessors. In one of his early addresses to newlyweds, he reconfirmed the traditional view that the wife was to be subject to her husband in love and that her husband was to exercise authority over her with love and respect. He even cited the misogynist defense of male authority found in I Timothy 2:13-14, which proclaimed that women were subordinate because they were the first to be deceived by the serpent.[181]

Designating Holy Scripture "misogynist" really takes some intestinal fortitude, if a misguided species of it. Nonetheless, the author's point cannot be denied: Pius XII agreed with Scripture that a wife owes obedience to her husband. The same author acknowledges the unsung fact that Pius XII's successor, the more liberal 261st pope John XXIII (AD 1958 – 1963) wasn't liberal about spousal power dynamics:

> His successor, John XXIII (1958-1963), essentially agreed. However popular he became as a symbol of the renewal of Church and society, his pronouncements on women proclaimed no revolution. In an address to representatives of a Congress on "Women and Social Life," for instance, he acknowledged that modern conditions tended to establish an "almost absolute equality of women with men," but he did not give unqualified approval to this trend. In words similar to those of his immediate predecessors, he asserted that a "parity of rights" had to be supported in all appropriate areas, but this did not imply a "parity of functions." On the contrary, the Creator gave women unique qualities and inclinations which fitted her for the vocation of motherhood. Some situations, he added, made

181 Camp, Richard L. "From Passive Subordination to Complementary Partnership: The Papal Conception of a Woman's Place in Church and Society since 1878." *The Catholic Historical Review*, vol. 76, no. 3, 1990, http://www.jstor.org/stable/25023342, Accessed 21 Apr. 2022, pp. 506–25,

> this vocation more difficult, the most serious of which was the employment of wives outside the home. "Anyone can understand that this prolonged absence from home and the attendant dispersion of energies creates a situation which prevents the wife from carrying out her duties of wife and mother, as she should." To enable the wife to alleviate this situation, he supported the principle of the family wage. He even urged women, in another address, not to allow their activities in the world outside the home to undermine their "open and delicate spirit." Fulfilling this promise might be very difficult, for women "are called to an effort perhaps greater than men, if you take into consideration women's natural frailty in certain respects."[182]

So it turns out, the popes wanting "renewal" in the Church did not want a reconfiguration of the created duality of human sexuality. Even the *more liberal*, second "Vatican Two pope"—the 262nd in total—Paul VI (AD 1963 - 1978), in *Inter Insigniores,* makes it painfully clear that the differences between the sexes remain unchanging, non-negotiable, non-negligible parts of God's will and plan for humanity:

> Could one say that, since Christ is now in the heavenly condition, from now on it is a matter of indifference whether he be represented by a man or by a woman, since 'at the resurrection men and women do not marry' (Mat.22:30)? But this text does not mean that the distinction between man and women, insofar as it determines the identity proper to the person, is suppressed in the glorified state; what holds for us also holds for Christ. It is indeed evident that in human beings the difference of sex exercises an important influence, much deeper than, for example, ethnic differences: the latter do not affect the human person as intimately as the difference of sex, which is directly ordained both for the communion of persons and for the generation of human beings. In Biblical Revelation this

182 Ibid.

> difference is the effect of God's will from the beginning: 'male and female he created them' (Gen 1:27).[183]

Further, Paul VI had this to say on the effect the equalization of rights has had on women:

> Equalization of rights must not be allowed to degenerate into an egalitarian and impersonal elimination of differences. The egalitarianism blindly sought by our materialistic society has but little care for the specific good of persons; contrary to appearances it is unconcerned with what is suitable or unsuitable to women. There is, thus, a danger of unduly masculinizing women or else simply depersonalizing them.[184]

Equally shocking to most traditional Catholics,[185] the issue of working mothers is tackled not only by the liberal "pope of the council" (or the anti-feminist heroes of tradition such as Leo XIII or Pius XI), but also by the liberalizing *Second Vatican Council* which he oversaw. As stated in one of Vatican Two's four sacred constitutions, *Gaudium et Spes*: "The children, especially the younger among them, need the care of their mother at home. This domestic role of hers must be safely preserved, though the legitimate social progress of women should not be underrated on that account."[186]

What the document's last line lacks in *clarity*— "legitimate social

---

183 Paul VI. *Inter Insigniores.* Papal Encyclicals. 26 Apr. 2017, Web. 23 Apr. 2021, Section 5.

184 Paul VI, "January 31, 1976, Speech to the Study Commission on Women," *The Pope Speaks*, 1976, pp. 164-165.

185 The Second Vatican Council is widely blamed among many traditional Catholics for introducing "modernism" into the Church and for inverting many traditional principles long held throughout the Church's history.

186 Paul VI. *Gaudium Et Spes*, 1965, https://www.vatican.va/archive/hist_councils/ii_vatican_council/documents/vat-ii_const_19651207_gaudium-et-spes_en.html, section 52. For this citation, and a handful of others in this chapter, I am indebted to the early research of my husband and his brother, David Gordon, in an early draft of what became my husband's book, *The Case for Patriarchy,* and also what will in the future become my brother-in-law's book forthcoming on St. Michael's Media, *No Christian Feminism.* That

progress"—its fine line makes up for in force—"need the care of their mother at home."

Similarly, to the chagrin of 21st century feminists, even ultra-progressive Pope Francis (AD 2013 – present), the 266th pontiff, offered some thornily traditional opinions on the value of sexual differences between men and women:

> Also, valuing one's own body in its femininity or masculinity is necessary if I am going to be able to recognize myself in an encounter with someone who is different. In this way we can joyfully accept the specific gifts of another man or woman, the work of God the Creator, and find mutual enrichment. It is not a healthy attitude which would seek to cancel out sexual difference because it no longer knows how to confront it.[187]

Advising women to keep Our Lady as our guide, Pope Francis stated in *Vultum Dei Quaerere*: "Mary Most Holy can serve as your example. She was able to receive the Word because she was a woman of silence – no barren or empty silence, but rather one rich and overflowing. The silence of the Virgin Mother was also full of love, for love always prepares us to welcome the Other and others."[188]

The Anti-feminist Declarations of Pope Pius XI

Pope Pius XI arguably delivers the most devastating onslaught against feminism.[189] Pope Pius XI greatly expands upon Aquinas's insight that a wife's "most noble office [equals her role as] a wife and

---

is, before their joint manuscript was split into two separate feminism books, I benefitted by reading a handful of citations included in this chapter.

187 Pope Francis. Encyclical letter *Laudato Si'.* 18 June 2015, No. 155.

188 Pope Francis. *Apostolic Constitution Vultum Dei Quaerere on Women's Contemplative Life.* 2016, Section 33.

189 Pope Pius XI wrote so extensively on the proper role of women that I felt it necessary to dedicate an entire section to his teaching.

a mother and a companion." The pontiff offers the following gloss, on wifely subjection:

> This subjection, however, does not deny or take away the liberty which fully belongs to the woman both in view of her dignity as a human person, and in view of her most noble office as wife and mother and companion; nor does it bid her obey her husband's every request if not in harmony with right reason or with the dignity due to wife; nor, in fine, does it imply that the wife should be put on a level with those persons who in law are called minors, to whom it is not customary to allow free exercise of their rights on account of their lack of mature judgment, or of their ignorance of human affairs. But it forbids that exaggerated liberty which cares not for the good of the family; it forbids that in this body which is the family, the heart be separated from the head to the great detriment of the whole body and the proximate danger of ruin. For if the man is the head, the woman is the heart, and as he occupies the chief place in ruling, so she may and ought to claim for herself the chief place in love.[190]

Pius states that the household emptied of its laboring mother greatly harms the family. In 1930's *Casti Connubii* the pontiff puts it this way:

> If, however, for this purpose, private resources do not suffice, it is the duty of the public authority to supply for the insufficient forces of individual effort, particularly in a matter which is of such importance to the common weal, touching as it does the maintenance of the family and married people. If families, particularly those in which there are many children, have not suitable dwellings; if the husband cannot find employment and means of livelihood; if the necessities of life cannot be

190 Pius XI. *Casti Connubii.* 1930, www.vatican.va/content/pius-xi/en/encyclicals/documents/hf_p-xi_enc_19301231_casti-connubii.html, Section 27.

> purchased except at exorbitant prices; if even the mother of the family is compelled to go forth and seek a living by her own labor; if she, too, in the ordinary or great harm of the home even extraordinary labors of childbirth, is deprived of proper food, medicine, and the assistance of a skilled physician, it is patent to all to what an extent married people may lose heart, and how home life and the observance of God's commands are rendered difficult for them; indeed it is obvious how great a peril can arise to the public security and to the welfare and very life of civil society itself when such men are reduced to that condition of desperation that, having nothing which they fear to lose, they are emboldened to hope for chance advantage from the upheaval of the state and of established order.[191]

Commenting on *Casti Connubii*, Helena Dawes writes:

> On the basis of this fundamentally antifeminist dogma, the Catholic Church continued to make pronouncements on issues affecting women. In February 1880 Leo XIII's encyclical on Christian marriage, *Arcanum Divinae Sapientiae*, stressed that Christianity had liberated woman from pagan servitude, yet reaffirmed the patriarchal values of Catholic dogma. Women's subordination was stated in even stronger terms in Pius XI's *Casti Connubii* of December 1930, which viewed demands for women's emancipation as debasing the womanly character and the dignity of motherhood.[192]

"Debasing the dignity of motherhood," indeed. Consider the following excerpts from *Casti Connubii* and say a prayer in thanksgiving for the clarity in which its pontifical author articulated the immutable truths of our Holy Mother Church.

On wifely obedience and the neglect of her womanly charges:

---

191 Ibid. Section 120.

192 Dawes, Helena. "The Catholic Church and the Woman Question: Catholic Feminism in Italy in the Early 1900s." *The Catholic Historical Review* July, 2011, pp. 484-526.

> The same false teachers who try to dim the luster of conjugal faith and purity do not scruple to do away with the honorable and trusting obedience which the woman owes to the man. Many of them even go further and assert that such a subjection of one party to the other is unworthy of human dignity, that the rights of husband and wife are equal; wherefore, they boldly proclaim the emancipation of women has been or ought to be effected. This emancipation in their ideas must be threefold, in the ruling of the domestic society, in the administration of family affairs and in the rearing of the children. It must be social, economic, physiological: - physiological, that is to say, the woman is to be freed at her own good pleasure from the burdensome duties properly belonging to a wife as companion and mother (We have already said that this is not an emancipation but a crime); social, inasmuch as the wife being freed from the cares of children and family, should, to the neglect of these, be able to follow her own bent and devote herself to business and even public affairs; finally economic, whereby the woman even without the knowledge and against the wish of her husband may be at liberty to conduct and administer her own affairs, giving her attention chiefly to these rather than to children, husband and family.[193]

Working outside of the home, he contends, debases the woman, her husband, and her family. He goes on to comment on how the dignity of motherhood is also adversely affected when the mother follows a diabolic inversion of liberty and emancipation:

> This, however, is not the true emancipation of woman, nor that rational and exalted liberty which belongs to the noble office of a Christian woman and wife; it is rather the debasing of the womanly character and the dignity of motherhood, and

193 Pius XI. *Casti Connubii. 1930*, www.vatican.va/content/pius-xi/en/encyclicals/documents/hf_p-xi_enc_19301231_casti-connubii.html, Section 74.

> indeed of the whole family, as a result of which the husband suffers the loss of his wife, the children of their mother, and the home and the whole family of an ever watchful guardian. More than this, this false liberty and unnatural equality with the husband is to the detriment of the woman herself, for if the woman descends from her truly regal throne to which she has been raised within the walls of the home by means of the Gospel, she will soon be reduced to the old state of slavery (if not in appearance, certainly in reality) and become as amongst the pagans the mere instrument of man.[194]

Pope Pius XI well understood that woman's abandonment of her duties to her home leaves the family bereft of warmth and togetherness:

> We see a woman who in order to augment her husband's earnings, betakes herself also to a factory, leaving her house abandoned during her absence. The house, untidy and small perhaps before, becomes even more miserable for lack of care. Members of the family work separately in four quarters of the city and with different working hours. Scarcely ever do they find themselves together for dinner or rest after work still less for prayer in common. What is left of family life? And what attractions can it offer to children?[195]

According to Pius, the mother cannot be replaced or placed into a non-domestic setting because her instincts are intrinsic to her female nature:

> It is clear that woman's task thus understood cannot be improvised. Motherly instinct is in her a human instinct, not determined by nature down to the details of its application. It

---

194 Ibid. Section 75.

195 Pius XII. *Questa Grande Vostra Adunata*. Woman's Duties in Social and Political Life, Address of His Holiness Pope Pius XII to Members of Various Catholic Women's Associations, 1945. http://catholictradition.org/Encyclicals/questa1.htm.

> is directed by free will and this in turn is guided by intellect. Hence comes its moral value and its dignity but also imperfection which must be compensated for and redeemed by education.[196]

Therefore, he leaves us to ponder the following question, with an insinuated answer:

> Has woman's position been thereby improved? Equality of rights with man brought with it her abandonment of the home where she reigned as queen, and her subjection to the same work strain and working hours. It entails depreciation of her true dignity and the solid foundation of all her rights which is her characteristic feminine role, and the intimate co-ordination of the two sexes. The end intended by God for the good of all human society, especially for the family, is lost sight of. In concessions made to woman one can easily see not respect for her dignity or her mission, but an attempt to foster the economic and military power of the totalitarian state to which all must inexorably be subordinated. To restore as far as possible the honor of the woman's and mother's place in the home: that is the watchword one hears now from many quarters like a cry of alarm, as if the world were awakening, terrified by the fruits of material and scientific progress of which it before was so proud.[197]

The website, *The Way*, urges women to look to Our Lady for guidance if they are struggling with an attachment to their true vocations as wives and mothers:

> On Christmas Day 1931, Pius XI issued an encyclical entitled *Lux Veritatis*. Pius addresses himself to how mothers, especially 'those mothers of our day who, wearied of childbearing, or of

196 Ibid.

197 Ibid.

> the matrimonial bond, have neglected or violated the obligation they assumed, should look and meditate intently upon Mary...' In doing so Pius hopes that these mothers will receive through the 'Queen of Heaven' the grace to 'become ashamed of the dishonor branded on the great sacrament of matrimony and be moved, as far as possible, to attain to her wonderfully exalted virtues'.[198]

Below is the full passage in *Lux Veritatis* referenced in the above commentary:

> Our predecessor, Leo XIII of happy memory, says: "Fathers of families indeed have in Joseph a glorious pattern of vigilance and paternal prudence; mothers have in the most holy Virgin Mother of God a remarkable example of love and modesty and submission of mind, and of perfect faith; but the children of a family have in Jesus, who was subject to them, a divine model of obedience, which they may admire, and worship and imitate." (Apostolic Letter, Neminem fugit, January 14, 1882.) But in a more special manner it is fitting that those mothers of this our age, who being weary, whether of offspring or of the marriage bond, have the office they have undertaken degraded and neglected, may look up to Mary and meditate intently on her who has raised this grave duty of motherhood to such high nobility. For in this way there is hope that they may be led, by the help of grace of the heavenly Queen, to feel shame for the dishonour done to the great sacrament of matrimony, and may happily be stirred up to follow after the wondrous praise of her virtues, by every effort in their power.[199]

Pope Pius XI also addresses the related question of the ramifications of women who work outside the home. As to be expected, he speaks

---

198 Leonard, Richard. "Beloved Daughters: 100 Years of Papal Teaching on Women." Melbourne, Australia: David Lovell, 2018, https://www.theway.org.uk/back/s093Leonard.pdf.

199 Pius XI. *Lux Veritatis*. Papal Encyclicals, 1931, Retrieved. 22 Apr. 2021, Section 49.

bluntly. In his encyclical *Quadragesimo Anno,* dated May 15, 1931, Pius makes mention that the husband ought to be paid a fair and just wage so that the household doesn't suffer an "intolerable abuse" by the wife working away from the home to compensate for her husband's low wages:

> In the first place, the worker must be paid a wage sufficient to support him and his family. That the rest of the family should also contribute to the common support, according to the capacity of each, is certainly right, as can be observed especially in the families of farmers, but also in the families of many craftsmen and small shopkeepers. But to abuse the years of childhood and the limited strength of women is grossly wrong. Mothers, concentrating on household duties, should work primarily in the home or in its immediate vicinity. It is an intolerable abuse, and to be abolished at all cost, for mothers on account of the father's low wage to be forced to engage in gainful occupations outside the home to the neglect of their proper cares and duties, especially the training of children. Every effort must therefore be made that fathers of families receive a wage large enough to meet ordinary family needs adequately. But if this cannot always be done under existing circumstances, social justice demands that changes be introduced as soon as possible whereby such a wage will be assured to every adult workingman. It will not be out of place here to render merited praise to all, who with a wise and useful purpose, have tried and tested various ways of adjusting the pay for work to family burdens in such a way that, as these increase, the former may be raised and indeed, if the contingency arises, there may be enough to meet extraordinary needs.[200]

---

200 Pius XI. *Quadragesimo Anno* (May 15, 1931). 1931, https://www.vatican.va/content/pius-xi/en/encyclicals/documents/hf_p-xi_enc_19310515_quadragesimo-anno.html, Section 71.

On the waning role of the "domestic environment" Pius writes in *Divini Illius Magistri:*

> The declining influence of domestic environment is further weakened by another tendency, prevalent almost everywhere today, which, under one pretext or another, for economic reasons, or for reasons of industry, trade or politics, causes children to be more and more frequently sent away from home even in their tenderest years. And there is a country where the children are actually being torn from the bosom of the family, to be formed (or, to speak more accurately, to be deformed and depraved) in godless schools and associations, to irreligion and hatred, according to the theories of advanced socialism; and thus is renewed in a real and more terrible manner the slaughter of the Innocents.[201]

After all, novel is the notion that a woman cannot be "fulfilled" by her domestic duties and therefore should occupy her valuable time with other endeavors. Throughout most of Christian history, there existed universal agreement that a godly woman remains at home to tend to the needs of her husband and any children that may come along.

The Pro- (and Anti-) Feminist Declarations of Pope John Paul II

Cue the 264th pope, John Paul II (AD 1978 – 2005), to attempt to undo the prolific anti-feminist teachings of Pius XI (and virtually all his forebears). *Sort of;* as we will see below, John Paul II seemed to harbor conflicting views on the sex revolution. Up to this point, Church Fathers, Scholastics, saints, martyrs, philosophers, doctors, and popes all agreed that women ought to remain at home by God's design. Then came Pope John Paul II and his modern *Catechism*, which attempted to resuscitate a proposition which never had life to begin with. But

201 Pius XI. *Divini Illius magistri.* Papal Encyclicals, 1929, Retrieved 19 Apr. 2022, from https://www.papalencyclicals.net/pius11/p11rappr.htm, Section 73.

even the "feminist" pope proved extremely ambivalent about his own embrace of feminism.

On wifely work, feminists find refuge from the onslaught of anti-feminist Tradition in a passage from Pope St. John Paul's *Familiaris Consortio:*

> Without intending to deal with all the various aspects of the vast and complex theme of the relationships between women and society, and limiting these remarks to a few essential points, one cannot but observe that in the specific area of family life a widespread social and cultural tradition has considered women's role to be exclusively that of wife and mother, without adequate access to public functions which have generally been reserved for men. There is no doubt that the equal dignity and responsibility of men and women fully justifies women's access to public functions. On the other hand the true advancement of women requires that clear recognition be given to the value of their maternal and family role, by comparison with all other public roles and all other professions. Furthermore, these roles and professions should be harmoniously combined, if we wish the evolution of society and culture to be truly and fully human.[202]

Pope John Paul II adds gloss to his confusing earlier statements in his Letter *to Women*, applauding women in various roles,[203] but most troublingly, for "women who work":

> Thank you, *women who are mothers!* You have sheltered human beings within yourselves in a unique experience of joy and

---

202 John Paul II. *Apostolic Exhortation Familiaris Consortio of His Holiness Pope John Paul II to the Episcopate, to the Clergy and to the Faithful of the Whole Catholic Church Regarding the Role of the Christian Family in the Modern World.* Ottawa: *Canadian Conference of Catholic Bishops*, 1982, Section 23.

203 I've included nearly the entire section here, not just the passage pertaining to "women who work," because Pope John Paul II has some valuable thoughts regarding *true* femininity worth reading.

> travail. This experience makes you become God's own smile upon the newborn child, the one who guides your child's first steps, who helps it to grow, and who is the anchor as the child makes its way along the journey of life. Thank you, *women who are wives!* You irrevocably join your future to that of your husbands, in a relationship of mutual giving, at the service of love and life. Thank you, *women who are daughters* and *women who are sisters!* Into the heart of the family, and then of all society, you bring the richness of your sensitivity, your intuitiveness, your generosity and fidelity.
>
> Thank you, *women who work!* You are present and active in every area of life-social, economic, cultural, artistic and political. In this way you make an indispensable contribution to the growth of a culture which unites reason and feeling, to a model of life ever open to the sense of "mystery", to the establishment of economic and political structures ever more worthy of humanity. Thank you, *consecrated women!* Following the example of the greatest of women, the Mother of Jesus Christ, the Incarnate Word, you open yourselves with obedience and fidelity to the gift of God's love. You help the Church and all mankind to experience a "spousal" relationship to God, one which magnificently expresses the fellowship which God wishes to establish with his creatures. Thank you, *every woman,* for the simple fact of being *a woman!* Through the insight which is so much a part of your womanhood you enrich the world's understanding and help to make human relations more honest and authentic.[204]

Many feminists argue that Pope John Paul II, in these remarks, gives his blessing for wives to work. However, he makes no specific reference to working women who have husbands or children. This is weaponized

---

204 John Paul II. "Letter to Women (June 29, 1995): *Letter to Women,* 29 June 1995, https://www.vatican.va/content/john-paul-ii/en/letters/1995/documents/hf_jp-ii_let_29061995_women.html, Section 2.

ambiguity in its classic form. But let's imagine for the sake of argument that this *one* pope is of the opinion that married women are permitted to abandon their domestic duties: what of it?

Catholic feminists argue that many of the above passages proscribing non-domestic wifely labor *also permit* working mothers simply because they mention the word "work" when referencing what a woman does around the homestead. It doesn't require much abstraction to distinguish that the "work" being done at home is licit and fundamentally differs from "work" being done away from the home—which is, in almost all cases, not licit. In one instance a woman cares for her own domestic duties and in the other she leaves her duties for others to complete.

During the papacy of Pope John Paul II "new feminism" was being hotly discussed within the hierarchy of the Church. So much so, that in 2004 the Roman Congregation for the Doctrine of Faith released *Letter to the Bishops of the Catholic Church on the Collaboration of Men and Women in the Church and in the World.* Theologian Gösta Hallonsten describes the letter as:

> The *Letter to the Bishops of the Catholic Church on the Collaboration of Men and Women in the Church and the World* of 2004 gives a good introduction to the basic traits of this new feminism. The document was issued by the Roman Congregation for the Doctrine of Faith, the Vatican's department for questions of doctrine and theology. Normally, this congregation only acts defensively, reacting to what is considered false teaching. To some extent this letter follows the traditional pattern, reacting to an alleged antagonism between men and women, promoted by radical feminism.[205]

However, Gösta's essay, "The New Catholic Feminism.: Tradition

205 Hallonsten, Gösta. "The New Catholic Feminism.: Tradition and Renewal in Catholic Gender Theology." *Christian Masculinity: Men and Religion in Northern Europe in the 19th and 20th Centuries*, edited by Yvonne Maria Werner, 1st ed., Leuven University Press, 2011, https://doi.org/10.2307/j.ctt9qdxtn.16. Accessed 15 Apr. 2022, pp. 275–92.

and Renewal in Catholic Gender Theology" goes on to describe startling modernization motives included in the above mentioned letter. It seems to me that "the alleged antagonism between men and women, promoted by radical feminism" wasn't the only goal of the letter:

> The document has three main parts, in addition to its preamble and conclusion. First, and most extended, is the treatment of 'Basic Elements of the Biblical Vision of the Human Person' (II). There follow two chapters on the importance of feminine values in society (III) as well as in the Church (IV). The biblical section testifies clearly to the reinterpretation of Genesis 1-3 undertaken within recent theology in regard to the traditional understanding. The main focus is on the statement in Genesis regarding the male-female relationship: "God created man in his own image, in the image of God he created him; male and female he created them" (Gen. 1: 27). Complementarities, not subordination, are the order of the day, as can be seen in the reinterpretation of the second creation narrative (Gen. 2: 4-25). 'Helpmate' is interpreted as partner, and it is underlined that the woman is of the same 'flesh', meaning on equal footing with the man, ontologically. Unity and communion is emphasised, through which Adam's 'original solitude' is overcome.[206]

Tying things back to Pope John Paul II, the same essay goes on to say:

> This is a prominent theme in John Paul II's meditations - the meaning of gender difference is to be seen in overcoming the solitude of human beings. Accordingly, the traditional bridal metaphors are a basic element in this line of thought. Epithets such as 'nuptial' and 'spousal' occur frequently. Nakedness, as mentioned in Genesis 2: 25, is an indication of the communal function of gender difference. In this way, the human body, marked with the sign of masculinity or femininity, includes *the*

206 Ibid.

> *capacity of expressing love, that love in which the person becomes a gift* and - by means of this gift - fulfils the meaning of his being and his existence. Continuing his commentary on these verses of Genesis, the Pope stresses that the body is "the expression of the spirit and is called, in the mystery of creation, to exist in the communion of persons in the image of God."[207]

It appears that the 2004 letter's supposed purpose of refuting radical feminism's objective of generating resentment between the sexes quickly morphed into denying the well-established hierarchy of the Christian household altogether!

Luckily for traditionalists, a pope (or, as in the above case: congregation or group of bishops), by dint of his office, is not necessarily correct in every utterance he makes. In fact, it is a Protestant notion to assert otherwise. It does not escape one's notice that I have also quoted Popes as an authority, but only because they are habitually consistent with Scripture and Tradition. Remember, popes can and *do* err from time to time. Popes are not restricted from expressing their own personal opinions. However, anytime a pope contradicts the thousands of years of Tradition and/or Scripture he is not speaking with authority. He cannot be doing so. Remember, the charism of papal infallibility does not encompass all a pontiff says and does:

> Hence an infallible Pope cannot be said to be one who can never err in his private conversation or teachings; or who cannot make any mistake in politics, government, etc. For the gift of infallibility, as held by Catholics, belongs to the Pope only in his official capacity, as supreme teacher of the church, and only when, in virtue of his Apostolic power, he defines a doctrine that belongs to faith or morals. This and no other is the subject matter of the Pope's infallible teaching.[208]

---

207 Ibid.

208 Brandi, S. M. "When is the Pope Infallible?" *The North American Review*, vol. 155, no. 433, 1892, http://www.jstor.org/stable/25102489. Accessed 16 Apr. 2022. pp. 652–60.

Further:

> A misconception is possible here. Every truth belonging to faith or morals may be infallibly defined by the Pope; but from this it does not follow that every truth infallibly defined by the Pope is a dogma of the Catholic faith, and, therefore, to be believed with a divine and Catholic faith. To be a dogma of Catholic faith, a doctrine must be a truth revealed by God, which the Pope defines to be such. If the doctrine or fact defined be not a revealed truth, then, although it too must be unhesitatingly believed, it is so believed only with an ecclesiastical faith, that is to say, with a faith that has for its motive "the authority of God's Church defining," not of God Himself directly revealing.[209]

Let us return to the private opinions of Pope John Paul II, who contradicts—or appears to contradict—all those named pontiffs before him on the issue of married women working outside of the home. In the below passage he even contradicts *himself*. In *Laborem Exercens* (1981) Pope John Paul II authored the following suggestively revolutionary language:

> Just remuneration for the work of an adult who is responsible for a family means remuneration which will suffice for establishing and properly maintaining a family and for providing security for its future. Such remuneration can be given either through what is called a family wage—that is, a single salary given to the head of the family for his work, sufficient for the needs of the family without the other spouse having to take up gainful employment outside the home—or through other social measures such as family allowances or grants to mothers devoting themselves exclusively to their families. These grants should correspond to the actual needs, that is, to the number of

209 Ibid.

> dependents for as long as they are not in a position to assume proper responsibility for their own lives. Experience confirms that there must be a social re-evaluation of the mother's role, of the toil connected with it, and of the need that children have for care, love and affection in order that they may develop into responsible, morally and religiously mature and psychologically stable persons.[210]

But just as the reader begins to suspect that the Pope has capitulated entirely to worldly feminism, his formulations take a relieving turn and (instead of contradicting) begin to affirm the timeless teaching of the Church, holding that it is still the inarguable Christian standard for society that must provide the conditions for the possibility of modern woman to:

> devote herself to taking care of her children and educating them in accordance with their needs, which vary with age. Having to abandon these tasks in order to take up paid work outside the home is wrong from the point of view of the good of society and of the family when it contradicts or hinders these primary goals of the mission of a mother.[211]

On an October 1979 visit to Limerick, Ireland Pope John Paul II gave the following helpful yet ambiguous counsel to mothers and young women in a homily:

> Do not think that anything you will do in life is more important than to be a good Christian father or mother. May Irish mothers, young women and girls not listen to those who tell them that working at a secular job, succeeding in a secular profession, is more important than the vocation of giving life and caring for this life as a mother. The future of the Church,

---

210 John Paul II. *On Human Work: Encyclical Laborem Exercens*. Office of Publishing Services, United States Catholic Conference, 1981, Section 19.

211 Ibid.

> the future of humanity depend in great part on parents and on the family life that they build in their homes.[212]

In other words, thank you to women who *don't* work...but it remains unclear whether John Paul believes with all of Catholic teaching that married women *must* not work outside the home.

The matter is never clarified much. In a February 1989 letter to the United States bishops, Pope John Paul II wrote:

> However, a radical feminism which seeks the rights of women by attacking and denying fundamental, clear and constant moral teaching does not reflect or promote the full reality and true dignity of women, who have not only a temporal worth but also an eternal destiny in the Divine Plan. Mary, Mother of Jesus, Mother of the Church, woman par excellence, embodies that radical dignity of women.[213]

And in his suggestive yet still-not-definitive 1994 *Letter to Families*, "the "toil" of a woman who, having given birth to a child, nourishes and cares for that child and devotes herself to its upbringing, particularly in the early years, is so great as to be comparable to any professional work."[214]

In Pope John Paul II's 1995 *Letter to Mrs. Gertrude Mongella, Secretary General of the Fourth World Conference on Women of the United Nations:*

> No response to women's issues can ignore women's role in the family or take lightly the fact that every new life is *totally*

212 John Paul II."1 October 1979: Visit to Limerick: John Paul II." *1 October 1979: Visit to Limerick,* 30 Sept. 1979, https://www.vatican.va/content/john-paul-ii/en/homilies/1979/documents/hf_jp-ii_hom_19791001_irlanda-limerick.html.Section6.

213 John Paul II. *Letter to the Bishops of the United States of America (February 22, 1989): John Paul II.* Letter to the Bishops of the United States of America, 22 Feb. 1989, https://www.vatican.va/content/john-paul-ii/en/letters/1989/documents/hf_jp-ii_let_19890222_vescovi-usa.html. Section: "Role of Women."

214 John Paul II. *Letter to Families Gratissimam Sane (February 2, 1994): John Paul II.* Letter to Families *Gratissimam Sane*, 1 Feb. 1994, https://www.vatican.va/content/john-paul-ii/en/letters/1994/documents/hf_jp-ii_let_02021994_families.html, Section 17.

> *entrusted* to the protection and care of the woman carrying it in her womb (Cf. John Paul II *Evangelium Vitae*, 58). In order to respect this natural order of things, it is necessary to counter the misconception that the role of motherhood is oppressive to women, and that a commitment to her family, particularly to her children, prevents a woman from reaching personal fulfilment, and women as a whole from having an influence in society. It is a disservice not only to children, but also to women and society itself, when a woman is made to feel guilty for wanting to remain in the home and nurture and care for her children. A mother's presence in the family, so critical to the stability and growth of that basic unity of society, should instead be recognized, applauded and supported in every possible way.[215]

On the topic of the necessity of a male, single-income household, Pope John Paul contends that "a workman's wages should be sufficient to enable him to support himself, his wife and his children. If through necessity or fear of a worse evil the workman accepts harder conditions because an employer or contractor will afford no better, he is made the victim of force and injustice."[216]

Clearly, John Paul II was not as revolutionary as the "Christian feminists'" proof texts make him out to be.

The point is: if popes can err or contradict themselves, they can certainly fall under worldly temptation to do so, and then alter course at the last moment. That is why we must look to Scripture and Tradition when papal discrepancies occur, rather than trusting our own or their biases.

---

215 John Paul II. *Letter to Mrs. Gertrude Mongella, Secretary General of the Fourth World Conference on Women of the United Nations (May 26, 1995): John Paul II.* Letter to Mrs. Gertrude Mongella, Secretary General of the Fourth World Conference on Women of the United Nations, 26 May 1995, https://www.vatican.va/content/john-paul-ii/en/letters/1995/documents/hf_jp-ii_let_19950526_mongella-pechino.html.

216 John Paul II. *Centesimus Annus,* 1 May 1991, no. 8.

But how does this work when catechisms are said to contradict one another? Can catechisms err? Again, one ought to remember that even catechisms are "guidebooks" or summaries of what we believe as Roman Catholics. They are not themselves infallible.

The Modern Catechism leaves out the "duties of wives" section while the older Catechism, the *Catechism of Trent,* does not. So which catechism should we use? Author Charles Coulombe provides us with the answer. Mr. Coulombe recently penned this article in response to the question of whether Pope Francis may change the catechism to renounce the death penalty and his answer offers insight to the authority of catechisms.

> At this point, one might well ask whether there is such a thing as an authoritative catechism. There is indeed—the *Catechism of the Council of Trent*, also called the *Roman Catechism*. Innumerable popes have praised it: Leo XIII called it "that golden book, the Roman Catechism," a "precious summary of all theology, both dogmatic and moral." For St. John XXIII, it was "the Summa of pastoral theology." St. John Paul II declared that "the Council of Trent . . . lies at the origin of the Roman Catechism, which . . . is a work of the first rank as a summary of Christian theology gave rise to a remarkable organization of catechesis in the Church." But its authority, as with the CCC, does not come from itself, but from the fact that for the most part it is made up of quotations from the infallible doctrinal declarations of the Council of Trent itself. Where it is not, there has been room for error, as shown in 1947 when Venerable Pius XII corrected its assertion that the Presentation of the Instruments is necessary for the validity of the Sacrament of Holy Orders. When not repeating prior infallible teaching, any catechism—including the Roman—is on its own.
>
> Does this mean that the *Catechism of the Catholic Church* is without value? By no means. It engages many questions not

> addressed by Trent, and in such areas also relies upon the faith and witness of the Eastern Catholic Churches. But it should be used in tandem with more authoritative works, such as the Roman—and discounted if it disagrees with them. Pope Francis may or may not be contradicting prior Church teaching in the changes he has made and apparently wishes to make in the CCC. If he is, it is not in a truly authoritative arena.[217]

Many feminist-modernists argue that the newer *Catechism* abrogates the older one (wherein we find the "duties of the wife" passage). (I suppose they are using the "what's newer is always better" fallacy.) Either way, it proves to be a non-issue because there is zero abrogation on the catechetical matter of duties of wives: the newer relies upon the older without changing it. Specifically, the newer *Catechism* abstains from saying a word on the matter, presumably in deference to the plenary expression of the Catholic teaching in the previous *Catechism*.

Even if the new *Catechism* contradicted the Roman *Catechism*—which it does not—one would have only to look at the words prefacing the newer one itself. Written in the beginning of the modern *Catechism* is a section "On the Publication of the *Catechism* of the Catholic Church" by Pope John Paul II. In anticipated response to the question of whether the newer one abrogates the older one are the words: "This *Catechism* is not intended to replace the local catechisms duly approved by ecclesiastical authorities, the diocesan Bishops and the Episcopal Conferences especially if they have been approved by the Apostolic See."[218]

Concluding Words on Magisterial Tradition

To recap, in the event a newer catechism contradicts an older one—such as is the case with the death penalty, but not the duties

---

217 Coulombe, Charles. "Can the Catechism Get It Wrong?" *Crisis Magazine*, 29 Nov. 2019, www.crisismagazine.com/2019/can-the-catechism-get-it-wrong.

218 Catholic Church. *Catechism of the Catholic Church*. 2nd ed., Our Sunday Visitor, 2000.

of wives—we must hold onto Sacred Tradition and Scripture. And this is precisely where feminists get themselves into the most trouble. Feminists attempt to retrofit Holy Scripture to excuse their lifestyle preferences. When that doesn't work, they recur to the old "pick and choose" routine of the cafeteria Catholic, when the "old fashioned" precepts of Sacred Scripture don't line up neatly with their personal economic plans.

Again, we turn to Pius X's *Oath Against Modernism*:

> Furthermore, I reject the opinion of those who hold that a professor lecturing or writing on a historico-theological subject should first put aside any preconceived opinion about the supernatural origin of Catholic tradition or about the divine promise of help to preserve all revealed truth forever; and that they should then interpret the writings of each of the Fathers solely by scientific principles, excluding all sacred authority, and with the same liberty of judgment that is common in the investigation of all ordinary historical documents. Finally, I declare that I am completely opposed to the error of the modernists who hold that there is nothing divine in sacred tradition; or what is far worse, say that there is, but in a pantheistic sense, with the result that there would remain nothing but this plain simple fact—one to be put on a par with the ordinary facts of history—the fact, namely, that a group of men by their own labor, skill, and talent have continued through subsequent ages a school begun by Christ and his apostles. I firmly hold, then, and shall hold to my dying breath the belief of the Fathers in the charism of truth, which certainly is, was, and always will be in the succession of the episcopacy from the apostles. The purpose of this is, then, not that dogma may be tailored according to what seems better and more suited to the culture of each age; rather, that the absolute and immutable truth preached

> by the apostles from the beginning may never be believed to be different, may never be understood in any other way.[219]

On trying the find error in Scared Scripture, Pope Paul VI adds:

> In the second place, we have to contend against those who, making an evil use of physical science, minutely scrutinize the Sacred Book in order to detect the writers in a mistake, and to take occasion to vilify its contents. Attacks of this kind, bearing as they do on matters of sensible experience, are peculiarly dangerous to the masses, and also to the young who are beginning their literary studies; for the young, if they lose their reverence for the Holy Scripture on one or more points, are easily led to give up believing in it altogether.[220]

Unfortunately, it's the modern woman who has given up her faith in Scripture and replaced it with the false idol of careerism. If you are one who is tempted to idolize one career or another, consider Pope Paul VI's words: "Work, too, has a double edge. Since it promises money, pleasure and power, it stirs up selfishness in some and incites other to revolt."[221]

And so a lowly housewife—standing on the shoulders of her Church's martyrs, Fathers, Scholastics, philosophers, doctors, popes, and saints—rests her case on the matter. The two or three dissenting voices in the course of thousands of years of Catholic Scriptural and Magisterial teaching won't topple this human pyramid.

I'll bow out of this chapter with the words of St. John Chrysostom:

> If it be asked, what has this to do with women of the present day? It shows that the male sex enjoyed the higher honor. Man

219 Pius X. *The Oath Against Modernism.* 1 Sept. 1910.

220 Leo XIII. *Providentissimus Deus (November 18, 1893): Leo XIII,* 1893, Retrieved 19 Apr. 2022, from https://www.vatican.va/content/leo-xiii/en/encyclicals/documents/hf_l-xiii_enc_18111893_providentissimus-deus.html
T, Section 18.

221 Paul VI. *Populorum Progressio. Catholic Truth Society,* 1967.

> was first formed; and elsewhere he shows their superiority. "Neither was the man created for the woman, but the woman for the man." (1 Cor. xi. 9.) Why then does he say this? He wishes the man to have the preeminence in every way; both for the reason given above, he means, let him have precedence, and on account of what occurred afterwards. For the woman taught the man once, and made him guilty of disobedience and wrought our ruin. Therefore, because she made a bad use of her power over the man, or rather her equality with him, God made her subject to husband. "Thy desire shall be to thy husband?" (Gen. in. 16.) This had not been said to her before.[222]

So, if you're a married woman who doesn't enjoy homemaking or one who finds it unfulfilling, then ask God to change your heart. More aptly, cope. Do your job (your real job): caring for *your own* home and family. Soon, you will find dignity and joy in it. You alone, by your own actions and decisions, can grant yourself the surest path to earthly happiness and even a heightened chance at otherworldly salvation.

And no, you can't hire another woman to do that for you, either.

---

222 Chrysostom, St. John. *Compete Works of St. John Chrysostom*, loc.132419.1 32426.

6

Wear What He Likes, Do What He Likes

Honoring Preferences Makes Marriage Great Again

It's no secret that in happy, healthy marriages, spouses ought to dedicate themselves to keeping their romance alive. This is especially true the longer you have been married, when rapport becomes more "comfortable", and the notorious rut threatens to set in. Below, I will identify one of the most common ways in which the husband and the wife tend to contribute to the marital rut.

Husbands, typically intentional and goal-oriented, frequently lose sight of this fact when they stop wooing their wives after the wedding day. A husband ought to pursue his wife like he did when their courtship was beginning, striving to earn her tender affections. He should take his wife on regular dates, show active interest in her day's triumphs and travails, proffer her meaningful tokens of his affection, and refresh her morale with sincere compliments. These sound like tokens, but they prove quite meaningful for his bride.

Wives, typically sentimental and present-tense-oriented, frequently lose sight of the fact that men remain the same visually-oriented creatures they were during courtship and haven't become "massive jerks" for maintaining and expressing their attraction to objective beauty. By way of example, Oxford scientists have theorized that babies were created to be "cute" so that their mothers are subliminally and constantly encouraged to care for them—even when the infant proves to be incredibly challenging.[223] Just as God created babies to be "cute" so their mothers would nurture them, God created women to be "beautiful" so their husbands would remain attracted to them. A wife can certainly help her husband's daily pursuit of her by looking pretty for him, and keeping in shape—more on this later. But exterior beauty ought not stop there. It should lead a husband to his wife's heart. Clearly, the best marriages are constituted by husbands and wives who remember these sex-specific challenges every day.

Because feminism has preponderated in the Western world, husbands are simultaneously chided colorfully for their own typical shortcomings and reproved for daring to address the husbandly grievances arising from their wives' shortcomings. Husbands today are presented with, literally, one of the worst double-standards on record, in our generation. Moreover, what realistically can a husband do to "feel better" if he is rebuked on all sides for attempting honest, respectful discussion with his wife in regard to maintaining her beauty so as to sustain an adequate degree of sexual intimacy (such as to nourish the average male's enthusiasm for his marital relationship)?

Once incentive to *give* has been removed from the give-and-take of the lifelong relationship, a marriage is in dire straits.

Both sexes would do themselves a great service to remember: *the key to keeping romance alive and well is to be mindful of your spouse's preferences.* If your preferences—or those of your spouse—differ from the stereotypical ones I referenced above, that's fine. Just honor each other's preferences.

The willingness to adapt yourself to impress your spouse is a good and holy thing. Naturally, such a practice is altogether scorned by the popular culture. Modernists and feminists have tried to convince us that no one but a woman has the right to express a marital preference—everyone besides women and wives should be utterly tolerant of those items of marital life which repulse them.

---

223 Jamieson, Sophie. "Why Are Babies and Puppies so Cute? Oxford Researchers Have the Answer." *The Telegraph, Telegraph Media Group*, 2016, www.telegraph.co.uk/news/2016/06/06/why-are-babies-and-puppies-so-cute-oxford-researchers-have-the-a/.

The reason for the wild success by the feminists in popularizing the "come as you are" platitude is the partial-truth it conveys: *yes, we all ought to be afforded unconditional love and dignity as human beings.* But intimacy and authentic happiness in marriage is far more complicated. Remember there was *one* perfect man and *one* perfect woman[224] and the rest of us have endless catching up to do.

Intimacy in exemplary marriages requires constant effort and sacrifice.

Catholics ought to be committed to making our marriages the strongest possible until we draw our last breaths. After all, matrimony is the chosen vocation for most of us. Regular appraisal of healthfulness in your relationship and modifying *what can reasonably be* modified to maximize intimacy is the easiest way to build your marriage quickly.

To be clear, I am not advocating "nit-picking" or derision by one spouse against the other. My advice presents a fine line to walk. Such sensitive matters ought to be handled with the utmost love, care, and respect. If your spouse gathers enough gumption to tenderly express to you a specific way you might easily improve upon, toward the increase of your relationship's intimacy, take heed. Listening wherever possible and satisfying your spouse's preferences is just plain courteous. So doing so will ensure a lasting marriage.

By way of example, a friend with the same first name as my own—a writer and contributor to several conservative Catholic weblogs—upset many people on social media after she declared that she refuses to wear pants, at the behest of her husband, who prefers that she wear skirts and dresses. Notwithstanding the fact that Stefanie even mentioned that this was a shared preference of hers, too, a full-throttle feminist melt-down ensued over Stefanie's declared "lifestyle preferences." (Bear in mind: this occurred on conservative Catholic social media.)

Hold the phone: weren't "lifestyle preferences" something the popular culture once—and even presently, in some corners—held sacred?

---

224 Jesus and Mary.

As noted above, even traditional Catholics expressed feminist objections to Stefanie's preferences. In some cases, the Catholics treated her more harshly than the secular mob did. Incidentally, if you are not a user of Catholic Twitter, there's a phrase I frequently employ to describe how Catholics regard other Catholics there: "Mother Trad Twitter eats her cubs." In other words, Catholic Twitter is a "nit-picking" dumpster-fire.[225]

When I still had the Twitter account *@AskYourHusband*—even as a pants wearer—I publicly supported Stefanie's no-pants stance.

What we were trying to impart was simple enough: as considerate wives, we care abundantly about each of our husband's preferences, because we love them and wish to please them. This was formerly known as "trying to be a good wife" in history's nobler times (eras with far healthier marital statistics than we enjoy now). For instance, in the 1950's:

> This time period saw younger marriages, more kids, and fewer divorces. In fact, the divorce rate was 2.5 divorces for every 1,000 people in 1950, and dropped to 2.3 in 1955. In 1958, the rate even slumped to 2.1, with 368,000 divorces.[226]

If you think that's good, consider the virtually non-existent divorce rate in the late nineteenth century: "In 1867, there were 10,000 divorces, and by 1879, there were 17,000 that year. However, the rate of divorce stayed at a very low 0.3 divorces per 1,000 Americans."[227]

In the category of "least surprising fact of the day," I present for your consideration today's divorce rate statistics: "About 40 to 50 percent of married couples in the United States divorce. The divorce rate for subsequent marriages is even higher."[228]

---

225 Hence, another reason I permanently logged off.

226 Olito, Frank. "How the Divorce Rate Has Changed over the Last 150 Years." *Insider*, 30 Jan. 2019, Web. 23 Apr. 2021.

227 Ibid.

228 "Marriage and Divorce." *American Psychological Association*. Web. 23 Apr. 2021.

The disgraceful state of man-woman relations was evident by the responses Stefanie received. Even her online defenders—myself included—received a feminist onslaught of baseless accusations: "your husband is a controlling misogynist," all the way to "you are self-loathing, weak-minded simpletons."

If the popular culture hates anything in this world more than a Christian man enjoying his headship over a grateful, happy, dutiful, and obedient wife, let me know. Conversely, if the left loves anything more than the universal abidance of *their preferences* (un-biological pronouns, various sexual debaucheries, murder of the innocent, etc.), let me know.

Long ago, a woman once viewed her wifely vocation as the highest art, the most noble calling. And she was right. Wifeliness entails the expenditure of no small effort to keep her husband's attention by magnificence in her cooking, homemaking, affection, and appearance. There was once a lovelier time when women knew how to do all of these things well. In that era, older wives were there to advise their newly married Christian sisters whenever they hit a snag. In brief, homemaking is that lovely art which Pope John Paul II's term "feminine genius"[229] ought to properly encompass.

Sadly, women today, myself included, have had to improvise because most of our elders have abandoned the art of homemaking in the period after the sexual revolution resulting in less shared wisdom.

Feminists can screech all they want—their shrill-sounding, overtaxed vocal cords will *really* get going if they read the next section—they'll never change what men *really* want: beautiful *homemakers* and beautiful *homemaking*.

229 St. Pope John Paul II is credited for making the term "feminine genius" popular.

Skip the Rest of This Chapter if You Aren't Ready to Hear What Men *Really* Want

Warning: if you subscribe to the incredibly selfish, unhealthy, and intimacy-killing "body positivity movement"[230] you're about to be genuinely offended by this entire section.

Ladies, if your husband has never sat you down to request, respectfully, that you honor his fashion-, exercise-, dietary-, or romantic-preference, you very likely have a *grave* marital problem. Since, like I have already mentioned, none of us is perfect, healthy marriages occasion many such conversations. Accordingly, such a taciturn husband (viz. one who never speaks up) can only be of the opinion that his wife would not handle such a conversation productively. Either such a man is the least assertive human being in the history of the world, or he's correct that such a conversation would prompt an unpleasant wifely tantrum.

I can't begin to tell you how many emails my husband and I receive (through my husband's apostolate) from faithful Catholic men asking how effectively to approach their wives about an unaddressed weight-gluttony issue. From any male's point of view, this proves to be the grandaddy of all intimacy-killers. It's probably one of the marital topics about which we receive the *most* emails. Before any gentlewoman loses her stately composure here, most of these men sincerely aim to sexually desire their wives. By reaching out for advice, they are seeking a way to fix failing intimacy due to their wives' "letting themselves go." It's apparent from the letters that these men truly don't want to hurt their wives' feelings. On the contrary, they convincingly seem terrified of hurting their wives' feelings (which is why they're struggling so poignantly and, in their hesitancy, failing to address this sensitive issue).

---

230 "Body positivity refers to the assertion that all people deserve to have a positive body image, regardless of how society and popular culture view ideal shape, size, and appearance." Cherry, Kendra. "Why Body Positivity Is Important." *Verywell Mind*. Web. 23 Apr. 2021.

Since so many men struggle with addressing this sensitive issue, I'll do it for them here. To my Christian sisters still reading along—those of you who didn't skip this section—know this: truth be told, I promised a *great* many husbands I would include this section in the book.

Wives who are the subjects—witting or unwitting—of this delicate discussion should know that in nearly all the emails we have received through the years, husbands regularly mentioned how something small like weight loss or increased wifely attention to general appearance (irrespective of age) would powerfully increase marital intimacy. These husbands, for the record, also have tended to mention their wives' natural beauty and their continued natural attraction to such wives... if only they could be pointed in the direction of healthy weight loss.

Hear me out before you curb my frank discussion and madly retort: "sexual intimacy should have little to do with weight! This is male vanity!" To submit to such reasoning constitutes an erroneous claim, perhaps a borderline dereliction of one's vows should a wife not take care of herself. We all know obesity is a big problem in America. It constitutes a cardiovascular health epidemic, and among the myriad problems it generates, it 100% adversely affects marital sexual intimacy. It's one of the most obvious threats to marriage, but sadly few want to address it.

Few want to address it, but some will. Take for instance this excerpt from *Social Psychology Quarterly:*

> Men, on the other hand, seem to emphasize physical appearance more strongly than do women when reflecting on the desirability of future spouses. This tendency is supported in the sex-specific listings of desirable characteristics in romantic partners (Nevid 1984) and in the sex-specific emphases placed on the perceived importance of physical attractiveness in forming judgments of people (Sprecher 1988). Moreover, wives' physical attractiveness is related to husbands' marital adjustment, but not vice versa (Murstein and Christy 1976).

> Changes in a wife's physical attractiveness (as measured by change in body type and by weight gain) affect her husband's sexual adjustment within the marriage (Margolin and White 1987). Using an evolutionary framework, Buss (1988) argues that the particular emphasis placed by men on women's physical attractiveness reflects men's need to select romantic partners on the basis of factors signaling reproductive capacity. Buss also argues that women emphasize men's ability and willingness to invest resources in their mates and offspring, and thus rely heavily on cues such as earning capacity, ambition, and status.[231]

For clarity's and charity's sakes, let's be Platonic about this and imitate a give-and-take dialogue, by addressing the most common objections women have to this issue.

Allow me to put myself under the microscope, with an uncomfortable admission. I've given myself this advice on several occasions. In fact, I'm giving it to myself right now before the birth of my seventh child. As a mother of seven children and a woman who enjoys a good meal, I find myself constantly in the position of having to mind my health and tend to the preferences of my husband. Understandably, he prefers a healthy, feminine frame. All men do, which is precisely why it's worth mentioning.

Objection #1: I have a disability (or am of advanced age) and cannot safely exercise.

If you have a legitimate disability, this advice certainly does not apply to you. Our husbands are called to love us in "sickness and health." For the rest of us, controlling weight can and must be a priority if we wish to keep intimacy alive in our marriages. For the severely

---

231 Stevens, Gillian, et al. "Education and Attractiveness in Marriage Choices." *Social Psychology Quarterly*, vol. 53, no. 1, 1990, https://doi.org/10.2307/2786870. Accessed 13 Apr. 2022, pp. 62–70.

disabled or the elderly, the lack of intimacy will prove an unavoidable cross your husband is called to bear. He is to treat you as Christ demands him to.

Objection #2: Sure, I have a weight issue, but I don't need to lose weight because my husband loves me no matter how much I weigh!

If you are telling yourself right now that your husband loves you no matter how much you weigh, then you're right (I hope). But that's actually beside the point. You ought to be asking yourself if he is *attracted* to you. The odds are, if you are currently overweight, his physical attraction to you is severely waning. After all, men, as we all know, are visually motivated creatures:[232]

> For example, male arousal, studies find, is strongly visual, and when men engage in sexual activity or even anticipate it, brain structures once thought to have little connection to sex spring into action. The same brain regions, however, remain relatively quiet when women are aroused.[233]

I'd respectfully invite you to *ask your husband* if he would support your weight loss. I'd bet you he has been wanting to broach this conversation, yet he just doesn't know how to do so without hurting your feelings. Initiating the conversation, on your part, would prompt the comfortable expression of his honest feelings on the matter. The tough part is: you just have to be willing to *listen* to it.

---

232 From Psychology Today: "As Ogas and Gaddam suggest, "Men's greater sex drive may be partially due to the fact that their sexual motivation pathways have more connections to the subcortical reward system than in women." "men's brains are designed to objectify females." Seltzer, Leon F. "The Triggers of Sexual Desire: Men vs. Women." *Psychology Today*. Sussex Publishers, 11 May 2012. Web. 23 Apr. 2021.

233 O'Connor, A. "In sex, brain studies show, 'La Différence' still holds." The New York Times. 16 Mar. 2004, Retrieved 19 Apr. 2022, from https://www.nytimes.com/2004/03/16/health/in-sex-brain-studies-show-la-difference-still-holds.html =.

Objection #3: Losing weight won't enhance my self-esteem. Why try?

Some women push back against weight loss because they esteem themselves lowly at their current weight and doubt that weight loss would improve anything. Again, this is simply not the point. Whatever your natural feminine assets may be, shedding those extra pounds will serve to amplify your husband's current attraction to you. Literally no one ever became less attractive by shedding excessive weight. Not to mention the health benefits of losing weight are manifold.

Those benefits are, according to Harvard medical experts: the lowering of cholesterol, blood pressure, knee pain, and the risk of diabetes. Weight loss increases self-esteem, sexual desire, quality sleep, and energy.[234] Again, putting all of the emphasis on "looks" puts us in danger of missing the wider issue. Losing weight has health benefits intended to increase the overall quality and length of your life. For married women, it will also naturally increase the desire of your husband (further, weight loss increases sexual desire on the part of the one exercising to lose weight).

Objection #4: I simply don't have the time to dedicate to exercise.

Even if your current weight is healthy, you ought to carve out time in your schedule to exercise. Doing so helps you to remain in good health. On average, it also enhances the odds that you will be around for your family for the long haul.

As the mother of many small children, I understand how difficult it is to find time to exercise amid your daily chores. When I am overwhelmingly busy, my husband and I load the kids into their strollers for a lengthy family walk (3-5 miles) after dinner. Doing so accomplishes several things at once.

By the time we are halfway done with our long walk, several of

---

234 Publishing, Harvard Health. "*The Far-Reaching Effects of a Little Bit of Weight Loss.*" *Harvard Health*, 2020, www.health.harvard.edu/staying-healthy/the-far-reaching-effects-of-a-little-bit-of-weight-loss.

the kids have already fallen asleep. Also, it's a time when my husband and I can enjoy extended conversation, with little or no distraction. Sometimes we even bring the dog, knocking out his daily walk, too. During the summer, when free time is most plentiful around my household, we change it up and routinely take daily, long, family bike rides with our Siberian husky attached on a bike-friendly dog leash. We often stop for a meal at an outdoor restaurant and also at the grocery store on the way back home for small incidentals. This means that literally, one single bike ride (albeit a lengthy one) accomplishes all the following during each summer day: exercise completed, an outing for the kids enjoyed, the Siberian husky's breed-specific exercise needs satisfied, everyone fed, (minor) grocery shopping done; and recreational, lengthy two-to-three-hour spousal conversation had. Arguably the most important facet of the bike ride is that everyone in our large family returns home in a happy mood, feeling as if we have "earned" the right to relax and watch a movie. It is the best routine, and we look forward to it each summer.

My cardiologist once informed me that raising the heart rate for 30 minutes per day, five days per week, is the *bare minimum* for the average person's heart-health.[235] So try your utmost to adjust your daily schedule to fit it in. It's not just about looking good: it's about putting yourself in a position to live a long, healthy life. You owe this to your spouse and children, and above all, God. After all, your body is meant to glorify Him. Long walks accomplish both ends at once.

Objection #5: Why should I lose weight if my husband is overweight, too?

You're right. You both should lose weight. Exercising together, toward a mutual goal, is a fantastic way to spend time together. I'm

---

235 The Heart Association says, "Get at least 150 minutes per week of moderate-intensity aerobic activity or 75 minutes per week of vigorous aerobic activity, or a combination of both, preferably spread throughout the week." "American Heart Association Recommendations for Physical Activity in Adults and Kids." www.heart.org. Web. 23 Apr. 2021.

not a "fitness junkie" by any stretch, but some of the fondest times of my life were when my husband and I would take night runs in Rome, Italy. After the children came along, we would put them all to bed (when they were newborns) and pay a local teenager to babysit as we went for an evening run. It's truly remarkable how working toward a mutual goal brings a husband and his wife together. Moreover, it's striking to note how helpful it is to have a workout buddy to help keep you motivated and accountable.

There have actually been studies done on the benefits of having an exercise partner:

> A study from Michigan State University, for one, found that doing aerobic exercise with a partner motivated subjects to work harder and longer, compared with those working out alone, thus improving overall fitness results.[236]

Objection #6: Ok, perhaps I should lose weight, but isn't this all just vanity?

According to Aristotle and St. Thomas Aquinas, you're using the term, "vanity," incorrectly. (But yes, some people exercise solely narcissistic purposes.) In Book Four of the *Nicomachean Ethics,*[237] vanity features as a vice—an excess—of the virtue magnanimity, which is defined as "claiming the correct amount of personal honor due." Properly understood, vanity entails claiming, by word or deed, more honor than is due to a person. Now, Aristotle does call the vain "foolish persons, who are deficient in self-knowledge and who expose their own defect"[238] by use of misleading physical indicia like "ostentatious dress and manner," aiming to appear better or more honorable than they are.

But Aristotle and St. Thomas Aquinas would have never considered

---

236 Latona, Valerie. "Exercising with a Workout Buddy Can Improve Results." *AARP*, 8 May 2019, Retrieved 23 Apr. 2021.

237 Goold, G.P., ed. *Aristotle XIX Nicomachean Ethics*. Vol. 73, Cambridge: Loeb Classical Library, 1926.

238 Aristotle, W D. Ross, and Lesley Brown. *The Nicomachean Ethics*. Oxford: Oxford University Press, 2009, Books IV., iii, 36.

physical fitness to be one of those false indicia, because fitness improves the *actual* state of one's bodily health, not just the *appearance* of it; and both thinkers thought extremely highly of physical fitness, in the first place. It is a moral virtue. Disapproval from either thinker would have been directed exclusively at *too much exercise* (i.e., hours upon hours per day) which would upset the "golden mean,"[239] or on the other hand, *improper motivation* for the exercise. An exercise regime of 30-45 daily minutes, motivated by health and marital concerns, is the right amount, for the right reasons.

Physical fitness was understood, even in Aristotle's day, to aid the health of women—even pregnant women. As he says in the *Politics*:

> Women who are with child should be careful of themselves; they should take exercise and have a nourishing diet. The first of these prescriptions the legislator will easily carry into effect by requiring that they should take a walk daily to some temple, where they can worship the gods who preside over birth. Their minds, however, unlike their bodies, they ought to keep quiet, for the offspring derive their natures from their mothers as plants do from earth.[240]

Objection #7: I recently had a baby, and I can't imagine focusing on my weight right now.

Resuming an exercise routine shorty after giving birth can feel similar to imagining having another baby right after birth. I've been there—seven times, actually. Having given birth myself (and all by cesarian section), I sympathize with and understand the tolls childbirth, together with caring for a newborn, have on post-partum women. Once a suitable time has passed to heal and rest from the strains of giving

239 Aristotle makes the "golden mean" the primary mark of virtue, in the *Nicomachean Ethics*. It rests between two extremes, both vices: the vice of excess and the vice of deficiency.

240 Aristotle. "Aristotle's Politics: Writings from the Complete Works: Politics, Economics, Constitution of Athens," Princeton University Press, 2016, pp. 208.

birth, start slowly integrating an exercise regimen into your schedule. This is precisely why jogging strollers exist, ladies!

As a matter of fact, the period of time after having a baby presents one of the greatest dangers to your long-term weight and appearance... precisely because it *is* such a good excuse to give up. This means that, provided what I said above, after a brief period of recuperation immediately after the baby is born, there's no time like the post-partum period to get to your exercise. Remember, with today's high-tech exercise equipment and advanced "sports science," everyday women like you and I are maintaining trim figures into their seventies.

Likely, your stamina will not be the same after childbirth as it was before, and you will have to build it back up again. Resuming regular activity also helps women struggling from post-partum depression. *The Journal of Women's Health* concludes its scientific study on the matter by stating, "Previous research indicates that mothers who are physically active during leisure experience lower levels of postpartum depressive symptoms than do inactive mothers."[241]

Regarding the mental-health benefits of exercise for post-partum women, *Healthline* states:

> Researchers in Australia explain that exercise may have an antidepressant effect for women with PPD. In particular, walking with baby in a stroller might be an easy way to get in some steps and breathe fresh air. In a study published in Mental Health and Physical Activity, walking was found to be a statistically significant way to ease depression. Can't fit in a long exercise session? Try working out for 10 minutes a few times during the day.[242]

---

241 Demissie, Zewditu, et al. "Associations between Physical Activity and Postpartum Depressive Symptoms." *Journal of Women's Health*, 2002, Mary Ann Liebert, Inc., July 2011, www.ncbi.nlm.nih.gov/pmc/articles/PMC3130516/.

242 Sullivan, Debra. "How to Deal with Postpartum Depression: Diet, Exercise." *Healthline*, 2020, www.healthline.com/health/depression/how-to-deal-with-postpartum-depression.

Note above how even just *reading* the multiplicity of exercise-scheduling suggestions proffered makes a girl feel better: getting an "attack plan" is half the battle. Again, begin with baby steps and then build from there.

Objection #8: What if my husband isn't being kind about my weight and is uncharitably pressuring me into slimming down?

If your husband is struggling to articulate his sexual frustration in a respectful and kind manner, you should tell him so. He probably needs to be reminded that you, like anyone who is attempting to make positive changes, require encouragement and patience. Derision and impatience are totally inappropriate. However, try to dismiss the temptation to postpone your need for positive health changes simply because your husband is behaving unkindly. Such changes are good for your health and marital intimacy no matter how much insensitivity your husband may be lacing his frustration with (remember, this is very important to him).

Try articulating to him how his insensitivity hinders, rather than encourages, your progress and how he needs to re-evaluate how he addresses you on the matter. Perhaps remind him of the *Catechism of Trent*'s exhortations to the husband, regarding how he ought to treat his wife (keeping in mind that he has the right to ask you to exercise, but you have the right to require that he conduct himself honorably when he asks):

> It is then the duty of the husband to treat his wife liberally and honorably: it should not be forgotten that Eve was called by Adam " his companion:" " The woman," says he, " whom thou gavest me as a companion." Hence it was, according to the opinion of some of the Holy Fathers, that she was formed not from the feet but from the side of man; as, on the other hand, she was not formed from his head, in order to give her to understand that it was not hers to command but to obey her

> husband. The husband should also be constantly occupied in some honest pursuit, with a view as well to provide necessaries for his family, as to avoid the languor of idleness, the root of almost every vice. He is also to keep all his family in order, to correct their morals, fix their respective employments, and see that they discharge them with fidelity.[243]

Keep in mind the last part of that passage, "He is also to keep all his family in order, to correct their morals, fix their respective employments, and see that they discharge them with fidelity." Your husband has the right to impose upon you binding requests pertaining to physical, marital, and spiritual health. But he is required by the faith to do so charitably.

Recall these words in *Casti Connubii*:

> This subjection, however, does not deny or take away the liberty which fully belongs to the woman both in view of her dignity as a human person, and in view of her most noble office as wife and mother and companion; nor does it bid her obey her husband's every request if not in harmony with right reason or with the dignity due to wife; nor, in fine, does it imply that the wife should be put on a level with those persons who in law are called minors, to whom it is not customary to allow free exercise of their rights on account of their lack of mature judgment, or of their ignorance of human affairs. But it forbids that exaggerated liberty which cares not for the good of the family; it forbids that in this body which is the family, the heart be separated from the head to the great detriment of the whole body and the proximate danger of ruin. For if the man is the head, the woman is the heart, and as he occupies the chief place in ruling, so she may and ought to claim for herself the chief place in love.[244]

---

243 *Catechism of the Council of Trent*. 1st ed., Baronius Press, 2018.

244 Pius XI. *Casti Connubii.* 1930, www.vatican.va/content/pius-xi/en/encyclicals/documents/hf_p-xi_enc_19301231_casti-connubii.html, Section 27.

In my experience, I've literally never once met a marital couple whose husband is *too* forward (as described above) about his wife's weight issue. In our era, the problem is precisely the opposite. But such a man is theoretically possible, and the previous advice should help in any such cases.

Objection #9: My husband prefers a bigger frame, losing weight would actually go against his preferences.

If you are married to a man whose preference is, legitimately, for "bigger gals," knock yourself out (within reason in regard to health standards). But the fact of the matter is that most men desire the opposite. The trick is finding out if your husband really feels this way or if he is lying so as to avoid a difficult conversation with you. Some men claim to be attracted to bigger women because they don't want to share their true feelings with their wives and by extension cause a huge altercation.

Opening yourself up to hear your husband's *true* preferences—allowing for the sake of argument that if he's used this line, there's at least a chance he's not been honest with you up to this point—will be difficult but doing so will not only increase your physical health, but the healthiness of the communication within your marriage. Listening to your husband without becoming indignant encourages him to be honest with you about his feelings in the future. After all, honest conversations are vital to maintaining a healthy and vibrant marital life, as hard as that may be sometimes.

Objection #10: What if I am currently at a healthy weight and my husband still wishes me to lose weight?

If your husband's preferences are contrary to what's advisable for your health, perhaps you could ask him to accompany you to your physician's office to discuss the matter with your doctor. Perhaps hearing your doctor explain the affects being underweight have on your health will help to put things into perspective.

Adverse health effects from being underweight include malnutrition, vitamin deficiencies, or anemia osteoporosis from too little vitamin D and calcium, decreased immune function, increased risk for complications from surgery, and fertility issues caused by irregular menstrual cycles.[245] Hopefully, once your husband understands how being underweight affects your overall health and the ability to bear children, he will defer to your doctor's recommendations.

In any case, you should probably discuss with your primary doctor whether taking in a few more calories a day would allow you to exercise so as to enjoy the many health benefits exercising provides (rather than avoiding exercise altogether).

Objection #11: It is a lie that being overweight is harmful to my health.

This is a tremendous lie generated and perpetuated by the so-called "body-positivity movement," and bizarrely enough, it's gaining traction. As with the other far-left social movements (gender theory, sexual-liberation, anthropogenic climate change, etc.), it is not rooted in fact. It is a biological given that being overweight is harmful to your health; more importantly, if you are a Catholic and the weight gain is voluntary, then it's also harmful to your soul.

Health care professionals have long agreed that "obesity puts you at greater risk for type two diabetes, heart disease, high blood pressure, arthritis, sleep apnea, some types of cancer, and stroke."[246]

Obesity in women is particularly devastating:

> Obesity negatively impacts the health of women in many ways. Being overweight or obese increases the relative risk of diabetes and coronary artery disease in women. Women who are obese have a higher risk of low back pain and knee osteoarthritis. Obesity negatively affects both contraception and fertility as

245 Ashley Marcin, "Underweight Health Risks: What You Should Know," *Healthline*, 15 May 2017, https://www.healthline.com/health/underweight-health-risks.

246 "Obesity and Overweight." *Stanford Health Care (SHC) - Stanford Medical Center*, 23 Oct. 2019, stanfordhealthcare.org/medical-conditions/healthy-living/obesity.html.

> well. Maternal obesity is linked with higher rates of cesarean section as well as higher rates of high-risk obstetrical conditions such as diabetes and hypertension. Pregnancy outcomes are negatively affected by maternal obesity (increased risk of neonatal mortality and malformations). Maternal obesity is associated with a decreased intention to breastfeed, decreased initiation of breastfeeding, and decreased duration of breastfeeding. There seems to be an association between obesity and depression in women, though cultural factors may influence this association. Obese women are at higher risk for multiple cancers, including endometrial cancer, cervical cancer, breast cancer, and perhaps ovarian cancer.[247]

More important than bodily integrity is moral integrity—which is also adversely affected by gluttony. Fortunately, the response to gluttony by moral theology affirms medical science. Yes, even today, gluttony *remains* a mortal sin, as unpopular as it *always* will be to remind sinners of their sin. The *Catholic Encyclopedia* says:

> Clearly one who uses food or drink in such a way as to injure his health or impair the mental equipment needed for the discharge of his duties, is guilty of the sin of gluttony. It is incontrovertible that to eat or drink for the mere pleasure of the experience, and for that exclusively, is likewise to commit the sin of gluttony.[248]

The Angelic Doctor, St. Thomas Aquinas, affirms that, notwithstanding what politically correct Catholics today suggest, gluttony can often indeed be a mortal sin:

---

247 Kulie, Teresa, et al. "Obesity and Women's Health: An Evidence-Based Review." *American Board of Family Medicine, American Board of Family Medicine,* 1 Jan. 2011, www.jabfm.org/content/24/1/75.

248 Delany, Joseph. "Gluttony." *The Catholic Encyclopedia.* Vol. 6. New York: Robert Appleton Company, 1909, 22 Nov. 2020, <http://www.newadvent.org/cathen/06590a.htm>.

> The vice of gluttony becomes a mortal sin by turning man away from his last end: and accordingly, by a kind of reduction, it is opposed to the precept of hallowing the sabbath, which commands us to rest in our last end. For mortal sins are not all directly opposed to the precepts of the Decalogue, but only those which contain injustice: because the precepts of the Decalogue pertain specially to justice and its parts, as stated above.[249]

A Catholic priest, Fr. Edward McIlmail, LC, adds his thoughts on the issue of gluttony:

> Gluttony is a disordered use of food and of the pleasure that eating and drinking gives us. The pleasure itself is part of God's plan. He made food to taste good. He gave us taste buds. It is no sin to enjoy food, to prepare good food, to have a cake at a birthday party, etc. The point is when we become unreasonable in our pursuit of this pleasure. This leads to a disordered attachment, damage to our health, and spiritual damage too. Perhaps you are asking the question because you sense that you might be crossing or being tempted to cross the line into gluttony. That might be a reason to pause and see if the Holy Spirit is calling you to a greater spirit of sacrifice. Forgoing a little food at each meal is a nice way to practice self-discipline and to show solidarity with the poor of the world. It can certainly discipline us to better stand up to other (and worse) temptations of the flesh. The Catechism briefly puts the danger of gluttony in context. No. 1866 says:
>
> Vices can be classified according to the virtues they oppose, or also be linked to the capital sins which Christian experience has distinguished, following St. John Cassian and St. Gregory the Great. They are called "capital" because they engender

249 Aquinas, Thomas. *Summa Theologiae*. II-II: 122: 1.

> other sins, other vices. They are pride, avarice, envy, wrath, lust, gluttony, and sloth or acedia.[250]

It is simply not rational for anyone to assert that obesity isn't catastrophic to the health of women. Denying this fact only puts women's health, souls, and marriages in grave danger. Anyone *truly interested* in the overall health of women ought to advocate that they maintain healthy figures and eating habits.

So, ladies, if your husband is asking you to focus more on your health—i.e. exercise and eating habits— don't be upset at him. Once you begin losing weight, I guarantee you'll be thanking him. I'll leave it to you to figure out the best way to do that…

Don't Act Like a Giant Contraceptive

Keeping a healthy appearance is one part of sustaining physical and emotional intimacy in a marriage. The other part lies in maintaining the right disposition. Accordingly, this section will address the *attitudes* and *behaviors* which objectively obstruct the potential for marital intimacy. In other words, don't act like a giant contraceptive.

It is an undeniable, objective truth that if the fundamentals of your marriage are not "up to par" in the marital bedroom, your relationship fails to be "up to par" everywhere else, too. After all, the Catholic Church has long referred to *coitus* as "the marital act."[251] Men and women must take particular care to look after the sexual needs of their spouses, and that means not blundering blithely through one's domestic routine, acting like a giant contraceptive. Among these avoidable states are acts and dispositions such as the "silent treatment," excessive solitary activities, excessive inactivity, nagging, bossiness, moodiness,

---

250 McIlmail, Fr. Edward. "Ask a Priest: When Does Eating Become Gluttony?" *RC Spirituality*, 25 Mar. 2018, rcspirituality.org/ask_a_priest/ask-priest-eating-become-gluttony/.

251 Duff, David M. "The Meaning of the Marital Act." *The Linacre Quarterly*, 1 Nov. 2004.

and the worst one of all (which seems to result from all of the above): closing yourself off sexually to your husband. It is the latter on which we will focus, momentarily. It is no surprise that relationships quickly spiral when the marital debt[252] is not being carefully attended to: again, the Church uses the term "the marital act" to designate the essential action—sexual union—which denotes the existence of the marital bond.

Those who are married made promises before God to dedicate their bodies to their spouses for the marital debt. This is why I dedicated so much time discussing the importance of bodily health in the previous section. But what good is bodily health if your behavioral health is foreclosing your marital affection?

Let's dive into the most controversial truth of married Catholic sexual ethics: spouses are not allowed to, without a just reason, deny the other the satisfaction of the marital debt. This applies to both the husband and the wife equally. The Angelic Doctor, St. Thomas Aquinas, in the *Summa* answers the question "whether one spouse is bound to pay the debt to the other at a festal time?", averring that:

> Since the wife has power of her husband's body, and "vice versa," with regard to the act of procreation, the one is bound to pay the debt to the other, at any season or hour, with due regard to the decorum required in such matters, for this must not be done at once openly.[253]

St. Thomas, then, goes on to say, "For it is ordained by God, on account of the weakness of the flesh, that the debt must always be paid to the one who asks lest he be afforded an occasion of sin."[254] Note how St. Thomas addresses neither sex in particular, but both together: the marital debt must be paid!

---

252 Marital debt, also known as conjugal debt, is the sexual obligation one spouse owes to the other.

253 Aquinas, Thomas. *The Summa Theologica of St. Thomas Aquinas.* London: Burns Oates & Washbourne, 1912, Question 64. Article 9 Ad 1.

254 Ibid.

Commenting on Aquinas's view on the marital debt, Philosopher Colleen McCluskey noted:

> Aquinas partitions these duties along the lines of the traditional division of labor according to which men operate in the so-called public sphere and women are responsible for the maintenance of the so-called private sphere (In NEVHI.12). Nevertheless, at least one of these duties is the same, and that is what comes to be called the marriage debt. The marriage debt requires that each partner acquiesce to a demand for sex by the other partner. In the later Middle Ages, it was commonly held that men and women were equal with respect to the marriage debt. Each partner was obligated to satisfy the debt, and each partner had the right to demand its satisfaction. Satisfying the partner's demand was never sinful, regardless of the other's motivation for the demand. Whether the demand itself was sinful depended upon the reasons one had for making it. Since in the eyes of most of the medieval theologians beginning with Augustine, the only proper motivation for sex, even within marriage, was procreation, any other reason would have constituted at least a venial sin on the part of the one making the request. Thus, it is within the rights of either party to request sex for whatever reason, and both parties have an equal obligation to satisfy that request. On Aquinas's view, equality with respect to the marriage debt falls under equality of proportion rather than equality of quantity the more active and therefore the more noble role. Once again, it is not entirely clear why the marriage debt is a matter of proportionality and not quantity, since both husbands and wives have exactly the same right to demand satisfaction of the marriage debt and exactly the same obligation to satisfy that debt.[255]

---

255 McCluskey, Colleen. "An Unequal Relationship between Equals: Thomas Aquinas on Marriage." *History of Philosophy Quarterly*, vol. 24, no. 1, 2007, http://www.jstor.org/stable/27745075. Accessed 13 Apr. 2022, pp. 1–18.

More importantly, Holy Scripture also tackles the issue, of course. In 1 Corinthians it is stated:

> But because of the temptation to immorality, each man should have his own wife and each woman her own husband. The husband should give to his wife her conjugal rights, and likewise the wife to her husband. For the wife does not rule over her own body, but the husband does; likewise the husband does not rule over his own body, but the wife does. Do not refuse one another except perhaps by agreement for a season, that you may devote yourselves to prayer; but then come together again, lest Satan tempt you through lack of self-control.[256]

Medieval historian, Dr. Elizabeth Makowski sums up the above Scriptural verses perfectly, "The apostle Paul was the earliest influential spokesman for a Christian view of marriage and sexuality. Marital sex was, for Paul, a safeguard against human weakness (1 Cor. 7.1-2)."[257]

On the topic of the marital debt being sanctioned by divine law, the 20th century encyclical *Casti Connubii* becomes again relevant:

> The second blessing of matrimony which we said was mentioned by St. Augustine, is the blessing of conjugal honor which consists in the mutual fidelity of the spouses in fulfilling the marriage contract, so that what belongs to one of the parties by reason of this contract sanctioned by divine law, may not be denied to him or permitted to any third person; nor may there be conceded to one of the parties anything which, being contrary to the rights and laws of God and entirely opposed to matrimonial faith, can never be conceded.[258]

---

256 1 Corinthians 7: 2-7.

257 Makowski, Elizabeth M. "The conjugal debt and medieval canon law," *Journal of Medieval History,* vol. 3, Issue 2, 1977, https://resources.saylor.org/wwwresources/archived/site/wp-content/uploads/2011/04/The-Conjugal-Debt-and-Medieval-Canon -Law.pdf, pp. 99-114.

258 Pius XI. *Casti Connubii.* 1930, www.vatican.va/content/pius-xi/en/encyclicals/documents/hf_p-xi_enc_19301231_casti-connubii.html, Section 19.

Due to the strong, mutual sexual desire designed by God within husbands and wives, it would be cruel for one spouse to deny the other the satisfaction of the debt. However, there *are* instances when one spouse can deny the other, like in time of severe illness or if a spouse is requesting sexual acts which are not licit. Common excuses like being "too tired" or "not in the mood" don't meet the standard for denying your spouse this fundamental right. If, like it is stated in Scripture, there is mutual agreement between spouses not to engage in sexual relations it should only be a short-term agreement, and the spouses should take to prayer until relations resume.

Unfortunately, some Catholics greatly misinterpret the marital debt as a license for an angry husband to force his unwilling wife to have intercourse with Church sanction. This is far from the truth. Common sense dictates that this scaremongering is, of course, nonsensical. The point is that, according to St. Thomas, the wife (or the husband) assumes a mortal sin upon her soul for denying what is rightly owed to her husband (or his wife) by God (unless she has a legitimate reason, as previously stated). Aquinas states:

> If the husband be rendered incapable of paying the debt through a cause consequent upon marriage, for instance, through having already paid the debt and being unable to pay it, the wife has no right to ask again, and in doing so she behaves as a harlot rather than as a wife. But if he be rendered incapable through some other cause, then if this be a lawful cause, he is not bound, and she cannot ask, but if it be an unlawful cause, then he sins, and his wife's sin, should she fall into fornication on this account, is somewhat imputable to him. Hence he should endeavor to do his best that his wife may remain continent.[259]

Many women deny their husbands sex for reasons they foolishly

---

259 Aquinas, Thomas. *Summa Theologiae.* Question 64, Article 1, Reply to Objection 3.

presume to be legitimate, like exhaustion from caring for children and housework. These do not constitute legitimate reasons. Further, a woman's daily schedule should be thoughtfully crafted to increase opportunities for marital intimacy.

I would be remiss if I didn't take a moment to briefly address a sad reality that many women currently struggling with: post-traumatic stress caused by past sexual abuse.

A minority of women deny their husbands sex from a multitude of graver reasons such as sexual abuse suffered earlier in their lives. You should know that this, while uncommon, is less uncommon than it seems. I receive many heart-breaking emails from women who were sexually abused and as a result have great difficulty enthusiastically enjoying sex with their husbands. As much as they want to enjoy the conjugal act, something holds them back. Until they got married, most of these poor souls were unaware of how their trauma would affect their marital intimacy. In other words, their husbands were the first they were *willingly* intimate with. I encourage such women to seek professional help now, so that you don't cause further suffering to your spouse by being unable to perform your wifely duties. Secondarily, I offer my prayers to any woman who is struggling in this regard. Seek St. Joseph's intercession for strength for you and your husband to bear this cross patiently until God sees fit to bring healing.

If you are a young, unmarried woman and foresee having these issues because of past abuse, communicate this with your future husband *before marriage* so that you can heal quicker. There is no shame in seeking help for past trauma—especially if your goal is to ensure a healthy future marriage for you and your husband—in fact, it's quite honorable. Marriage presents enough challenges on its own. For your sake and your husband's, don't enter into it with a handicap which might have been remedied earlier.[260]

---

260 *Focus on the Family* published an excellent article, "Sexual Trauma and its Effect on Marriage," for those looking to read more on this topic: https://www.focusonthefamily.com/marriage/sexual-trauma-and-its-effect-on-marriage/.

Making Time for Marriage (No Matter How Many Children You Have!)

Even if you are a woman with ten plus children, you ought to be putting your husband first. Too many wives falsely claim this to be a preposterous notion since children, unlike grown men, require constant care and attention (usually, moreover, those making this claim do *not* have thirteen children). They miss the point: it's not so much the husband who needs constant care, *but rather the marital relationship*. In fact, the healthiest marriages are the ones curated and tended to most frequently, and with the most concern. Some find it counterintuitive that team MVPs—e.g. Kobe Bryant—not the team's weakest players, always show up at practice first and stay the longest. Tireless improvement is what made Kobe Bryant the MVP, not solely natural talent. The same principle applies to marriages: stronger couples put constant effort into their relationships; weaker couples haplessly act as if there is no such thing as improvement. For instance, it really refreshes the romance to be alone with your husband for a late-night date: conversation, movie, dessert, game, book read aloud. Try it. Truly, it makes both spouses feel like a priority, in one another's eyes.

In our marriage, we try to make time in the evening and morning for just us. (I'll explain how we do so later in this section.) This quality time really helps to keep frustrations and annoyances at bay. In so doing, it keeps my husband and me "in lock step" for longer periods between inevitable disagreements.

However, since having seven children, one with a severe medical issue, I have been guilty on a few occasions of claiming exhaustion and thereby putting my spousal relationship temporarily on the side. After all, caring for young children and housework is not only physically exhausting, but also *emotionally exhausting*. Sometimes I found myself becoming short-tempered with my husband over trifling matters, which led me to become even more "intentional" about correcting these strong tendencies against intimacy. Instead, I tried to initiate a "come-to-Jesus" moment (inclusive of self-reflection, prayer, and spousal conversation—usually in that order) to re-evaluate and re-work my schedule. In fact, I've had to re-evaluate my schedule with each new addition to our family (usually around the time the new baby turns 12 or 18 months).

While in an Italian hospital with my newborn first child for over a month, my mother-in-law once gave me some wise advice. She insisted upon watching the baby, so that my husband and I could grab a coffee together in the hospital food court (which also sold delicious Roman-style pizza and biscotti). I initially thought she was crazy: why in the world would I leave the bedside of my ailing, post-operative child to go do something as insignificant as grabbing a beverage I could get from the hospital room? As it turns out, a rejuvenating coffee and enlivening inter-spouse conversation proved to be *exactly* what my husband and I needed. Time together, "just the two of us,"[261] for emotional re-connection and the sharing of our deepest thoughts (about the medical mayhem besetting us both) was exactly what we needed. In that hour, we were able to reimagine a portion of our former normalcy. Every time Abby undergoes a periodic serious surgery, we recall the lesson of that day and carve out time to re-connect with one another. Even an hour goes a long way.

It is obvious that domestic duties become subjectively *harder* when a wife is not connecting emotionally with her husband. When we become too focused on our wifely schedules, duties, chores, and bills, we naturally begin relating to our husbands more like roommates and less like Christian spouses. When this inevitable drift occurs periodically in my household, either my husband or I always notice the phenomenon early and address it quickly. Yes, even a small problem shakes up our marriage. Therefore, my husband and I are on guard against the slightest threat to our intimacy.

Learning the art of "cutting corners" on small tasks throughout the day is one way we have recouped time for our marriage (see my list

---

261 "...you and I."

below). Even though many of us have been told not to cut corners, you cannot put a price on quality time with your husband and children. These precious moments quickly add up.

Focusing time and attention on my marriage while simultaneously keeping a tidy home, happy children, and solid homeschool routine still isn't easy. Only after much trial and error did I settle upon a list of tasks that could be truncated or amended without sacrificing quality homemaking. When I was a new childless wife, I could afford to dust the furniture every morning. Now that I'm wearing so many additional "hats," I have to do some such trivial tasks less frequently.

In other words, if forced to choose between Lazarus's two sisters, I want to be like Martha, not Mary. Recall the story of Martha in Scripture and you'll get my meaning:

> As Jesus and his disciples were on their way, he came to a village where a woman named Martha opened her home to him. She had a sister called Mary, who sat at the Lord's feet listening to what he said. But Martha was distracted by all the preparations that had to be made. She came to him and asked, "Lord, don't you care that my sister has left me to do the work by myself? Tell her to help me!"
>
> "Martha, Martha," the Lord answered, "you are worried and upset about many things, but few things are needed—or indeed only one. Mary has chosen what is better, and it will not be taken away from her."[262]

Being a "trad wife" doesn't require the butchering and de-feathering of your own hand-raised chickens. Nor does it require the beating of your laundry with a quartz crystal in a sparkling, alpine stream—especially if such ideal luxuries detract from your quality time with your husband. Such things prove to be paradigm instances of the "pyrrhic victory," something which takes such a heavy toll that it negates

262 Luke 10: 38-42.

any true sense of achievement and damages long-term progress. The "crunchy mom movement" or those who prefer to make or do everything themselves can easily be *hampered* by such pyrrhic victories.

The first mark of a happy home is not organically, hand-washed laundering but rather the close union of its head and its heart. One of the goals of life is learning to make the difficult look easy; too many housewives are doing the opposite. Work smart, not hard, after all. Common sense, people: learning how to do simple chores efficiently proves key to caring for a large family and making sure to fit in lots of time for your husband.

Below is my unfashionable "cutting-corners-laundry-list." I'm sure many of you have developed lists similar to mine. Like many of you, over time I've added incrementally an item or two to my list—usually after a new child is born.

1. Instead of doing laundry every other day, I do it once every week—but I know how and where to conceal my Mount Everest of clothes (as do all mothers).
2. My kids re-wear their play clothes throughout the week (and on wintry days of inclement weather, on which we don't leave the house, sometimes play in their pajamas), such as to lessen the laundry load.
3. I serve my kids almost all their meals on paper plates, with the noteworthy exception of special meals on feast days or holidays. (This was something that hilariously caused quite a stir on Catholic social media a few years back when a woman like-minded to myself made a similar declaration; some women were aghast at this practice and a full-fledged war ensued).
4. I fit all our young kids in our master bathtub at bath time—they love it, too.
5. I have six daughters and you better believe that the able-bodied ones "pull their weight" around here. All of the elder girls are fully capable of mopping floors, changing diapers, feeding pets,

loading and unloading dishwashers—before they hit six years old. They earn a fair wage for it, too, propping up the local dollar-store economy singlehandedly with their earnings. It proves a good practice for everyone.

6. Speaking of dishwashers, I am notorious among my friends for loading my dishwasher like I'm playing a game of Tetris. Our electric dishwashers also earn their keep around here.
7. You know why all my little girls have short little bobs? It's certainly not for fashion, it's because it's far easier and faster to brush all of their hair (and to dry it). Do you know how long it takes to brush out seven heads every morning? I do, which is why we prefer the bob.
8. In addition to pedagogical lessons, I assign self-guided lessons in homeschool so that I get some light housework done as the older kids "teach themselves" an hour each school day.
9. I typically depend heavily on my crock-pot throughout the week. It's an excellent time-saver, cooking meals to perfection throughout the live-long day. The crock-pot has family meals hot and ready to serve. I have long employed the same tireless, ceramic servant which was gifted to me at my wedding. When it finally "kicks the can," I will be providing it with a full-honor burial, complete with 21-gun salute, for its unparalleled service to the Gordon household.
10. I order my groceries online and schedule them for free "pick-up" so that I don't have to spend hours walking around the grocery store…or days locating all fourteen of my kids' individual shoes, hidden in fourteen separate corners of my home.
11. I order several household staples through on a thrifty online subscription and automatic delivery service. This way, I never run out of items like diapers and wipes.
12. When I make doctor's appointments for my kids, you better believe I schedule all seven of them for their check-ups at the same appointment.

13. All of my kids go to bed a bit later than most. That way, they don't rise at the crack of dawn demanding *Lucky Charms*. Instead, they wait until a decent hour to do so. This affords my husband and I the time to enjoy our coffee and conversation, alone, in the morning before they arise for their *Lucky Charms* (no child in the history of humanity has willingly eaten the oat pieces).

This brings me to the most *prominent* and *intentional* way we choose to save time in the Gordon household: we rarely enroll our offspring in organized children's activities. Instead, we spend *nearly all* of time together actively doing fun things at home and outdoors. We regularly play outdoor sports together, do outdoor gardening, play board and video games, take lengthy walks and bike rides, do group readings aloud, have outdoor bonfires, do drawing and painting—not to mention family vacations and homeschooling field trips to museums and aquariums, theme parks, and pro sports games. As a matter of fact, we even bought an RV to do these things, all around the country (especially in summertime).

Household intimacy is the fruit of time together: time spent playing, praying, working, reading, resting, and even getting bored together. In order for great intimacy to occur, families must maximize the twenty-four hours they have together. It's *staggering* to note how many families squander entire weekends (and many weekday nights) shuttling children around town, to some trifling activity. Most of these activities are self-evidently meaningless to both kids and parents—just a way of wasting valuable time. Time spent as a family proves comparatively far more valuable (which is far less true in the case of older boys' sports,[263] but luckily, six-sevenths of our children are the other sort).

263 None of this is to categorically suggest that we *forbid* our children from participating in such activities. We would, of course, allow an exceptional activity like a sport our son commits himself to, so long as it's not just some fleeting fancy. We believe this also helps the children to learn a) priority and b) follow-through. How frequently do these parents pack out their weekends with puerile group activities not because the

Shamefully, family time is being systematically eradicated in favor of "busying the kids" with outside activities. Hopefully, now my reader understands the problem: how do husbands and wives find time to spend with one another as they're each carting around a divided group of their kids from one activity to another? (Honestly, I've asked my kids what they prefer, and they regularly report to us that they'd rather partake in family activities.)

Not only are such at-home activities great for family togetherness, but they offer lots of opportunities for the husband and wife to flirt and be together throughout the weekend. This transitions our examination of the homeplace rather nicely to the next subsection: refreshing the intimacy of your marriage through frequent, nearly constant mutual flirtation.

Flirt with Your Husband Every Day

You don't cease to be your husband's girlfriend after you become his wife. As odd as that may sound, all it means is that you should try to be as demonstrative of your affections as you were when you were his girlfriend. It's not complex. Dressing up how he likes, taking an interest in his day, complimenting him, showing him how much you need him (for small and large things), and flirting with him are "to do" list items that should be done far more frequently than just on special occasions. These things should be happening literally every day. As a wife, it's actually your job.

Too many women—ever mindful of "getting their share" of adulation, praise, and visible tokens of affection—forget that men need affirmation as well.

---

child has shown any sincere interest whatsoever in them, but rather because parents have thoughtlessly christened the unimaginative activities "something positive for the kids to do ." Should any of my children show a veritable, lasting interest in pursuing a hobby, I would gladly reevaluate how to incorporate it into our family schedule. But, for our part, we will never willingly be the family whose entire weekend is spoken for with insipid activities.

Aside from all the obvious means listed above, there are additional ways to maximize the natural flirtation lying dormant within your marriage. It's not all coquettish banter, high heels, and cinematically saucy looks and expressions—though these things certainly qualify. Far more often, flirtation is constituted in subtler ways by taking an active interest in *his* work, *his* hobbies, and *his* interests. So doing offers many increased opportunities for daily intimacy. Don't just take an interest, actually join him in such interests.

For example, I assist my husband with many of his apostolate's technological functions. The apostolate is a job and hobby on which he works from home, so I am fortunate to assist him rather conveniently—just one room removed from our children. At present, I contribute to my husband's gig by the following: editing his videos, setting up his studio and audio, helping run his online classes and website, and making show notes. I do so because I am interested in what he does; and we love spending time with each other. Also, assisting him in his work helps us to stay more connected throughout the week. Even if your husband doesn't work from home, perhaps you could carve out some time in your week to assist him with something he has on his plate. I can vouch for the fact that doing so affords many opportunities for the two of you to bond while you are working toward a shared goal.

A few years ago, I helped my husband to rework his first published book, *Catholic Republic,* after it had been rejected by its first publisher.[264] We sat at our kitchen table each day with snacks and tea and did a big-time makeover on it together while our kids played in the yard.

If it's not possible for you to participate in assisting your husband with his workload, participating in his hobbies counts as a fine substitute. Even if his hobbies aren't formfitting to your taste, tag along and try to make the best out of it. You'll be surprised how your interest waxes. For instance, my husband enjoys all things basketball related. As a person with absolutely no athletic ability, I would be a nightmare to

264 Gordon, Timothy. *Catholic Republic: Why America Will Perish without Rome.* Manchester, NH: Crisis Publications, 2019, pp. 209-54.

play with. What I *can* do is tag along with him to the local park, sit on a blanket, and watch and chat as he practices shooting free throws. The children are perfectly capable of playing on the playground equipment nearby without their mother hovering over them every second. As a matter of fact, that's the arrangement they like best.

I have friends who accompany their husbands to the shooting range, to go duck hunting, to spend the day at the racetrack, and even one friend who tags along with her husband to *Comic-Con*[265] in *full costume* each year. Another friend of mine learned how to lay tile to tag along with and to assist her husband with his trade.

Truly, the little things count when trying to impart to your husband that you still find him alluring, interesting, and fun to be around. It's incredibly simple.

As well as working toward a shared goal, or taking an interest in his hobbies, wives should also compliment their husbands often and tell them what they're *doing right*. What a foreign notion. Have you noticed, like I have, that men have become the focus of everyone's derision? Men are being told that their masculinity is offensive—that heading their own rightful households is misogynistic. They're being propagandized, along with the rest of us, that consecrating their lives to these goodly things is innately violent or sexually deviant.

Even if you don't subscribe to such nonsense, ask yourself when the last time was that you told your husband he was doing something you appreciate. Perhaps many of you have acquired this lovely habit already. If so, I am sure you already see the fruits of doing so.

I make mention of it here because, I'm sad to announce, I've been around mostly women who do the exact opposite. Wifely complaints about husbands, in social settings, has gotten *totally out of hand*. (Recall my related trauma from Disneyworld!)I hear it everywhere, and I'm even hearing it in traditional Catholic circles. If one hears a wife running her husband down in public, the only proper response is declaring,

---

265 Comic-Con is a multi-day comic book convention. Fans of various entertainment media congregate and often dress in costume.

"I'm sorry, I cannot be party to this," while exiting the room. This should be obvious, but men have feelings too and *everyone* likes approval. Men, like women, need encouragement and affection. In some ways, I have learned after almost two decades of marriage, men need it more.

Again, besides the obvious ways of flirting with your husband, heartfelt praise can be incredibly flirtatious.

I encourage wives to stop what they're doing each day when your husband returns from work, meet him at the door, and give him a kiss. When mapping out your meal plans for the week, ask your husband if there's some special meal he'd like you to cook. Don't indulge sour attitudes such as, "he'll take what I give him!"

Men *also* appreciate gifts, compliments, and love letters. I try to write my husband a long letter every now and again to tell him, specifically, how much I love him and in what ways I am proud of him. Instead of sending him text messages with requests, reprimands, and other boring material, send him spontaneous compliments or tell him how much you miss him when he's away. If your husband is like mine, he makes himself a cup of coffee and always lets it get cold before he starts to drink it. Why not warm it up for him and bring it to him with a kiss?

Also, "fill in his gaps" by completing tasks he hates. For example, my husband *loathes passionately* organizing and is always forgetting to write down his many appointments. So, I bought him a dry erase calendar—and maintain it for him—to help keep him on schedule and organized.

None of the above ideas are intellectually ground-breaking. They need not be: old formulae work. Nor were the items of my list intended to be articles of boasting. On the contrary, many of them were passed humbly along to me from other married women. Those which were my original inventions were just simple, impromptu gestures of heartfelt love. I simply proffered them to my reader to pay back that grace which was given to me by the good advice I once received. Little acts of kindness and flirtation throughout the day—properly implemented—send your husband the irrepressible message that you are still attracted to him and remain deeply honored he chose you to be his wife.

Conclusion

The ideas expressed throughout this entire chapter—and throughout this entire book—are concisely articulated in the following closing remarks from the *Opus Dei* founder, St. Josemaría Escrivá:

> If a marriage is to preserve its initial charm and beauty, both husband and wife should try to renew their love day after day and that is done through sacrifice, with smiles and also with ingenuity. Is it surprising that a husband who arrives home tired from work begins to lose patience when his wife keeps on and on about everything she thinks has gone wrong during the day? Disagreeable things can wait for a better moment when the husband is less tired and more disposed to listen to them.
>
> Another important thing is personal appearance. And I would say that any priest who says the contrary is a bad adviser. As years go by a woman who lives in the world has to take more care not only of her interior life, but also of her looks. Her interior life itself requires her to be careful about her personal appearance; naturally this should always be in keeping with her age and circumstances. I often say jokingly that older facades need more restoration. It is the advice of a priest. An old Spanish saying goes: 'A well-groomed woman keeps her husband away from other doors.'
>
> That is why I am not afraid to say that women are responsible for eighty per cent of the infidelities of their husbands because they do not know how to win them each day and take loving and considerate care of them. A married woman's attention should be centered on her husband and children as a married man's attention should be centered on his wife and

> children. Much time and effort is required to succeed in this, and anything which militates against it is bad and should not be tolerated.
>
> There is no excuse for not fulfilling this lovable duty. Work outside the home is not an excuse. Not even one's life of piety can be an excuse because if it is incompatible with one's daily obligations it is not good nor pleasing to God. A married woman's first concern has to be her home. There is an Aragonese saying which goes: 'If through going to church to pray a woman burns her stew, she may be half an angel, but she's half a devil too.' I'd say she was a fully-fledged devil.[266]

Win your husbands every single day, ladies. Every. Single. Day.

266 "Conversations with Monsignor Escrivá de Balaguer," Ecclesia Press, Dublin, 1968, 1a.

7

The Obligatory Complimentary Chapter on Women

By now you may feel a bit challenged, perhaps picked on, dear female reader. I have spent a great amount of time advising women, myself included, to consider improving their: bodies, minds, schedules, choices, behaviors, habits, marriages, mothering, and clothing. In this chapter I intend to focus on the beauty of femininity and how it has been indispensable to society from the very beginning.

Although many today seek to distort a woman's role in the family, every woman was created by God for specific and immutable purposes. In Aristotle's *Nicomachean Ethics*, specifically in his recurring "function argument," Aristotle addresses how creatures are only "good" to the extent that they fulfill the function for which they were created. This is one of Aristotle's many items of sheer common sense. To refresh your memory:

> Nicomachean Ethics is a philosophical inquiry into the nature of the good life for a human being. Aristotle begins the work by positing that there exists some ultimate good toward which, in the final analysis, all human actions ultimately aim. The necessary characteristics of the ultimate good are that it is complete, final, self-sufficient and continuous. This good toward which all human actions implicitly or explicitly aim is happiness in Greek, "eudaimonia," which can also be translated as blessedness or living well, and which is not a static state of being but a type of activity.

> To discover the nature of human happiness it is necessary to determine what the function of a human being is, for a person's happiness will consist in fulfilling the natural function toward which his being is directed.[267]

In light of Aristotle, what "good" did God create women and how does fulfilling their purpose add to their happiness? Using Aristotle's reasoning, we might recur to the example of a hammer to help clarify matters. If a hammer is used according to its design, which aims to optimize its function—forcing nails into hard substances—it will be a productive tool. If, for instance, a hammer is used as a crude brush-tip to paint with, it will not be nearly such an efficient tool.

Women today are denying their proper functions and accordingly—if you recall the study on woman's happiness in an earlier chapter[268]—are finding themselves more miserable than ever. Then they ask why! Understanding their husband-aiding functions within the family (or priest-aiding functions in the case of nuns) is the only way women can find the happiness they seek. "True femininity" can be defined very simply: doing the feminine things we were designed by God, within nature, to do. The Lord gifted woman to man so that she may enrich his life and be his faithful companion. In doing so, God gave woman to all of humanity for its betterment—akin to how Jesus offered Mary to us all as He hung on the cross:

> When Jesus saw his mother and the disciple whom he loved standing beside her, he said to his mother, "Woman, here is your son." Then he said to the disciple, "Here is your mother." And from that hour the disciple took her into his own home.[269]

---

267 Aristotle, et al. "Aristotle: Nicomachean Ethics Summary." *Grade Saver,* www.gradesaver.com/aristotles-ethics/study-guide/summary.

268 Aggeler, Madeleine. "Women Are Unhappier Than Men, But Only Until We're 85!" *The Cut,* 14 Dec. 2017, www.thecut.com/2017/12/study-women-are-unhappier-than-men-but-only-until-were-85.html.

269 John 19: 26-28.

The natural gifts bestowed upon each woman are not meant for herself alone; rather, she, in turn, offers them freely to the common good. Civilization is dependent upon women—but not in the way feminists would have you believe. Instead, humanity depends on women in the intrafamilial ways *God* intended: he wanted us at home taking care of our husbands and children.

To illustrate my point, let's conduct a simple thought experiment: I want you to think of the three most important women in your life and the *one reason* why each one is so meaningful to you.[270] I'd bet that none of the reasons you listed had anything to do with how successful these women were in their careers (assuming they had one). Instead, I'd wager that each of your three reasons center around one facet of *true* femininity which will be articulated in one or more of the sections below.

Truly Feminine Women Are Indispensable as Mothers

Woman by her very nature is maternal – for every woman, whether ... married or unmarried, is called upon to be a biological, psychological or spiritual mother – she knows intuitively that to give, to nurture, to care for others, to suffer with and for them–for maternity implies suffering – is infinitely more valuable in God's sight than to conquer nations and fly to the moon.
—Alice von Hildebrand

As a species we would be nowhere without the life-giving biology of woman. Only once you reflect upon the fact that for nine months, a woman's body is capable of incubating and nourishing an entirely delicate, dependent human being, can you *truly* appreciate women. It is the only thing we do that is truly *sui generis* or unique. God designed woman—as he designed all His creatures—so thoughtfully: she can even carry multiple babies in her womb and nurture them both with her body, after birth.

270 If any are still alive you might take the nearest opportunity to tell them they made your top five list and why.

And yet the feminists, who badly mimic the manly virtues, snub the miraculous life-giving power only *our* bodies are capable of. Such women are ashamed of their sacred purpose, bartering it away in exchange for superficial ambitions that can't possibly be realized except in a society which lies to them. How shamefully ignorant. Feminists search relentlessly for some imagined "purpose" when it's hiding in plain sight, right under their noses—inscribed in their very bodies. As a woman, what can be more glorious than bringing new life to the world? It's a sublime honor. It astounds me to see so many women chemically inhibiting their bodies' natural life-giving, life-affirming excellences.

Moreover, it's not just enveloping and developing an infant in the womb which make mothers indispensable to society. Rather, it's the indispensable nurturing they provide to their children—for no one will ever be on your side more than a loving mother. And those children who grow up without such a mother carry this wound for the rest of their lives, sometimes passing it along to their offspring.

A truly feminine mother sacrifices *greatly* during her pregnancy. She undergoes Herculean levels of physical pain bringing her beloved child into the world. After birth—before the body of the mother has even had a brief pause for recuperation—she further exhausts her body and mind caring for her newborn. And shortly thereafter, she *still* wants to do it all over again. This can only reduce to the purest love of life.

I can speak from experience in this regard. My first-born daughter, Abigail Francis, couldn't conceivably have been born under more stressful circumstances. As a first-time mother, I had no idea what to expect from childbirth. At eight months gestation, in Rome, Italy, little Abby was born via emergency cesarian section: sometime between month seven and month eight of gestation, the little dear had suffered several brain hemorrhages *in utero*. Even after an extremely painful recovery, weeks spent waiting outside of the NICU, and a month of hospitalization subsequent to her first (of many) brain surgeries, I was thrilled to do it all over again.

Two years later I became pregnant with my second-born, Olivia

"Maggie" Magdalene. Back in the States, my doctors were convinced that history might well repeat itself, so I was hospitalized for some uncomfortable weeks to receive some *ultimately needless* plasma transfusions. I won't bore you with the unpleasant details, but I had some rough weeks. The doctors thought that my husband and I might have a rare genetic incompatibility that may have caused Abby's brain hemorrhages, necessitating that they test us to prevent our second child from having the same emergency. While in the hospital, I found (through their testing) that I had a severe case of gestational diabetes, necessitating that I give myself insulin shots several times a day. In the meantime, I was undergoing the preventive treatments assuming the genetic incompatibility, just in case the test came back positive. And there was only one lab in the country that regularly ran the needed diagnostic test. Weeks passed before I received my results, causing some distress and uncertainty. But by the grace of God, it came back negative. And even though we never discovered what had happened to Abby, we felt relieved that her condition would not replicate in future pregnancies. Maggie was also born via cesarean section because my first cesarean wasn't performed properly, and I could no longer safely deliver babies naturally.

Because of these two difficult pregnancies, some women, especially feminists, would see this as a valid reason to cease having more children. However, being avidly pro-life, my husband and I eagerly looked forward to our next child. My third pregnancy occurred between two and three years later. I looked forward to bringing life into this world one more time…via cesarean…and this time with twins. So, my track record of complicated pregnancies continued unblemished. My record for gestational trouble was fated to go undefeated through the birth of my third and fourth children. After a backbreaking pregnancy, at the end of which I could hardly walk—or control another bout of gestational diabetes with insulin—Peregrine "Pippin" Gianna and Charlotte "Charlie" Anselm were born…via cesarean, for good measure.

At this point my doctors were pleading with me to not become pregnant again, claiming they didn't think I could safely have another cesarean. Two to three years after the birth of my twins, I became pregnant with my first son, Gabriel Ambrose. If you were hoping that my track record of difficult pregnancies finally came to an end, not quite. Although, no genetic tests were run and no stowaway "bonus" children sprang from my womb at the last minute, I was still hit by gestational diabetes. To cap the fun of another long diabetic pregnancy, Gabe's delivery went perfectly smoothly—*not*: halfway through my cesarian section, my spinal anesthetic wore off. Following his delivery, I wanted to cry out "Freedom!" from the famous Braveheart scene.

At this point, I had four complicated pregnancies versus zero normal ones. My sixth child, Miriam Josephine, maintained my difficult pregnancy streak by evincing multiple markers for *Down's Syndrome* which appeared on ultrasound. Naturally, we waited until after her birth to confirm that she did not have it, but the frightening proposition haunted the last five months of the pregnancy. Not to mention, my less-than-pro-life doctors had been scaring up catastrophic images in my head of uterine rupture throughout my last two trimesters. Not surprisingly, I had another bout of gestational diabetes. Good times. And as I sit here typing—with the "baby" of the family toddling around on chubby legs—I can candidly express that I will do it all over again if Providence wills it. I'll gladly go for baby number seven, on a 7-0 record, if the Lord wills it.[271]

Truly feminine mothers are our first fans, first teachers, and first loves. God designed mothers to interweave their very existence with

---

271 Right before the publication of this book, I found out that I had become pregnant with our seventh child—our sixth girl, to be named Penelope Pius. Some left-leaning Catholics have argued that women, like me, who have dangerous pregnancies are reckless by continuing to allow themselves to get pregnant. They argue that illicitly using contraception is *actually the responsible thing to do* since it will prohibit the possibility of leaving behind prior children should the mother die in childbirth. To them I say: "A witless worm have you become. Therefore be silent, and keep your forked tongue behind your teeth. I have not passed through fire and death to bandy words with a serving-man till the lightning falls." Which is a Tolkien nerd's way of saying, "stay in your lane and learn your faith."

that of their children. To wit, there is an old saying about maternity: "Motherhood is your heart forever walking around outside of you."[272]

Truly feminine women have an enormous capacity for motherly love. Such women can have dozens of biological children and *still* maintain the ability to share unmitigated love with an adopted child, her husband, neighbors, friends, and extended family members.

Truly feminine women maintain and perfect their nurturing abilities—even and especially into their very advanced age. Years back, when I had given birth to the twins, I brought them to a retirement home to raise the spirits of the elderly residents. Upon entering, we immediately found ourselves surrounded by a group of elderly women all waiting patiently for their turn to hold one of the babies. A hauntingly common and deeply felt remark made by these ladies was: "enjoy every moment, it goes by way too fast."

Truly feminine mothers share a singular sort of sagacity to younger women, as St. Paul admonished. They assist younger women in the cultivation of holiness and gentleness—especially within the context of the marital relationship. Such women number a precious few in our day, rendering them an even more invaluable commodity. They help us to become better wives, mothers, and sisters. When a young wife (or mother) confronts a high fever in her newborn, a first Thanksgiving turkey, or an early marital spat with her husband, she seeks *honest* council. Only an unwise woman seeks or proffers empty, false platitudes. Sadly, in our day, foolishness abounds amongst seekers and grantors: I mourn the loss of such women in society today—the society by and for aging feminists.

Even truly feminine women *without* children can share, in an equivocal sense, their natural maternal gifts to society. They are our religious and unmarried sisters who spend their time serving our communities of faith and extended family. (I can't even count how many times my single friends or family stepped in to help us at a moment's notice when my eldest daughter had a medical emergency.)

---

272 This quotation could not be attributed to an author.

Our nation used to depend greatly upon religious sisters to run orphanages, schools, hospitals, and poor houses. We will cover women religious later in this chapter, but a brief mention proves worthwhile here. These dauntless women were the first to run to those with unknown and horrifying medical sicknesses. Religious sisters like Mother Teresa (St. Teresa of Calcutta), cradled and comforted those dying from AIDS, when it was new and with hyperinflated prescriptions of danger (rendering the act of charity one of genuine courage as well). Keep in mind, it was a time in history when we still weren't sure how AIDS was transmitted:

> Mother Teresa, who won the Nobel Peace Prize in 1979 for her work among the poor in Calcutta, India, opened an AIDS Hospice in Greenwich Village on Christmas Eve in 1985. Mother Teresa was the founder of the Order of the Missionaries of Charity, a Roman Catholic congregation of women dedicated to helping the poor. Considered one of the 20th century's greatest humanitarians, she was canonized as Saint Teresa of Calcutta in 2016.
>
> In 1985 AIDS was still very much a disease with unknown, unresearched implications. Many were dying and the illness was highly stigmatized. Community opposition at the time forced cancellation of plans for other AIDS centers in New York City. It makes perfect sense that Mother Teresa, known for her work with the poor and lepers of Calcutta, was called to help those suffering under extreme discrimination for their illness and that St. Veronica's in Greenwich Village opened its arms to the terminally-ill patients.[273]

Like priests, nuns are celibates, free to submit themselves to heightened danger—compared against the danger to which laymen can

---

273 Stephens, Lannyl. "When Mother Teresa Opened an AIDS Hospice in Greenwich Village." *Village Preservation,* 17 July 2020, www.villagepreservation.org/2018/12/24/when-mother-teresa-opened-an-aids-hospice-in-greenwich-village/.

reasonably expose themselves. Although they don't have their own children to care for, it still constitutes true grit.

Truly feminine women, if they remain celibate, prove to be "virgin mothers" by reference to our collective Virgin Mother. These women magnify the Lord through their holy maternal service to their brothers and sisters in Christ and their willingness to sacrifice their own comforts to attend to those around them.

Because truly feminine women keep a healthy prayer life, I'll end each of the following sections with a specific prayer (or two) corresponding to the role discussed. On the importance of prayer, *The Catholic Girls Manual and Sunday Missal* says the following:

> Prayer is a means as efficacious as it is necessary, for obtaining help from God. Our blessed Lord has urged us often to have recourse to it, and has given us the model of the perfect prayer—the Lord's Prayer. To this prayer, Holy Mother the Church usually joins the Angelical Salutation or the *Hail Mary,* so as to render homage to the Blessed Virgin Mary. Prayer is necessary for salvation, victory over temptation, is the practice of virtue, and perseverance of grace. If the proper things are asked for, and the prayer is made with attention, humility, confidence, sincerity and perseverance, God will certainly grant our petitions. We do not always obtain what we pray for, either because we have not prayed properly or because God sees that what we are asking would not be for our good.[274]

The following two prayers may be recited daily by Christian mothers. A truly feminine mother ought to remind herself often that her children are "on loan" from God, and that her children are His in the first place.

274 Fearns, John M. S.T.D. *Catholic Girl's Manual.* Catholic Book Publishing Co., N.Y., 1952, pp. 33.

The Christian Mother's Daily Prayer for the Children

O Mary, Immaculate Virgin and Sorrowful Mother, commend our beloved children to the Most Sacred Heart of Jesus, who refuses nothing to His Mother.

Holy Guardian Angels: Pray for them.
St Joseph: powerful patron, pray for them.
St. John: beloved disciple of the Heart of Jesus, pray for them.
St. Augustine: pray for them.
St. Anthony: pray for them.
St. Aloysius: pray for them.
St. Anne, Mother of Mary: pray for them.
St. Elizabeth, pray for them.
St. Monica, pray for them.

My Queen! My Mother! I give you all myself, and to show my devotion to you, I consecrate to you my eyes, my ears, my mouth, my heart, my entire-self. Wherefore, O loving Mother, as I am your own, keep me, as your property and possession. Mary, please help me to be a good mother today and always. Mary, most sorrowful Mother, of Christians, pray for me and my family. St. Joseph, foster-father of our Lord Jesus Christ and true spouse of Mary, the Virgin, pray for my husband and me. AMEN.[275]

A Mother's Prayer to the Guardian Angles of her Children

I humbly salute you, O you faithful heavenly Friends of my children! I give you heartfelt thanks for all the love and goodness you show them. At some future day I shall, with thanks more worthy than I can now give, repay your care for them, and before the whole heavenly court acknowledge

275 Franciscus, Rev. Pius, O.F.M. "Mother love, A Prayer Book for Christian Wives and Mothers." *Archconfraternity of Christian Mothers*, 1979, pp. 8-10.

their indebtedness to your guidance and protection. Continue to watch over them. Provide for all their needs of body and soul. Pray, likewise, for me, for my husband, and my whole family, that we may all one day rejoice in your blessed company. AMEN.[276]

Truly Feminine Women Are Indispensable as Wives

Christian wife! Follow the footsteps of the ideal of all womanhood, the Blessed Mother of God; in joy and sorrow, she will be your advocate at the throne of her Son.
—Saint John Vianney

The truly feminine woman is not only her children's most faithful devotee, but also her husband's. As Scripture states,

> The Lord God formed man from the dust of the ground and breathed into his nostrils the breath of life, and man became a living being. ... The Lord God took the man and put him in the Garden of Eden to work it and take care of it. ... The Lord God said, 'It is not good for the man to be alone. I will make a helper suitable for him.' ... He brought them to the man ... But for man no suitable helper was found. So the Lord God caused the man to fall into a deep sleep and while he was sleeping he took one of the man's ribs and closed up the place with flesh. Then the Lord God made a woman from the rib he had taken out of the man and brought her to the man. The man said 'This is now bone of my bones and flesh of my flesh; she shall be called 'woman' because she was taken out of man.' For this reason a man will leave his father and mother and be united to his wife, and they will become one flesh.[277]

276 Ibid.
277 Genesis 2:7, 15, 18-24.

The truly feminine wife takes it to heart that her duty in marriage will be multifarious.

She is her husband's best friend, lover, cook, cleaner, secretary, and biggest fan. A wife who takes her role seriously is her husband's greatest advocate—helping him to tackle all of life's adversities with gentle good humor, fidelity, and affection. She understands that, though her husband is her head, she is the heart (and in a sense, the neck—which supports the head in all of its many functions). To help him accomplish whatever God calls him to accomplish, she keeps him well-loved, well-fed, and well-organized as he discharges his duties to provide for their family.

A man with his faithful wife by his side can weather any storm. The truly feminine wife *never* seizes upon her husband's defeats to "teach him a lesson" or to deride or chide him. Instead, she, through her tireless praise and admiration, encourages him to "try, try again." A truly feminine wife understands that she can breathe new life into her defeated husband with a few supportive words and some affectionate reassurance.

Describing, once more, the friendships of unequals—of which the spousal friendship is the holiest instance—Aristotle makes it perfectly clear that nature was designed such that the wife has the infused instinct to show more affection to her husband (than vice versa): "inequality is redressed by affection."[278] In other words, it is not "sexism" which accounts for the husbandly expectation of superlative wifely affection, but nature itself. Husbands bear the brunt of the world; accordingly, they need and deserve more affection than wives. Wives are protected from the brunt of the world in their docility and domesticity; accordingly, they owe more affection than husbands.

Aristotle writes, "affection seems to be the mark of a good friend; hence it is friends that love each other as each deserves who continue to

278 Goold, G.P., ed. *Aristotle XIX Nicomachean Ethics*. Vol. 73, Cambridge: Loeb Classical Library, 1926, pp. 481 translator's liner notes.

be friends and whose friendship is lasting."[279] Note Aristotle's key words, "as each deserves." The marital friendship, according to Aristotle, is "lasting" when justice is apportioned according to nature. This apportionment is ensured when wifely affection is constant.

At the end of the day, truly feminine wives are, amazingly, able to juggle the *many* duties of the household and still be their husband's friend and sweetheart. The truly feminine wife understands how to rejuvenate the daily romance by remembering always to be her husband's adventure-affirming girlfriend as well as his faithful spouse. She can do this even when her day is wrought with the stresses of childcare, homeschool, or tedious housework.

I've known elderly women who still dress up—complete with regular manicures, pedicures, and salon appointments—so as to impress their husbands. Is it a coincidence that these are the women I know with the happiest and longest-lasting marriages?

Everyone has *that* older female relative who volunteers unsolicited, explicit marital advice to all of the family's newlyweds. Laugh as we all might at such a woman's transgressions into "TMI,"[280] we have to all admit that she knows how to keep a man happy.

For my part, I was made to blush by an audacious grandmother during my wedding shower. Grandma's advice was strikingly similar to the following hilarious conversation taken from the movie, *My Big Fat Greek Wedding.* On the eve of her big, fat, Greek wedding, protagonist Toula, is shamelessly advised by her mother, Maria Portokalos, in the following way:

> Maria Portokalos: Toula, on my wedding night, my mother, she said to me, "Greek women, we may be lambs in the kitchen, but we are tigers in the bedroom."

---

279 Aristotle, W D. Ross, and Lesley Brown. *The Nicomachean Ethics.* Oxford: Oxford University Press, 2009, Books VIII, viii, 4.

280 "Too much information."

> Toula Portokalos: Eww. Please let that be the end of your speech.[281]

Humorous as the scene is, it ranks among the best marriage advice any new bride could receive on the eve of her wedding (as off-putting as it is to get it from a mother…or, in my case, a grandmother).

A truly feminine Catholic wife enthusiastically becomes both her husband's lover and friend, but also the heart of their home. The presence of such a woman is the very reason the home is warm, inviting, well-appointed, and cheerful. Without such a woman, the house is not a home. This is why everyone likes to be wherever mom is at for Christmas, Thanksgiving, and Easter. A truly feminine wife pours her heart and soul into tending her home—even the unpleasant tasks—such as to present her husband with a tranquil place to rest his head at the end of a difficult day. Ask any man: he'll tell you that his primary short-term incentive on the toughest days at work comprise a cheerful wife, well-appointed home, and fragrant dinner awaiting him upon his arrival. The mind is boggled by the amount and diversity of tasks accomplished by the truly feminine wife throughout the day; this list of tedious chores (inclusive of the beautification of self, home, and even the kids) must be discharged in its entirety such as to present the wife, the home, and the children to a world-weary husband.

From the days of the "honeymoon phase," well into the golden days as the elderly matriarch of the family, the truly feminine wife *never stops* adoring her husband and believing he can accomplish great things—even when his body grows old and frail. To her, he remains the daring lad who won her heart all those many years ago.

Never forget that even though the wife is not the equal to her husband in the Aristotelian sense, she can still enjoy a meaningful "friendship of unequals" with him. As a reminder:

---

281 Zwick, Joel. *My Big Fat Greek Wedding*. Gold Circle Films, 2003.

> There is a different kind of friendship, which involves superiority of one party over the other, for example, the friendship… between husband and wife.[282]

Mother Love, a Catholic woman's prayer book, also proves a valuable source of uncommon advice ("uncommon" by today's standards). I frequently turn to this small book when I'm seeking inspiration to improve upon my vocation. In it, one finds a challenging yet useful questionnaire, *A Spiritual Checkup*, which helps women to identify the ways in which they may be lagging as wives or mothers. As the old adage goes: *correct a wise woman and she will thank you for it.* Try as we all might, slipping into ruts and bad habits proves inevitable. When it does, all of us must "up our game." I present this questionnaire here in the submissive spirit of the helpful servant, because my aim is to help the helpers, those truly feminine wives and mothers out there:

A Spiritual Checkup

1. Have I tried to be a source of encouragement and inspiration to my husband?
2. Have I impaired the authority of my husband with the children regarding obedience?
3. Have I belittled him before the children or his friends by revealing his faults?
4. Have I been indulgent, obedient, and conciliatory to my husband?
5. Have I tried to be neat in my appearance when my husband comes home from work?
6. Have I frequently discussed with my husband the character formation of the children?
7. Have I every day recited the *Christian Mother's Daily Prayer for the Children*?

---

282 Aristotle, W D. Ross, and Lesley Brown. *The Nicomachean Ethics.* Oxford: Oxford University Press, 2009, Books VIII, vii, 1.

8. Have I prayed with my children and taught them their religion?
9. Have I been reading and studying how to train my children to be good Catholics and loyal citizens?
10. Have I taken an interest in the studies of my children and made sure that they use their talents?
11. Have I tried to mention items of a religious nature in my remarks, or is the family conversation limited to the movies, sports, styles, television and the weather?
12. Have I corrected the faults of the children, especially stubbornness, selfishness, disobedience and untruthfulness?
13. Have I used unbecoming language in their presence, cursed or abused them when angry?
14. Have I allowed my children to bring their friends home, even though the furniture and rugs are given rather rough treatment?
15. Have I permitted my sons or daughters to date too young in life? To "go-steady" with no prospect of marriage in the near future?
16. Have I permitted the children to visit dangerous places of amusement, or allowed them to go to entertainments without sufficient supervision?
17. Have I been supervising the use of the radio and television set, or are my children at times being subjected to trashy programs?
18. Have been checking the reading material of my family and the movies they watch at home or away from home?
19. Have I studied about the misuse of drugs, and worries that teenagers say to adults: "You have drinks, we have drugs"?
20. Have I taught my family to assume responsibility in parish, civic and political matters?[283]

---

283 Franciscus, Rev. Pius, O.F.M. "Mother love, A Prayer Book for Christian Wives and Mothers." *Archconfraternity of Christian Mothers*, 1979.

In order to maintain a vibrant marriage, as noted above, minding the relationship's physical *and* spiritual health matters. After all, the spiritual and physical health of human bodies are intertwined with one another; why should it be any different in the case of marital relations, within the single "cell"[284] of the mystical body of Christ (i.e. the family)? Because women are multi-taskers by our feminine nature, we sometimes calculate too ambitiously and thereby assume too many tasks at once. In this vein, we can easily become preoccupied with the corporal demands of homemaking, and overlook the requirements of our spiritual health. A house can only *truly* become a home when the woman tends to her spiritual health as much as her physical health. Her husband and her children will be better loved if she keeps the Lord at the center of her life. The following daily prayer may be used to regularly renew our wifely invitation of God into our hearts as the animating principle of our vocation:

A Wife's Prayer

> Most Holy Trinity, Father, Son, and the Holy Spirit, You instituted marriage in the earthly Paradise and in the New Law, You elevated it to the dignity of a sacrament, attaching to it many graces. Grant to my husband and me the grace to live holily in so sacred a state and, by the practice of Christian virtues, to act always as is becoming a Christian couple. As Your minister joined our hands at the holy altar, so may we journey through life with one heart and soul, tasting its pleasures with moderation, enduring its sorrows with resignation and, at all times, mutually assisting and consoling each other.
>
> May Your true and holy fear strengthen us to serve You uprightly with pure heart and eyes and lips, in mutual esteem and forbearance! Grant that the children born of our union may be pure of heart and well-disposed in mind, and that they

284 CCC #2207.

may gladly walk in the way of Your Commandments. Teach us to be faithful images of the Holy Family of Nazareth, of the blessed foster-father Joseph, of the most devout Mother Mary, and the Child Jesus, that we may be made worthy to live under their protection, to die in their favor, and to be forever blessed in their company. AMEN.[285]

Truly Feminine Women Are Indispensable as Friends

There is nothing I would not do for those who are really my friends. I have no notion of loving people by halves, it is not my nature.
—Jane Austen, *Northanger Abbey*

Truly feminine women act like operators of "emergency hotlines" to our downcast friends, supplying rapid counsel, encouragement, and support at all hours of the day and night. You are blessed to have just one of these women in your life. If you do, you are certainly proud to call her "friend." She is the first person (beside your husband) whom you call when exciting (or even not so exciting) news presents itself. She's the one who brings your family a pre-made meal when you just had a baby—and after you eat, holds your newborn for a few hours while you grab a quick nap.

This is the friend who encourages you *earnestly* and *credibly* when you're at your lowest—she actually says affirmative things which you believe, or which re-convince you that you're lovable. By contrast, when phony or less profound friends try to buck you up, they invariably overshoot their mark or give you a fake compliment you know immediately you don't deserve. (This only makes you feel worse.) A perfect (and simultaneously, quite funny) example of this kind of perennially loyal friend is *Parks and Recreation's*[286] Leslie Knope, in regard to her friend Ann Perkins. (As with all modern sitcoms, there's a fair amount

---

285 Franciscus, Rev. Pius, O.F.M. "Mother love, A Prayer Book for Christian Wives and Mothers." *Archconfraternity of Christian Mothers*, 1979, pp 155-156.

286 Daniels, Greg. *Parks and Recreation*. All seasons. NBC, 2015.

of feminist claptrap needing to be filtered out, throughout the series.) One of the more charming aspects from the show is how much Leslie Knope admires and stands by her Ann. Leslie's admiration reaches such levels that she is incapable of addressing Ann without adding in glowing compliments. I compiled the eleven best compliments and honorifics Leslie gives Ann, throughout *Parks and Recreation*'s seven seasons:

> "Ann, you poetic, noble land mermaid."
> "Ann, you're a genius! Your brain is almost as perfect as your face."
> "Ann Perkins, you perfect sunflower."
> "Ann, you beautiful, rule-breaking moth."
> "Ann is the greatest human being ever invented."
> "Ann, you're such a good friend. You are a beautiful, talented, brilliant, powerful musk ox."
> "Ann, you beautiful, sassy, mannequin-come-to-life."
> "It is the most beautiful object I've ever seen. It is like the Ann Perkins of dresses. It is amazing." (Leslie making reference to her own wedding dress)
> "Ann, you cunning, pliable, chestnut-haired sunfish."
> "He's so beautiful! And you're so beautiful. I mean, you're always beautiful, but right now you're the most beautiful, glowing, sun goddess ever." (To Ann and Ann's newborn)
> "Now I have two best friends, Ann and Ann. Each one more beautiful than the other."[287]

Wouldn't we all appreciate a friend who candidly admires us as much as Leslie admires Ann? However, the underdeveloped aspect in Leslie's friendship with Ann involves the moral and even practical challenges true friends issue one another from time to time; that is, this dimension of true friendship seems wholly lacking between Leslie and Ann. Truly feminine friends are those who, in a manner similar to that of your husband, will help you to get back on the path to heaven

287 Ibid.

when you stray from it. They will tell you when you're wrong because they understand that admitting your faults makes you a better wife, mother, friend, and disciple of Christ.

I speak of friendships which endure trial by (occasional) fire. This is a friend whom you can depend on for *honest* counsel. The litmus test for such a quality is that its possessor won't blindly take your side, knowing as she does that a real friend will never withhold a dose of reality when needed. Such a true friend is willing to incur your anger rather than lie to pamper your feelings. In the end, she knows you will appreciate her honesty and moral courage.

Edmond Dantes tells Luigi Vampa[288] that "a man is always in need of a good friend." He's right. It is true in different ways of women.

These friends are also the women in your life who know how to defer: viz. that *your best friend is your husband.* She understands that the healthier your marriage is, the happier you will be. She is jealous of neither your husband nor you. Accordingly, she encourages you to spend quality time with your spouse (even if it means not seeing you as much as she'd like), even offering occasionally to babysit your kids so that you can have a romantic evening with your husband. Such a friend recognizes that your husband and children are your top priorities and operates on a tacit "no compete" clause: she will never compete with either party for your love. She knows she has already secured it, albeit in a disparate way.

A truly feminine friend is a woman you can safely confide in—almost like you would with a priest—and thereafter, trust that she would never betray your confidence through gossip. She understands when to give counsel and when to listen quietly. As wise as our husbands are, women benefit by the input of other women when examining an array of female-only issues: childbirth, wifeliness, mothering, etc.

Truly feminine friends are those who are *genuinely* happy for you when you have triumphs. They are never competitive or bitter when learning your good news. No matter what their station is in life, they

288 Reynolds, Kevin. *The Count of Monte Cristo.* Buena Vista Pictures, 2002.

are heartened to see your station improve. These are the kind of women who throw impromptu parties for you when you have a big victory… or know just the right gift to send.

Also, where would we be in Christendom without truly feminine women who enthusiastically step in, as friends, to care for those who do not have family to depend on. Across the world, rightly ordered women care for the lonely souls within their communities via a good meal or gentle word, reaffirming their dignity as children of God. Yes, truly feminine women excel at opening their homes and hearts to those in need of God's mercy and love. I can't tell you how many times I witnessed a complete stranger being doted upon at my grandmother's kitchen table. Grandma was *convinced* that her postman needed a daily rest, snack, and cold beverage *at her table*, before continuing on his route. I'm not joking: she would even go so far as to leave the postman's daily snack—complete with a Coke—in her mailbox if she had an appointment when he came by. When I moved back in with her as a young adult—having lived there once for a time as a child and returning briefly during my young-adult courtship with my husband—I was startled to find a half-cool Sierra Mist in the mailbox on the first day I checked our mail!

Grandma's kitchen table and spare rooms were seldom empty because she was a friend to so many.

All of this is very Aristotelian. Remember, Aristotle laid out three kinds of friendship: friendships of utility, of pleasure, and of virtue.[289] The latter kind is the only one Aristotle considered a *true* friendship because personal affections and connections based on moral virtues help us to habituate those qualities—which is for Aristotle and the Catholic tradition *the* distinctly human function (namely, habituating virtue). And in turn, friendships based upon the function argument—as it is applied to humanity—prove the strongest and most durable.

By contrast, friendships of utility and pleasure are fleeting and

289 Aristotle, W D. Ross, and Lesley Brown. *The Nicomachean Ethics.* Oxford: Oxford University Press, 2009, Books VII and IX.

self-serving to one or both of the friends. Friendships of utility are the most superficial. These relationships are akin to befriending that kid in your neighborhood with a pool…only because he has a pool. Friendships of pleasure are somewhat deeper—at least in such relationships, you enjoy the person's company—but these center not around virtuous pleasure, but rather the sort of accidental pleasure which mischievous adolescents too often seek in one another's company.

When two women view their friendship in its proper context—shared virtue—the friends mutually will the highest good of the other, in the course of their durable bond. Such a durable bond can and occasionally does withstand the aforementioned "tough love" mentioned above.

Society would be a dull place, indeed, without female fellowship. I'll conclude with this quote from *Charlotte's Web* by E.B. White, which nicely summarizes the selfless love truly feminine women offer as friends:

> "Why did you do all this for me?" he asked. "I don't deserve it. I've never done anything for you." "You have been my friend," replied Charlotte. "That in itself is a tremendous thing."[290]

A Prayer for Our Friends

O God, Who by the grace of the Holy Spirit, hast poured into the hearts of thy faithful the gifts of charity; grant to Thy servants, for whom we implore Thy mercy, health both of body and soul; that they may love Thee with all their strength, and cheerfully perform those things which are pleasing unto Thee. Through Christ our Lord Jesus Christ. AMEN.[291]

---

290 White, E.B. *Charlotte's Web*. 1990.

291 Fearns, John M. S.T.D. *Catholic Girl's Manual*. Catholic Book Publishing Co., N.Y., 1952, pp. 526.

Truly Feminine Women Are Indispensable as Daughters

To an old father, nothing is more sweet than a daughter.
—Euripides

Anyone who has a daughter understands what it feels like to be wholly believed in—no matter how deserving we are of such devotion. Very young daughters mark the epitome of true feminine optimism, because they have not been corrupted by the evils of feminism. When they are young, daughters help us to cultivate our behaviors in order to become the people they already esteem us to be. Is there anyone who admires you more than your daughter? Our daughter's admiration provides us with the necessary fuel to power us though our tribulations, dispelling whatever lingering temptations to quit dwell darkly in our souls.

When they are young, daughters help each of their parents to refine their vocations as husband and wife. Young daughters help their mothers to cultivate proper wifely behaviors. Truly feminine mothers realize that the manner in which they fulfill their duties profoundly influences how their daughters will eventually fulfill their own. Moreover, little girls depend on their mothers to "lay the foundation" within their young minds, establishing how vital to society the wifely vocation is. If the daughter chooses marriage in her adulthood, as most do, she will be inclined to imitate her mother's example—for better or worse. This is why the truly feminine woman fills the role of a good wife for the sake of her husband...*and daughters.*

As a mother of six young daughters, their constant watch motivates me to cultivate my abilities as a wife and mother. After all, the cheerful wife's dedication to her vocation conveys to her daughters the grave significance homemaking still bears, whether or not it receives the recognition it deserves. For, if the mother tears down the family through nagging, the daughter will soon follow (or else spend a great amount of her marriage laboring to rectify the mother's bad influence). This proves an especially pernicious pitfall since even in families *without* snippy nags, the husband more easily earns the reputation, among the children, as "the fun one" through roughhousing, souvenirs and surprises brought home to children from work, and the manly dismissal of smaller rules which wives have a predilection for following in a doctrinaire manner.

Young daughters also help their fathers to become better husbands and fathers, of course. A young daughter's devotion to her father inspires him to cultivate higher and higher levels of protection and moral-spiritual leadership—two of the foremost ways men head society. It is true that a truly masculine man accepts the responsibility to protect and lead, from the moment he takes a wife. But it is only when a man has a daughter that he comes fully to understand how essential his masculinity is for the preservation of Christianity, and indeed, for the life of the world. Daughters who enjoy the "luxury" (from today's perspective) of masculine fathers tend to marry young men cut from the same goodly cloth—this way lies the preservation of the Christian family. Maintaining the admiration of a young daughter helps to incentivize a man to further cultivate noble leadership by uniting strength and empathy—the qualities for which we venerate Saint Joseph.

Astute men with daughters possess a more lucid understanding of femininity—and by extension, their own wives—since young daughters encompass the most innocent version of their wives' feminine attitudes and predispositions. Summarily, I've noticed that my own husband has developed gentler ways of communication since our daughters were born. He more fully understands in what ways females are naturally motivated to submit themselves to male leadership. Women who are doing their part as truly feminine deserve a strong leader who understands how to interact with a woman's gentler demeanor. Male householders, as I have stated many times, have the more difficult job because they have to protect like the warrior class, yet lead their families to heaven like the priestly class. Daughters play a pivotal role in society by inspiring our leaders—with their beauty and docility—to discharge their duties with compassion and fortitude.

The old adage, "I'm not your friend, I'm your parent" actually turns out false. The friendships parents cultivate with their children—although friendships between unequals—ought to be intimate real friendships. On the parent-child friendship let us look, again, to Aristotle. He says:

> The friendship of a king for those who live under his rule depends on his superior ability to do good. He confers benefits upon his subjects, since he is good and cares for them in order to promote their welfare, just as a shepherd cares for his sheep. Hence, Homer spoke of Agamemnon as "shepherd of the people." The friendship of a father is of the same kind, but it differs in the magnitude of benefits bestowed. For he is the author of their being, which is regarded as the greatest good, and he is responsible for maintaining and educating them... furthermore, it is by nature that a father rules over his children, ancestors over their descendants, and a king over his subjects. These kinds of friendship depend on superiority, and that is why we also honor our parents. Accordingly, in those relationships the same thing is not just for both partners, but what is just depends on worth or merit, and the same is true for friendship.[292]

The roles frequently change when those daughters become grown women, i.e. truly feminine daughters now provide their parents with the same compassionate care they were given as children. They are often the caretakers of their elderly parents and even sit in constant vigil at the deathbed of their dying parent. Sometimes, as is the fate for my daughters, a daughter's role as caregiver doesn't end with the death of her parents but will continue in service of a severely handicapped sibling. This is, incidentally, yet another reason why my influence over the type of caregiver my daughters become is so vital: they will be

292 Fearns, John M. S.T.D. *Catholic Girl's Manual.* Catholic Book Publishing Co., N.Y., 1952, pp. 526.

responsible for the health and happiness of their eldest sister someday. Not only does Abby require constant care, but since she is immobile, she also requires constant social interaction. Our daughters understand that Abby cannot seek them out for companionship or assistance, so they must routinely seek her out. In instances where I am occupied with the needs of a newborn or other household duties, my daughters can easily step in and assist Abby.

Early on, my daughters learned the importance of caregiving in two distinctive ways: firstly, insofar as they are sisters to a handicapped sister; secondly, as they were great-granddaughters to my grandmother, who lived with us when she was very ill. My husband and I wanted to lead by example, showing our daughters that we aren't asking them to do anything that we weren't willing to do first.

Goodly daughters are especially attuned to the needs of others; in sum, they help us to be honorable stewards to all who depend upon us.

Prayer for Our Parents

> Lord, I surrender to You my family. Lord Jesus, I pray for my parents. Though you blessed them abundantly, today they are in need of your help. Give my parents joy and strength. Fill them with your strengthening presence. Lord, give them real thirst and hunger for the Holy Spirit and for the Word of God. Give them health in spirit, soul and body.
>
> Even though they may feel that all the trouble they took for their children are being wasted, help them to see the great reward waiting for them in Heaven. Help my parents to forgive themselves and forgive everyone else.
>
> Even though as parents they may have failed to fulfil their duties, Lord, set them free from sadness and sorrow, regrets and sense of guilt. Jesus fill them with your Holy Spirit. Thank you, Jesus. AMEN.[293]

---

293 Aristotle, W D. Ross, and Lesley Brown. *The Nicomachean Ethics*. Oxford: Oxford University Press, 2009, Books VIII.11, 1161a11.

Prayer of a Wife or Mother for Her Sick Relative

O heart of Jesus, merciful and compassionate Heart, look with an eye of pity upon my sick [name of relative]. O You, who endured upon earth all that was most painful, relieve [name of relative] sufferings! In memory of the bitter desolation, You endured in the Garden of Olives, console [name of relative] in their misery. For the sake of Your cruel scourging and frightful crowning with thorns, grant [name of relative] patience in their tribulations. By Your most wearisome carrying of Your cross, grant [name of relative] unshaken constancy in this trial and perfect resignation to God's holy will. By Your cruel death, grant [name of relative] a calm and peaceful departure from this life, if so it is best for [name of relative] eternal welfare.

But if, O sacred Heart, it be not opposed to Your greater honor, grant [name of relative] a prolongation of life and restoration to perfect health. I beg this of You by Your own infinite goodness and mercy. It was for [name of relative] welfare that You cast [name of relative] upon this bed of sickness. Give [name of relative] light to discern Your loving designs and, greater ardor, to seek the salvation of [name of relative] soul. Take from them their former tepidity in Your service and fill [name of relative] with a loving zeal for Your honor. Grant that in this present tribulation they may understand how insignificant and transitory are all earthly joys. Strengthen [name of relative]'s heart to live henceforth solely for You and heaven, O God; and when You have given health to [name of relative] soul, restore likewise the strength of body. O Jesus, You Who healed so many sick, heal [name of relative] also, that [name of relative] may gratefully magnify Your name and, after a long life of piety and good works, depart happily in You, O lord, to love You and praise You and glorify You forever and ever! AMEN.[294]

---

294 Franciscus, Rev. Pius, O.F.M. "Mother love, A Prayer Book for Christian Wives and Mothers." *Archconfraternity of Christian Mothers*, 1979, pp. 199-201.

Truly Feminine Women Are Indispensable as Sisters (Big and Small "S")

God has not called me to be successful; He has called me to be faithful.
—attributed to Mother Teresa

As sisters (big or small "s"), truly feminine women extend their maternal talents to the needs of those within their nuclear family,[295] and as religious sisters, to the needs of everyone. Naturally infused female talents have already been thoroughly covered in this chapter. However, society tends to overlook the women who quietly serve humanity in their vocations as religious sisters.

Perhaps you know some heroic religious sisters. But the vast majority of such sisters of Christ carry out their service to humanity unnoticed in orphanages, hospitals, schoolrooms, slums, and cloistered convents. For centuries, these unmarried women have filled the vacancies left open in society by women who chose the married vocation of homemaking.

This is precisely why religious women are so vital to society. And it is why we all must pray for more vocations. Many of my detractors will point out that it is "necessary" for women to fill certain jobs—especially those jobs which serve children and other women. The midwife, the nurse, and the elementary teacher typically top the professional list—proffered by feminists as "counterexample"— whereupon a woman is typically preferred over a man.

As noted in previous chapters, married women must not neglect the duties of their own homes in order to fill such jobs. This is unacceptable. Religious sisters, however, could fill those same jobs without neglecting the duties of their vocation.

Mother Teresa once gave this account of the importance of the religious vocation:

> The sisters care for forty-nine thousand lepers. They are among the most unwanted, unloved, and neglected people. The other

---

295 "Nuclear family" is usually a reference to a married couple and their dependent children.

> day one of our sisters was washing a leper covered in sores. A Muslim holy man was present, standing close to her. He said, "All these years I have believed that Jesus Christ was a prophet. Today I believe that Jesus Christ is God since he has been able to give such joy to this sister, so that she can do her work with so much love."[296]

This is precisely why it is vital to train our young daughters to serve the needs of others. Perhaps if we encourage our daughters to be become religious sisters instead of prompting them to chase some tacky career and a buck, we could swell the ranks of religious sisters. Unlike the training required for today's professional work, becoming a religious sister is less expensive and more rewarding. Moreover, if a woman was raised within the confines of a *properly functioning* Christian household, then much of the training has already been undertaken. In properly run Christian homes, daughters are already being trained compassionately to meet the needs of their family members. By the time a young woman reaches the age-appropriate level for her vocation, she ought to be fully prepared to either become a religious bride of Christ or a bride to a young man.

Just as sisters in a nuclear family assist their mother, so do sisters in a convent help their Mother Superior. Both types of sisters revere and learn from their mother's good example, so as to one day replace her function. Sisters of both kinds are able to discharge their duties *so well* that they may elevate themselves to the rank of saint (and many have done so—see the next section).

Litany for Vocations

> God, our Father, Creator who calls us to life: Have mercy on us.
> God the Son, Faithful Servant: Have mercy on us.
> God the Holy Spirit, Life-Force of Courage: Have mercy on us.
> Mary, Mother of Jesus, our High Priest: Pray for us.

---

296 Kelly-Gangi, Carol (editor). *Mother Teresa: Her Essential Wisdom*. Fall River Press, 2006, pp. 23.

St. Joseph, her spouse: Pray for us.
St. Peter and St. Paul, First Apostles: Pray for us.
St. Benedict and St. Scholastica: Pray for us.
St. Dominic, St. Francis, St. Ignatius: Pray for us.
St. John Vianney: Pray for us.
St. Elizabeth Ann Seton: Pray for us.
All holy men and women of God: Pray for us.
Lord, give the gift of a generous heart to parents and those called to priesthood and religious life. We ask this through Christ, Our Lord. AMEN.[297]

Truly Feminine Women Are Indispensable as Saints

Let go of your plans.
—St. Teresa Benedicta (Edith Stein)

This chapter would be incomplete without the inclusion of those most special women who certainly achieved their eternal reward. The following saints exemplify one form or another of true femininity. Of course, the Blessed Virgin, the perfect woman, is the Catholic woman's consummate exemplar for femininity. However, the following women—having not always been perfect in their lifetime, unlike Our Lady—deserve their own mention. The saints fill the role of showing us, in their multiplicity, how each temperament has a place in the kingdom of Heaven.

The imperfect lives of each of the following women reveal to us that imperfect women can actually—not just theoretically—elevate their habits and lives by the grace of God.

As such, female saints are indispensable to society. In regard to extricating beauty and goodness from this fallen life below, these holy women have "been there and done that." They are eminently relatable insofar as they, like us, operated from within a framework of moral and

297 "Prayers for Vocations and Seminarians." St. Thomas Aquinas Catholic Church, www.stacharlotte.com/95.

temperamental vices, sins, doubts, practical shortcomings, insecurities, and even phobias.

In other words, some women have foolishly argued that the Virgin Mother's example proves worthless since her perfection sets an impossible standard to emulate. Indeed, hers was a tough act to follow; no one is doubting that. We will most certainly come up short, they say, so why even try? Of course, this is nonsensical. The Marian paradigm example provides the "textbook" (whereas saintly examples provide the handbook). Not to mention, the Virgin's perfect example confers us with insight concerning God's conception of the perfect woman. Is it not His idea of perfection which ought to be our Morningstar and Eveningstar (however difficult to satisfy)?

In a September 1963 letter, J.R.R. Tolkien said the following of our aim for perfection: "To ourselves we must present the absolute ideal without compromise, for we do not know our own limits of natural strength (+ grace), and if we do not aim at the highest we shall certainly fall short of the utmost we could achieve."[298]

So bear in mind that the following saints had many imperfections. Women fatally intimidated by the perfection of the Virgin Mother deprive themselves of all the good reasons to follow the path of the saints. Since we now live in gravely immoral Western societies—conceptually united by a globalism which seem to tighten its grip by the day—studying the lives of holy women proves an indispensable resource. It is an unfortunate fact that as society worsens, the modern woman is increasingly robbed of encountering the most practical antidote: truly holy women to "mentor" us by the witness of their lives. And so, studying these female saints encourages us women to do battle against our culture's toxic threats. As seen in the following accounts, we too can be victorious like these holy women by embracing our crosses.

Let's begin with St. Monica (AD 332-387, feast day August 27), who can lend inspiration to the dutiful Catholic mother, seeking to go even

298 Carpenter, Humphrey. *The Letters of J.R.R. Tolkien.* Houghton Mifflin Harcourt Publishing Company, New York, N.Y., 1981, pp. 326.

deeper in the faith. In particular, how can a modern woman—who is also a dutiful Catholic mother—convert the beloved hearts of her wayward children or husband through prayer and penance?

It is relatively unsurprising that St. Monica is the patroness of married women: difficult marriages, disappointing children, victims of adultery or unfaithfulness, victims of (verbal) abuse, and conversion of relatives. All of these make her a narrowly tailored model for today's Christian wives and mothers.

The brief account, below, fails to articulate the many sufferings Monica endured by the outrageously wayward lifestyle of her very famous son, St. Augustine. (If you don't know, she desperately followed her wayward son, St. Augustine, from town to town in attempt to get him to abandon his debauchery and to get him to convert to Christianity—which he, of course, eventually did.) Instead, the account focuses on those travails she suffered by her husband, Patritius:

> Sorrow played a big part in the life of Saint Monica, the sorrow of a loving wife for a harsh spouse and a devoted mother to a wayward son. Life was not kind to Saint Monica. Her husband, Patricius, was a pagan. Though naturally generous and kindhearted, Patritius was a harsh and unfaithful husband. His mother and servants took their cue from him in their treatment of his young wife. Monica bore her difficulties with patient cheerfulness and her conduct profoundly influenced Patritius, finally bringing him to the gift of faith after twenty years of married life.
>
> Wife beating was common among the pagans and Monica's neighbours marveled that not once did Patritius strike his wife.[299]

As a saintly wife and mother, St. Monica, prompts modern women to never give up on the hearts of our husbands and children. Let us

299 "Our Patron / St. Monica." St. Monica Catholic Church, www.stmonica-edmond.org/our-patron-st-monica.

always remember that our sufferings provide us with an opportunity to draw nearer to Christ.

Next, let us examine the case of St. Catherine of Siena (d. 1380, feast day April 29), patroness of the dying and Doctor of the Church. St. Catherine can inspire the modern woman to use her intellectual talents to bring peace to our families and our communities:

> As a mystic and Doctor of the Church, St Catherine used her gifts of philosophy and theology to encourage peace among the Italian territories of her time. She worked tirelessly for the crusade against the Turks and for peace between Florence and the Pope and was instrumental in restoring the Papacy to Rome. She also established a monastery for women in 1377 outside of Siena. During her time St Catherine also composed over 400 letters which became so influential that she was later declared a Doctor of the Church.[300]

St. Catherine, patroness of miscarriages; people ridiculed for their piety; sexual temptation; and the sick. Let us all seek to become the intellectual peacemaker. Please guide modern women to devote ourselves to learn about our Catholic faith so that we may also bring Christ's teachings to our children. The world desperately needs the truth of Christ. St. Catherine, please protect us as we bring His commandments to the most sinful and troubled among us.

The life of St. Katharine Drexel (AD 1858-1955, feast day March 3) reminds us to reject materialism and to use our wealth to assist those in need:

> St. Katharine Drexel was born into high society and wealth. Her estate would have been worth about $400 million in today's standards, but after a surprise suggestion that she become a

---

300 Theodore, Amy. "20 Women Saints Who Made a Mark on the Catholic World." MNnews Today, Mnnews.today Your Local Source of Catholic News for Newcastle, Maitland and the Hunter, 2 Mar. 2018, mnnews.today/church/2018/27971-20-women-saints-who-made-a-mark-on-the-catholic-world/.

> sister from the Pope, Katharine reconsidered her marriage proposals and discerned that the religious life was, indeed, for her. She gave everything to God, including her entire inheritance, and dedicated the remainder of her life to educating and caring for the Native Americans and Black Americans. By the time she died, she and her religious sisters had established about 50 Indian missions in the United States. As women, we are often tempted toward materialism and the security that marriage affords. Katharine's heart was so full of charity that she renounced everything in order to give her all to others.[301]

St. Katharine Drexel, patroness of philanthropy, pray for our culture that we may realize there is infinitely more to life than gaining material wealth. Show us how to open our hearts to God's call to service to others (even if that means abandoning our own goals for His). Please open the closed eyes of the modern woman. Enlighten her that her success is not measured by her bank account, or how many degrees she acquires, but rather by how she serves her family.

Sts. Felicity and Perpetua (d. 203, feast day March 7 in the Ordinary Form and March 6 in the Extraordinary Form) by their martyrdoms encourage the modern woman to never to deny the Lord. Sadly, many women deny Christ—together with His teachings—out of cowardly self-preservation. They prefer denying Christ and compromising their morals for fear of persecution at the hands of the anti-Christians on the ascent. Give us strength for speaking and living "hard-truths." The modern woman ought to reflect on the example of Sts. Felicity and Perpetua who were:

> two of the earliest Roman martyrs, these saints are honored together because Felicity was the slave of Perpetua, a young noblewoman who was nursing a newborn. Pregnant herself,

301 Ewing, Jeannie. "20 Most Inspiring Woman Saints to Know and Love." *The Writings of Cora Evans,* The Mystical Humanity of Christ Publishing, www.coraevans.com/blog/article/20-most-inspiring-woman-saints-to-know-and-love.

> Felicity gave birth to her daughter only moments before her execution. They were martyred because they refused to apostasize their Christian faith, so they were sentenced to die in the "celebration games" in honor of Roman Emperor Septimus Severus' birthday. Their heroism in the face of such barbarism, especially as they entrusted their babies to God's care, is unprecedented, which is why we hear of them in the Litany of Saints on high feast days in the Church.[302]

Saints Felicity and Perpetua, patronesses of mothers and expectant mothers, pray for your modern-day sisters: that we will remember never to compromise our faith or morals such as to "fit in" with the anti-Christian culture. Inspire us to be willing to accept the public persecutions that surely follow those who refuse to compromise.

St. Edith Stein (AD 1891-1942, feast day August 9) abandoned the secular world and converted from Judaism to Catholicism, before dying in a gas chamber in Auschwitz. She should inspire the modern woman to abandon the secular world and to turn her life over to Christ. Atheism ensnares many souls simply because so few people in the modern age bother to seek the truth. Accordingly, they fall for the devil's lies. St. Edith Stein, an intellectual in her own right, opened her heart and mind to the truth of Christ and converted to Catholicism in 1922:

> After leaving her Jewish faith and becoming an atheist, St. Edith eventually converted to Catholicism through her discovery of the True Presence of Christ in the Eucharist and joined the Discalced Carmelites. When the Nazis conquered Holland, St. Edith and her sister were arrested and sent to the concentration camp at Auschwitz where she died in the gas chambers. St. Edith is remembered for a life of dedication, consecration, prayer, fasting and penance.[303]

---

302 Ibid.

303 Theodore, Amy. "20 Women Saints Who Made a Mark on the Catholic World." MNnews Today, Mnnews.today Your Local Source of Catholic

St. Edith Stein, patroness of Europe, pray for the conversions of our fallen away sisters in Christ. Pray for all souls who, either by arrogance or stubbornness, have denied Christ and the One True Faith which He instituted. Motivate these lost souls to seek answers from holy resources and people; prompt such lost lambs to decipher when they are being served half-truths by false shepherds.

St. Mary of Egypt (d. fifth century, feast day April 1) struggled from an early age with sins of the flesh. In the modern age, it is no secret that sexual licentiousness has been both permitted and encouraged. Many women—even at very young ages— are manipulated to believe that they are free to make sinful choices regarding their bodies. Such "choices" nearly always are those which, unrepented and uncorrected, will lead a woman's soul to hell. St. Mary of Egypt, by her own conversion from sexual debauchery, realized that her body was not her own. She came to understand that the "choices" she elected either took her away from God or brought her closer to Him. Her conversion story should be a powerful motivator for the modern-day woman to abandon her sexual immorality and thereby save her soul. Specifically, it is related about her life:

> Mary of Egypt became a prostitute at the age of twelve and devoted her life of promiscuity to "anti-pilgrimages," where she made it her goal to lure holy men away from the path and into a life of sin. She encountered an icon of the Blessed Virgin Mary at the Church of the Holy Sepulcher and spent the rest of her life living in the forest, doing penance for her past sin.[304]

St. Mary of Egypt, patroness of chastity, pray for us that we may not be so easily deceived by the culture of lies. Prompt that all women will understand the dignity in which they were created; help them to

---

News for Newcastle, Maitland and the Hunter, 2 Mar. 2018, mnnews.today/church/2018/27971-20-women-saints-who-made-a-mark-on-the-catholic-world/.

304 Langr, Chloe. "25 Women Saints Who Prove Every Day Is Women's Day." *EpicPew*, 11 Mar. 2016, epicpew.com/25-women-saints-prove-every-day-womens-day/.

treat their bodies as God expects them to do. St. Mary of Egypt pray that all women currently abusing their bodies with sexual sins reclaim the sanctity for which God has created them.

These holy women, defenders of true femininity, remind us to intercede and stand by our husbands and children, grow in our faith, resist sexual temptation, renounce materialism, refuse to deny Christ, seek the truth, and repent of our sins. Their lives represent the positive attributes we seek to emulate for they sought authentic friendship with God and with their fellow brothers and sisters in Christ. Some were indispensable biological and spiritual mothers, but all were indispensable sisters of charity to a world in desperate need of love. The modern woman has a choice: to wander aimlessly or to follow the path God has inscribed in her very body, the path of peace and happiness. I pray this last chapter provides that compass, guiding her to that blessed path.

8

The Leader Who Won't Lead

Throughout the many burden-laying chapters of this book, many female readers probably asked themselves: do I *really* have to submit to a husband who isn't fulfilling *his* vocation. The quick answer is yes, though it needs some serious unpacking and careful clarification.

These same women often follow up with the natural question, "Then what can I do to fix my husband?". Doubtless, the state of bondedness to a captain who is deficient in some serious manner or another is a non-negligible problem. The plain—if not easy—answer is that you cannot under your own power fix him, and nagging him to change will only worsen your situation (and his). In a disparate context, the toxic historic influence of feminism swindled women into believing they can take matters into their own hands and shame their husbands into compliance. How utterly foolish—in either case. I would wager much of the public marital discord we're all witnessing today comprises a spectrum of varying instances of this same illogic. Women who adopt this approach attempt to usurp God's unique role: holding men accountable, while forgetting their own accountability, which continues to be, namely, *honoring their husbands* (yes, even though they are profoundly flawed).

However, there exist plenty of *truly feminine* practices a wife may employ to convert her wayward husband's heart.

Chiefly, a wife who finds herself in such an unfortunate situation must pray unceasingly for her husband. She must have fervent faith that God will move her husband's heart. Like St. Monica, she must bear patiently with her husband's rebellion and stubbornness. *Expect the longest conversion-timeline; be hopeful for the shortest.*

I have seen firsthand how the Lord often employs a wife's faithfulness in prayer, patience, understanding, and even her example of fealty to inspire her husband's conversion. A wife freely embracing her suffering cannot but "sound the clarion call" for her husband to fulfill his obligations to her. There are no guarantees that such wifely heroic sacrifice will bear immediate fruit in this life—certainly the next. Whatever the outcome, the wife's love, faithfulness, patience, and devotion to prayer will earn her notice from Her Savior. For no earthly reward is greater than hearing Christ's words, "Well done, good and trustworthy servant"[305] upon your death. (Of course, her holy desires *may* be fulfilled on earth through her prayers: namely, her husband also dedicates himself to Christ. We cannot understand from within time which prayers will be answered and which will not.)

Despite a wife's fervent prayers to convert her husband, there are common situations when the husband refuses to fulfill his duties as head of the household. Let's explore these areas. We will begin with the most severe instances, keeping in mind that I am merely offering the Church's point of view in regard to what a Christian woman can, cannot, and ought to do in such dire situations.

One final important note: submission to one's husband does not extend to subjecting yourself and your children to harm.

Less Common and More Important: Submission When There Is Abuse, Neglect, or Addiction

Up to this point this book has assumed that wives ought to be submitting to their rightly ordered (or *largely* rightly ordered) Christian husbands. Once more, I tender the question for the careful consideration of the reader: does a wife have to submit to a husband who is not living out Christian principles?

---

305 Matthew 25:23.

We have already stated the answer is "yes," but there are important distinctions which need to be made. Husbands *are not* allowed to order their wives to violate Church teaching. Nor are husbands allowed to violate Church teaching themselves. Remember, as the husband is the head of the wife, Christ is the head of the husband (because the husband is a constituent part of "the Bride of Christ"). The wife may, according to Church teaching, protect her soul and body in instances where the husband is putting either in grave danger.

Many faithful Catholic women wonder what course of action they are licitly allowed to take if their husbands put them (or their children) in grave danger. Keep in mind, grave danger doesn't always mean physical danger. There are women with husbands who aren't posing a physical threat but rather grave spiritual peril. A small minority of faithful Catholic women operate under the misconception that being submissive to one's husband extends to subjecting themselves to dangerous living conditions. This is absolutely false; the Church teaches the exact opposite.

Catholic women ought to know that they may licitly remove themselves (and any children present) out of danger by leaving the home if there is a real threat to their safety. Canon law states:

> A spouse who occasions grave danger of soul or body to the other or to the children, or otherwise makes the common life unduly difficult, provides the other spouse with a reason to leave, either by a decree of the local ordinary or, if there is danger in delay, even on his or her own authority.[306]

Catholic Answers provides the following additional commentary on when the common life ought to be restored:

> The canon does go on to state that once such a danger has passed, common life should be restored, but given the unique

306 *Code of Canon Law: Latin-English Edition*. Washington, DC: Canon Law Society of America, 1999, #1153.

> difficulties of abuse cases (e.g., promises to reform are all too often broken), an abused spouse may wish to allow an independent specialist such as a priest or a psychologist to determine if and when it is safe to resume common life. The Church considers civil divorce in such cases to be the ecclesial equivalent of a legal separation and tolerates civil divorce sought for just cause (such as to ensure personal safety and/or the safety of children) to settle estate and child custody arrangements. The divorced person is still considered validly married and may not remarry in the Church unless and until an annulment is granted.[307]

In sum, a married woman who finds herself in a grave situation actually has the moral responsibility—to herself and her children—to separate physically from her husband. However, exercising the authority to separate *physically* from her husband does not mean that she has the authority to separate *spiritually* from him.

As you probably know, the Catholic Church does not permit divorce. The Church may declare that a marriage which was never valid at its inception is and always has been null and void, through a "declaration of nullity." Specific qualifications must be met in order for a spouse to obtain the declaration of nullity. The *United States Conference of Catholic Bishops* itemizes those qualifications:

> "Annulment" is an unfortunate word that is sometimes used to refer to a Catholic "declaration of nullity." Actually, nothing is made null through the process. Rather, a Church tribunal (a Catholic Church court) declares that a marriage thought to be valid according to Church law actually fell short of at least one of the essential elements required for a binding union. For a Catholic marriage to be valid, it is required that:

---

307 Catholic Answers Staff. "Is Divorce a Sin When One's Spouse Is Abusive? "*Catholic Answers*, 23 Feb. 2019, www.catholic.com/qa/is-divorce-a-sin-when-ones-spouse-is-abusive.

1. the spouses are free to marry;
2. they are capable of giving their consent to marry;
3. they freely exchange their consent;
4. in consenting to marry, they have the intention to marry for life, to be faithful to one another and be open to children;
5. they intend the good of each other; and
6. their consent is given in the presence of two witnesses and before a properly authorized Church minister.

Exceptions to the last requirement must be approved by Church authority.[308]

Obviously, only the Church has the power to decide if a marriage was *ab initio* valid or not. Individuals may not make that judgement for themselves.[309]

If there must be a physical separation, the wife ought to find herself in frequent prayer for the conversion of her husband and not take occasion to behave as a single woman. Even though the wife is not living under the direct watch of her husband she *is still married* to him in the eyes of the Church and should honor and love him even in his deficiency. Usually this means praying for his conversion, encouraging him to seek professional help, fasting for him, and having Masses said for him.

Many people argue that such a woman ought to "cut her losses" and move on to another marriage so that she may "achieve happiness" in her life. This is nonsense. Happiness— misdefined by many

---

308 "Annulment." USCCB, www.usccb.org/topics/marriage-and-family-life-ministries/annulment#tab--how-can-a-couple-who-has-been-married-for-many-years-present-a-case.

309 A Catholic who erroneously believes he possess the power to dissolve his marriage (either by his own power or by the court's) behaves similarly to the character Michael Scott from the comedic sitcom, *The Office*. In the season 4 episode, "Money," Michael finds himself in financial ruin and merely declares bankruptcy by shouting the word "bankruptcy" to a startled group of his employees (instead of going through the actual, legal process of bankruptcy). Lieberstein, Paul. "Money." *The Office*. NBC. New York, New York, 18 Oct. 2007. Television.

in the culture to mean pleasure-seeking[310]— was never the goal of life. Following the rules and beatitudes Christ has laid down for us so that we can achieve Heaven, on the other hand, is. Frequently, following Christ's teachings proves difficult and can make us temporarily miserable. We simply cannot go around bending the rules the moment they promise not to afford us an easy path. In life, our crosses can be unbearably heavy, but we must carry and embrace them, nonetheless. For the cross is the only way to Heaven and the only way to true happiness.

Women living apart from their husbands (for the aforementioned safety reasons) who have not sought annulments should be taken as an inspiration to the rest of us. They ought to be helped accordingly. It sounds strange to say—after seven chapters of railing against married women in the workforce—these women must go to work to provide for their children. In addition to which, they are deprived of marital intimacy. In addition to which, they must witness their children suffer the practical loss of a father. In addition to which, they must attempt impossibly to be both mother and father to the children. Such is the enormous shame of the husband: no matter how hard his wife may try to mitigate the damage he wrecks, his family will suffer for his absence.

These gritty women show us how *not* to take the easy way out of our comparatively minor sufferings. They inspire us to follow Christ's commandments, Scripture, and perennial Church teaching even during our greatest tribulations. Moreover, their example constitutes a living, breathing call to their husbands to abandon their wantonness and thereby become the men Christ expects them to be. It is far easier for a man to continue in his debauchery if his wife palliates his conscience by engaging in some herself. On the contrary, if a man has a holy wife who suffers faithfully in his absence, like St. Monica going about her days in fervid prayer for his soul, then he is far less likely to make

310 The Church accepts the natural goal of life as Aristotle's eudaimonia, which is properly defined happiness. The supernatural goal of life is, of course, union with Christ.

excuses for himself. His wife, by her persistent holy example, is always calling his soul into account.

Once more, this isn't to say that the wife will always be victorious in converting her husband. The proposition bears repeating. Because we all have free-will,[311] some men will remain resolute in their depravity. Nevertheless, the wife in such situations must lead her children to Heaven by her example alone.

It is the obligation of a Christian society to care for the abandoned married woman, seeking where possible to lessen her undue burdens. Her neighbors, friends, and family ought to regularly check in with her to offer their time, labor, or financial assistance. Lacking a man around the house leaves many chores and repairs undone. Moreover, her Christian employer ought to be deliberately lenient with her volatile schedule. Subsidiarity[312] dictates that local individuals—far better than laws and governments—should contribute, in spontaneously relevant ways, to help her out (e.g., her single co-workers ought to offer to fill in for her, when she inevitably has to miss work occasionally to care for the needs of her children).

If any of you poor abandoned women are reading this right now—I know several personally who may be—should your husband take the proper actions to create a safe home environment, I hope that you will forgive him and reunify your marital home. But if he doesn't improve, please know that your suffering serves a purpose: it works toward your own sanctification in the same sense that your marriage does. Indeed, you remain in the sacrament, however solitarily. Christ will never

---

311 "Free will" is the freedom to choose between different possible courses of action without the constraint of necessity or fate.

312 CCC #1884: "The principle of subsidiarity, one of the basic tenets of Catholic social doctrine, promotes governance at its smallest level based on the natural law tenet that 'God entrusts to every creature the functions it is capable of performing, according to the capacities of its own nature...the way God acts in governing the world, which bears witness to such great regard for human freedom, should inspire the wisdom of those who govern human communities."

abandon you as your husband did. Keep the faith, and your reward will await you on the other side of the eschaton.

The following prayer may be useful for wives in many difficult situations (not limited to substance abuse problems):

Wife's Prayer for Help with a Drinking Husband

> The worry that keeps pressing on my mind concerns my husband. He is drinking much more than he used to. The children have noticed that their father at times is not quite himself. Please, Lord, help me to handle this problem the right way. Keep me from nagging him. I know that nagging will not cure him but may drive him to drink even more. Help me to be patient with my husband as You have so often been patient with me. Give me the courage to seek professional advice. AMEN.[313]

Most Common Situation: No Alpha in Your Beta Soup

The most common problem Christian wives encounter with their husband's leadership is the near-total lack thereof. The political and cultural left's favorite portrayal of the Christian husband is that of a bullying, male-chauvinist alpha: utter poppycock. If anything, Christian men could stand to become a *great deal* more alpha. The reality of our cultural situation is that feminism has infiltrated the Christian household so efficiently that a majority of otherwise masculine men are going about their affairs behaving like cowering (if embittered) betas, not macho alphas. Which is to say, many modern men are followers, not leaders. Maddeningly and unwittingly, these men keep feminism evergreen by failing to take initiative within their households—in turn, this leaves a void typically (read: disastrously) filled by the wife.

And so, we've come to the most common problem with the

313 Franciscus, Rev. Pius, O.F.M. "Mother love, A Prayer Book for Christian Wives and Mothers." *Archconfraternity of Christian Mothers*, 1979, pp. 167-168.

husband's acting like a beta: the wife's acting like the alpha, in response. "But surely," these women plead, "I must take charge if my husband won't?"

This is mostly, yet not entirely, incorrect. If, for instance, your husband refuses to work or to take the family to Mass, you must "step up" in his stead. Yet problems invariably arise when a wife starts *believing* that she is the rightful head of her household, rather than merely "filling in" temporarily, from necessity. "What's the distinction?" you may ask. The distinction lies squarely in the attitude of the wife.

Wives who adopt the appropriate attitude of substituting *only as necessary* for derelict husbands—while still enthusiastically acknowledging the husband as head of the household—are to be commended. To be fair, this is difficult to negotiate. Such women prefer not to be displaced to the helm of the ship in the first place. They would candidly prefer to return to their domestic duties. Women of this caliber will never opportunistically "take charge" in all areas of life. In short, such restrained women prove *exceedingly* rare. Most women in this situation are tempted by the allurements of the power grab, electing the opposite approach to the timely power return. That is, they actually believe that they are bosses just because they had to fill in for the boss, during his crisis of leadership.

It's a form of subtle marital-transgenderism.[314] That is, just because a person (whether in necessity or not) adopts the characteristics of a person of the opposite sex, it doesn't actually mean the substitution can be accomplished within nature. A woman may behave as a man all she wishes, but she will never convince anyone, save for herself (nor will she enjoy the God-given male bestowals).

To determine whether they usurp their husband's headship or perhaps are in danger of incrementally doing so, wives must ask themselves the following questions:

---

314 I define this concept as husband and wife "swapping" roles.

1. Do I secretly enjoy heading my household in my husband's stead?
2. Would I resent giving my husband back the controls if he took initiative to improve?
3. Am I expanding upon the opportunities left in the wake of his deficiencies, scooping up *all* the family decisions (and not just those which are most vital and necessary, in my husband's absence)?
4. Am I privately and gently encouraging—not nagging at—my husband to lead the household?
5. Do I resent my husband for his shortcomings? Do I talk badly about him or treat him poorly, in public or private?
6. Am I docile, or am I—by my poor responses—preventing my husband from taking charge? Have I given him reason to believe I will respond adversely if he ever attempts to return to his rightful leadership?

Most women today would likely fail the above questionnaire because they are already acting as *in persona husband* in *most domains,* not just the areas where he is most absent. A wife ought to frequently check in with her husband, reminding him that he is the head of the household even if he is remiss in a few of his duties; she must pray and gently request him to accept his proper role as the priest of the home. She should remind him how attractive she finds him whenever he takes charge over household matters. (Again, she shouldn't nag him into compliance—which never works and only sows more division.)

A wife should never disparage her husband or talk badly about his shortcomings in public, especially in front of their children. Instead, she ought to treat him with the most profound respect. At the same time, her enthusiastic reactions to his leadership must signal that she will happily comply.

Of course, these principles double for the woman who is neglecting her duties to the household. No one can take her place, either: not nannies, babysitters, day-care workers, extended family members, or even the husband himself. A man's attempted surrogation for his absent wife no more renders him the heart of the home than it makes her the head of the house when she steps in for him.

Again, to assert otherwise is a form of transgenderism: it stands for the proposition that without regard for a person's biological sex, he or she can serve any function of the opposite sex, at any time and for any reason. It stands, in other words, for the elimination of Christian complementarity: the special fittingness of the two sexes and their "dovetailing" roles within the Christian family and society. One living according to this disordered credo will always be living an illusion, and never living their true vocation.

The household is already suffering from the loss of its rightful head. The suffering of the household doubles when the heart gives out. Neither organ can serve the other's function; either will give out twice as fast when inefficiently trying to cover for the other. (It proves impossible for a woman to lead *and* follow.) Children must follow the example of one leading male, and one following female. There is no other ideal. The household run by a father-surrogating mother is deprived of its head and heart; headless and heartless, the home lies in the shadow of a play-acting, frustrated tyrant. Consequently, family and friends start encountering awkward social interactions with the disordered couple because disfunction is impossible to conceal.

"It's Dignity! Gah! Don't You Even Know Dignity When You See It?"[315]

By now, you know I love to illustrate my cultural critiques with humorous pop-culture references, particularly *The Simpsons.* The following scene comes from the hallowed episode, "A Millhouse Divided." I'll set the stage for you: Marge and Homer have decided to heighten

---

315 Groening, Matt. "A Milhouse Divided." *The Simpsons.* Dir. Steven Moore. Fox, New York, New York, 1 Dec. 1996. Television.

their family's sense of culture by hosting a dinner party for several of their married friends. In attendance are Kirk and Luann Van Houten; throughout the dinner party each member of the Van Houten couple takes occasion to air their dirty laundry. Immediately, it becomes painfully apparent to all the guests that they are miserable in their marriage.

Even during a lighthearted game of *Pictionary,* Luann and Kirk have a hard time concealing their contempt for one another. The couple has the following exchange in full view of all the Simpsons' house guests:

> [Kirk and Luann's turn at Pictionary]
> Kirk: Ah, come on Luann, you know what this is.
> Luann: Kirk, I don't know what it is.
> Kirk: [sighs] It could not be more simple, Luann. You want me to show this to the cat, and have the cat tell you what it is? 'Cause the cat's going to get it.
> Luann: I'm sorry, I'm not as smart as you, Kirk. We didn't all go to Gudger College.
> [the timer dings]
> Kirk: It's dignity! Gah! Don't you even know dignity when you see it?
> Luann: Kirk, you're spitting.
> Kirk: Okay, genius, why don't you draw dignity. [Luann does so; everyone gasps in recognition, but viewers can't see it]
> Dr. Hibbert: Worthy of Webster's.
> Reverend Lovejoy: Now, Kirk, it's only a game. Sometimes, we...
> Kirk: Aw, cram it, churchy!
> Kirk: [to Luann] Why don't you tell them one of your little bedtime stories, huh? Like the one about how rotten it is to be married to a loser. Or how about the one about how I carry a change purse? Yeah, a purse!
> Homer: Shut up and let the woman talk!
> Luann: Okay, Kirk, I'll tell a story. It's about a man whose

> father-in-law gave him a sweet job as manager of a cracker factory.
>
> Homer: Bo-ring!
>
> Luann: A man whose complete lack of business sense and managerial impotence...
>
> Homer: Ooh, here we go!
>
> Luann: ...sent the number one cracker factory in town into a tie for 6th with "TableTime" and "Allied Biscuit."
>
> [Marge hides a box of "Allied Biscuit"]
>
> Kirk: You want to hear a secret, everybody? Luann loves it, loves it when I fail.
>
> Luann: Oh yes, Kirk. I love having to borrow money from my sister. I love having to steal clothes from the church donation box.
>
> Reverend Lovejoy: [quietly] Oh, sweet Jesus.[316]

"Okay," you may retort, "but that's fiction." Believe it or not, I've actually been around plenty of couples *nearly* this unhinged in real life. It's actually not that rare (after all, nothing's shocking today).

What's quite common is something like the following. My husband and I are attending an event with several other couples. The location doesn't matter. Sometime throughout the evening, we meet *him* and *her*. I'm sure you all will recognize the picture of the couple I am describing.

Let's start with *her*. She's the woman who deigns it appropriate (or funny) to start whining about her husband's deficiencies to complete strangers. She is the type of woman who will pounce upon another woman's mostly unrelated anecdote and will apply it to her own husband, who comes up short in something *remotely like* that area. I could be at a pool party describing to a small group of women how, at my husband's adult-league basketball game, the referee's pants fell down while he was making a call. And this Luann Van Houten-type would

---

316 "A Milhouse Divided/Quotes." *Simpsons Wiki*, Web. 19 Apr. 202, www.simpsons.fandom.com/wiki/A_Milhouse_Divided/Quotes.

seize upon my funny anecdote as an opportunity to share with us how horribly her relationship (and her husband) is. For example, she would say something like: "Gah! Sports! My husband is too weak to play sports." See how she's subverted not only my delightful story, but also the gaiety of the entire pool party? I'm always tempted to respond to such unhappy women: "well, you picked him, sweetheart—what does that say about you? Also, thanks for dampening the mood!"

These women see an open invitation to besmirch their husbands anytime the topic of family-life comes up, which kills *the single* conversation topic virtually all females enjoy together. When such a woman is around, the group has to switch to comparatively *less* awkward conversation topics like everyone's stance on abortion or which religion is the true one.[317]

Moving on to *him*: according to my husband (and all his buddies) the Kirk Van Houten-type is the man who is so accustomed to being henpecked that he has lost all ability to relate to other men. When such types attempt to sound macho, they overshoot their mark or just say hilarious things. Later in the same episode, Kirk—who has by now separated from Luann—engages in the following dialogue with Homer:

> Kirk: Singles' life is great, Homer. I can do whatever I want. Today I drank a beer in the bathroom.
> Homer: The one down the hall?
> Kirk: Yeah! And another great thing, you get your own bed. I sleep in a racing car, do you?
> Homer: I sleep in a big bed with my wife.
> Kirk: Oh. Yeah.[318]

Emasculated, he is more like a child than a man. He will undoubtedly be the weakest member in his group of male friends. Yet, because his home-life is so unbearable, he insists on spending all his free-time

317 Irony intended.

318 "A Milhouse Divided/Quotes." *Simpsons Wiki*, Web. 19 Apr. 202, www.simpsons.fandom.com/wiki/A_Milhouse_Divided/Quotes.

with "the guys." Since human beings are naturally social, the domestic lack of the husband-and-wife intimacy renders him all the more dependent on his male companions. His friendship with his wife suffers even further because he puts so little effort into leading her. And he cannot escape the vicious, negative cycle he helped create—no wonder he prefers to spend time away from the mess he created.

Instead of resolving his marital difficulties, this man holds his tongue at home—only to unleash it around his buddies during social gatherings. So, he, like his wife, poisons the environment with his tactless and deficient social awareness. Since the man, not the woman, is the head of the household, the social awkwardness of the couple reflects his failed leadership. Some people may take objection to such wide-sweeping stereotypes. So, here's my disclaimer about stereotypes: they're usually true.[319]

And yet, seeking out the counsel of a professional, priest, close family member, or friend is a far different situation than tarnishing the reputation of your spouse to a group of random people. All of us have been in situations where we needed the fresh, objective advice from someone trusted. Still, we must keep in mind, though, that when we are seeking out counsel to never use it as an opportunity to gossip about our spouses: one can still actually be guilty of the sin of detraction. *The Catechism of the Catholic Church* says of detraction:

> Respect for the reputation of persons forbids every attitude and word likely to cause them unjust injury. He becomes guilty:
>
> - of rash judgment who, even tacitly, assumes as true, without sufficient foundation, the moral fault of a neighbor;
> - of detraction who, without objectively valid reason, discloses another's faults and failings to persons who did not know them;
> - of calumny who, by remarks contrary to the truth, harms the

319 Which is why they're funny.

> reputation of others and gives occasion for false judgments concerning them.[320]

It's a good rule of thumb to pretend that your spouse is sitting in the room with you as you characterize your marital difficulties. (Or alternately, just have him sit there, and consult a counselor together; this is probably best.) It is an axiom that human beings loathe to hear someone gripe about his spouse in a group setting. However, I've almost never resented someone with good-will seeking out my advice in the appropriate setting.

My intention with the above section was not to be callous to those in troubled marriages. Instead, I would urge such people to take the appropriate measures for amending their marriages behind closed doors (and to save us all from awkward social interactions if they opt against this). On the rare occasion whereupon I've felt a friend has misused my counsel as an opportunity to gossip about her spouse, I owe (and gave) her the reminder that her husband is owed her loyalty and confidence above all others. As bad as it is for spouses to publicly badmouth each other, it is especially destructive when they do so in front of their shared children.

Following the "Leader"

For a leaderless household, ensuring the proper formation of one's children must be greatly daunting at times. For the leaderless woman, a careful balance exists between trying to protect the children from their father's bad example and exercising caution not to foster contempt of him.

Naturally, children have a right not only to love each of their parents generally, but also to be specifically insulated against having to "pick sides" during disagreements. But what should a woman to do if

---

320 Catholic Church. *Catechism of the Catholic Church.* 2nd ed., Our Sunday Visitor, 2000. #2477.

her husband is providing such a bad example that his behavior must be addressed and warned against?

As we saw with marital counsel-seeking, there's a fine line between appropriate and inappropriate expression and exposition of the problem to small children.

In such situations where a father's example must be warned against—or even removed from the family home altogether—his wife must be near-scrupulously careful not to divulge needless details. Naturally, it is impossible to hope that one's (even) very young children won't take notice when something proves to be seriously remiss with their father. Accordingly, a heart-to-heart conversation with them is indispensable. When such a conversation does occur, the mother ought to explain that the father needs desperate love and prayers. Even if a husband and wife are temporarily separated, she must always tell her children that she still loves their father and prays ceaselessly for his conversion and return. Basically, the mother is fostering an environment maximally conducive to the husband's dignified return to the bosom of the family (should he make the appropriate changes).

Any alternative will be disastrous for the family. Women who belittle their children's father seldom win the allies they seek. A child's love for even a deficient father is profoundly ingrained. The mother exposes only her own selfishness when she attempts to create a wartime ally out of her child; in turn, the child loses respect for both parents, while usually siding with the father.

Teenaged and adult children require just as much parental sensitivity, if in differing ways. Older children will be more finely tuned to the signs of dysfunction in their parents' relationship. When children are younger, the parents may have an easier time hiding their arguments or explaining the father's periodic absences. On the other hand, adult children ask more probative questions and prove vastly more perceptive. Mothers may be tempted to treat teenaged children like confidants by dint of the fact that such offspring are capable of reasoning, communicating, and showing empathy akin to peers. As a matter of fact, inquisitive older children may even *demand* to be afforded details on the state of their parents' marriage.

Even with such older children, a mother in her loneliness must resist the natural temptation to treat them as her equals. She still must do her best to preserve the reputation of their father at all times. She must keep in mind that her marriage is a model after which her children will craft their own romantic relationships. Even if their parental model of marriage was less than ideal, or if the parents are living separately, the children can still learn from their mother how to respect an imperfect spouse. Indeed, even if the children find more successful relationships than their parents, they still benefit from having learned patience from a longsuffering mother. And all humans should learn from their mothers how to suffer with dignity and grace: namely, via the power of prayer, fasting, and self-denial.

A mother who displays charity during her tribulations by upholding her spouse's dignity and protecting her children from the injurious politics of parental feuding will, in the end, earn her supporters. Her children will rally to support her simply because she will have behaved so admirably during her misfortunes.

The "B Word"

It's all fine and good to lay out sweeping propositions expressing proper wifely behavior during times of crisis, but how realistic is any of this advice? How can a woman who is suffering the loss of a leader and protector combat becoming the dreaded "b-word?"

By "b-word," I, of course, mean "bitter."

Bitterness and female disappointment go together like a wink and a nod. A well-formed Christian woman does her utmost to combat this, however. How does the most robust Christian woman keep bitterness at bay as she faces the most wounding disappointment a woman can bear, in the form of an absent husband?

It has been attributed to Queen Catherine of Aragon—who ought to be the patroness of jilted wives—once quipped, "None get to God but through trouble." Queen Catherine knew better than most what it's like to be in a *very* troubled marriage.

If you are unfamiliar of the tragic fate of Queen Catherine (AD 1485-1536), she was the first wife of the infamous womanizer and wife-beheader, King Henry VIII. Queen Catherine was the first of the king's six wives to be cast aside, as he chased woman after woman in search of a son and heir. King Henry not only cast aside his wives, but *also* cast aside his Catholic faith—in order to rid himself of his first wife, Catherine of Aragon. The Pope (Pope Clement VII) forbade his requests to divorce Catherine to marry his Protestant mistress, Anne Boleyn (who became the first wife he had beheaded):

> For seven years the pope avoided issuing the annulment because he could not alienate Catherine's nephew, the Holy Roman emperor Charles V. Finally Henry separated from Catherine in July 1531. On May 23, 1533—five months after he married Anne Boleyn—he had his own archbishop of Canterbury, Thomas Cranmer, annul the marriage to Catherine. Parliament passed the Act of Supremacy repudiating all papal jurisdiction in England and making the king head of the English church. Although Catherine had always been loved by the English people, Henry forced her to spend her last years isolated from all public life.[321]

As a devout Catholic, Queen Catherine's pain redoubled when King Henry VIII rejected his Catholic faith over the matter. (Instead of persevering in the faith, he made up yet one more new form of Protestantism: Anglicanism.) The tragic life of Catherine of Aragon ended with an even more profoundly tragic death. Before dying, she had to endure being forcibly removed from the king's estate, inclusive of separation from her only child (who would later become the

---

321 "Catherine of Aragon." *Encyclopædia Britannica*. Encyclopædia Britannica, Inc. Web. 28 Apr. 2021.

infamous Queen "Bloody Mary"). She died prayerfully in secluded, sub-par living conditions:

> Until the end of her life, Catherine of Aragon would refer to herself as Henry's only lawfully wedded wife and England's only rightful queen. Her faithful servants continued to address her by that title. In 1535, she was transferred to the decaying Kimbolton Castle in the wilds of Huntington. Confining herself to one room, leaving it only to attend mass, Catherine prepared to meet her end. While she was permitted to receive occasional visitors, she was forbidden to ever see her daughter Mary. She was also forbidden to communicate with her, but discreet sympathizers ferried secret letters between mother and daughter. Henry offered them both better quarters and the company of one another if only they would acknowledge Anne Boleyn as his new queen. Neither did.[322]

Catherine endured all these perjuries and insults, while her husband openly flaunted his Protestant floozy, Anne Boleyn, in her absence. She merits serious respect as a jilted, yet constant Catholic wife.

The point is that Catherine provides an exemplary—no, an outright heroic—figure that today's women may look to. Throughout her separation from the King, Catherine kept constant vigil for their reconciliation. She forbore the relentless embarrassments of her husband's public attempts to divorce her, time and again. One of the last actions she took before her death was to pen this touching letter to King Henry VIII on January 7, 1536. In it, she heartfully beseeches him to quit his debauchery. Also, she sincerely seeks to remind him of her wifely love. She even jokingly sprinkled in a few wifely "honey-do" requests, within her last correspondence:

---

322 "Catherine of Aragon." *Catherine of Aragon - New World Encyclopedia*. Web. 28 Apr. 2021.

> My most dear lord, king and husband,
>
> The hour of my death now drawing on, the tender love I owe you forceth me, my case being such, to commend myself to you, and to put you in remembrance with a few words of the health and safeguard of your soul which you ought to prefer before all worldly matters, and before the care and pampering of your body, for which you have cast me into many calamities and yourself into many troubles. For my part, I pardon you everything, and I wish to devoutly pray God that He will pardon you also. For the rest, I commend unto you our daughter Mary, beseeching you to be a good father unto her, as I have heretofore desired. I entreat you also, on behalf of my maids, to give them marriage portions, which is not much, they being but three. For all my other servants I solicit the wages due them, and a year more, lest they be unprovided for. Lastly, I make this vow, that mine eyes desire you above all things.
>
> Katharine the Quene[323]

Catherine is a fine example of suffering mortifying indignities while keeping our eyes fixed upon the Lord and *our* lords— our husbands. Any modern woman who finds herself in marital trouble ought to read a biography of Catherine to draw inspiration from her strength in great marital adversity. Her marital troubles were so extreme that movies, books, and even comedies have retold it. Catherine wisely understood that to stave off bitterness, she had to throw her sufferings at the feet of Our Lady and our Lord. So much forbearance requires *supernatural* heroism.

To combat bitterness, women should try, as Catherine did, to view their husbands as Christ does—that is, as lost souls in need of rescue.

---

323 Hanson, Marilee. "Letter of Katharine of Aragon to her husband, King Henry VIII 7 January 1536." https://englishhistory.net/tudor/letter/letter-of-katharine-of-aragon-to-king-henry-viii/, 8 Feb. 2015.

There is a great deal of pity to be mustered for someone who is acting so wickedly that he has cut himself off from the sacraments. In short, empathy for the husband's separation from Christ becomes a wife's opportune ally in combating bitterness.

For, as the husband is estranged from his wife, he has also estranged himself from Christ. This is the very point of it all: the Church elevated matrimony to a sacrament. In alienating the wife, the husband alienates Christ. And since there is no life outside of the sacraments, such a man deserves his family's most desperate compassion. None of this suggests that bitterness can be eliminated altogether. But it should stand for the proposition that such jilted women ought to try to convert their bitterness into more productive passions like concern, empathy, and holy fear for the sake of another.

After all, a bitter woman has almost no chance of converting her husband. Besides, bitterness if indulged makes life unduly difficult for her and her children. Living with such an extra psychological burden proves detrimental to one's physical and spiritual health. Some women who indulge the temptation to become bitter simply give up taking care of themselves. Bitterness can also have an adverse spiritual effect, leading some women to give up attending Mass altogether—following their husbands' unholy example. I have met many women who sadly have taken the opposite approach to that of Catherine of Aragon. In so doing, they lost faith in God because they mistook His allowance for human error through free will for abandonment: "He should have prevented my hardship," as all other apostates utter in exodus from the One True Faith. It's an unmitigated tragedy when a woman loses her faith because of an unfaithful husband—who has twice betrayed her: leaving her side and then tempting her to leave the sacraments. Such women must at all cost avoid the bitterness from their failed marriage, and thereby obviate the apostasy which would constitute their own doom.

Without a devout father *or* mother in the home, the children become more likely to abandon their own faith. I implore Christian wives and mothers to never abandon Christ. However unjust your situation may be, it would be infinitely more wicked for you to leave Christ who sustains you perfectly.

Stay the course and you will find that your faith will get you through these trials. Surrendering to bitterness is a temptation to walk away from God. By all means, use everything you can to combat this temptation. The abandoned woman may find this prayer particularly helpful to recite when feeling disheartened about her marriage:

Prayer in An Unhappy Marriage

> O God, Lord and Director of my life, You have placed me in the state of marriage. In it I hoped for joy and happiness, but now I experience only problems. Much of my trouble is my own fault. But, it is Your will, O heavenly Father that my husband and I stay together. May Your will be done! You place before my eyes Your only Son, whose whole life here below was the hard way of the cross. You call upon me to follow Him. I will do, O Lord, what You demand of me. I thank You from my heart for your love in treating me as You treated Your well-beloved Son. But I am weak! Have pity on my cowardice!
>
> I know that without Your special grace, I shall be unable to bear my cross as I should. Give me what You demand of me, and then ask what You will. Give me Your most lovable Son, as You gave Him to the most Blessed Virgin Mary, that He may be always with me, to counsel and assist me in Your love. Place in me the open wound of His Heart. Fill me with His forgiveness, meekness, and humility. Grant me a share in His fortitude, and I shall be able to endure all things.
>
> Lord, send me sufferings, trials, and tribulations as numerous and as heavy as seems good to You; but, at the same time, increase my patience and resignation. Teach me, after the example of my sweet Savior, to repay evil with good, angry

> words with silence or gentle replies; to merit Your favor by a strict fulfillment of duty, and, by ready obedience and constraint, faithful love, regain my husband's heart for myself and for You.
>
> Preserve us, Almighty God, from the deceits of the evil spirits and from the malicious, or perhaps well-meant though foolish language and counsel of silly people. Grant us peace and harmony, rue affection and forbearance, devout sentiments and holy fear, that we may cheerfully labor, pray, and suffer with and for each other. May we walk together the way of Your holy Commandments and together reap the reward of our good works for an endless eternity! Grant us this, Heavenly Father, for the love of Jesus, Mary and Joseph, as also of all the saints who, in the married state, sanctified themselves and attained eternal life. AMEN.[324]

No family should suffer from the egocentrism of a derelict leader. Often, well-meaning people offer insipid platitudes during a friend's time of crisis because they lack answers. Unfortunately, their advice centers on trifles such as "happiness" and "moving on," rather than underscoring the importance of staying on the narrow path of righteousness. The best advice I've always received was initially the hardest to hear. Sisters in Christ can laugh, disagree, cry, debate, and empathize all in one afternoon gathering and emerge better friends for it. Perhaps *Ask Your Husband* might be the fodder for such a get-together.

Remember, it's primarily your husband who will have to stand before God and account for the state of your family. Still, a wife must do her part, even if it be secondary.

---

324 Franciscus, Rev. Pius, O.F.M. "Mother love, A Prayer Book for Christian Wives and Mothers." *Archconfraternity of Christian Mothers*, 1979, pp. 164-167.

One Letter about a Good Husband, and One Letter for a Bad One

The following two letters are resources to help women. The first letter will help you understand the mind of men in regard to marriage. And the second letter appeals to a husband who is derelict in his duty.

I'll start with the good letter. Actually, the following constitutes carefully selected *excerpts* from a letter, penned by a kingly Catholic, husband, and father: J.R.R. Tolkien. In March 1941,[325] Tolkien penned the following advice to his twenty-year old son regarding common apprehensions men face in their prospective travails in love and marriage. The letter's excerpts are organized into six subtopics within the general topic of married relations. This correspondence proves as helpful to women as it is to men because it aids women's dim understanding of how men regard intimate relationships.

1. True Love is about More than Sex

Sex, Tolkien noted, is the element which brings life and vitality to love. But the true lover is one who brings more than sex to the table:

"A 'lover': "engaging and blending all his affections and powers of mind and body in a complex emotion powerfully coloured and energized by 'sex'."

2. Friendship with the Opposite Sex is Impossible

According to Tolkien, our life in a "fallen world" is what prevents deep, platonic friendships between male and female persons. The desire may be there, but it always seems to go awry:

"To ordinary folk it can only rarely occur: two minds that have

325 Carpenter, Humphrey. *The Letters of J.R.R. Tolkien.* Houghton Mifflin Harcourt Publishing Company, New York, N.Y., 1981, pp. 48.

really a primarily mental and spiritual affinity may by accident reside in a male and a female body, and yet may desire and achieve a 'friendship' quite independent of sex. But no one can count on it. The other partner will let him (or her) down, and almost certainly, by 'falling in love'. But a young man does not really (as a rule) want 'friendship', even if he says he does. … He wants love: innocent, and yet irresponsible perhaps."

3. Chivalric Love is Dangerous

While most women find the idea of chivalric knights and fair maidens quite romantic, Tolkien believed the concept detrimental to women because it places them at the center of the relationship. This sets them up as a god-like figure and only leads to future disappointment and disillusionment:

"[Chivalry] takes, or at any rate has in the past taken, the young man's eye off women as they are, as companions in shipwreck not guiding stars. (One result is for observation of the actual to make the young man turn cynical.) To forget their desires, needs and temptations. It inculcates exaggerated notions of 'true love', as a fire from without, a permanent exaltation, unrelated to age, childbearing, and plain life, and unrelated to will and purpose."

4. Women are More Practical than Men When it Comes to Love

Tolkien explains that women are much more prone to desire the practical elements of love – such as building a home and family – than they are the romantic parts. As a result, the female heart is more easily damaged if the male was simply toying with her affections:

"A man has a life-work, a career, (and male friends), all of which could (and do where he has any guts) survive the shipwreck of 'love'. A young woman, even one 'economically independent', as they say now (it usually really means economic subservience to male commercial employers instead of to a father or a family), begins to think of the 'bottom drawer' and dream of a home, almost at once. If she really falls in love, the shipwreck may really end on the rocks."

5. Marriage Does Not Cure Sexual Desires

According to Tolkien, those who believe marriage will enable them to live in effortless purity in regard to sexuality are dead wrong. It is possible – and a state to be sought earnestly – but it takes great "grace," "self-denial," and "mortification" to achieve it:

"No man, however, truly he loved his betrothed and bride as a young man, has lived faithful to her as a wife in mind and body without deliberate conscious exercise of the will, without self-denial. Too few are told that – even those brought up 'in the Church'."

6. Marriage is Not about Soulmates

The quest for a soulmate, Tolkien implies, can go on for a lifetime. Tolkien infers that the idea of the soulmate is at the root of the divorce culture:

"When the glamour wears off, or merely works a bit thin, they think they have made a mistake, and that the real soul-mate is still to find. The real soul-mate too often proves to be the next sexually attractive person that comes along."

The way to break this cycle is to recognize the following:

"But the 'real soul-mate' is the one you are actually married to. You really do very little choosing: life and circumstance do

> most of it (though if there is a God these must be His instruments, or His appearances)."[326]

Tolkien's fatherly advice is unparalleled in terms of its depths and non-token qualities. Because few men have such fathers to advise them thus, the women of the world now need a more somber letter.

The letter below—a modern to nod Queen Catherine of Aragon's last letter to her King Henry VIII—is intended for desperate Christian wives to share with their derelict husbands (those who are deficient in their duty but who are not so grossly deficient as to be unsafe to be around). A wife ought to use this tool to remind her husband of his duties toward his family. It also serves as constant reminder concerning his obligations to God, particularly the preservation of his own soul. Over the years, many women have asked me via email how to address such husbands *privately* and *lovingly*. Though I have no personal experience in this regard, I attempted here to compile the many sufferings women in this unfortunate situation have expressed to me. Hopefully, it will also provide a modicum of hope to the wayward husband: "all is not lost," after all, if he should only do what's necessary to regain his home.

> Dear Husband,
>
> When all of the years of your life have spent, and you stand before God Almighty, how do you suppose He will judge you? As you stand at your eternal judgment, will you attempt to peddle the same hackneyed excuses for your wantonness as you did during the most ignoble hours your life?
>
> Please don't be so foolish. Don't you know you stand before Him who heard all my prayers and pleas? He knows me as His faithful daughter and as your neglected wife and mother of our

---

326 Holmquist, Annie. "Tolkien's Fatherly Advice to His Son on Sex." *Intellectual Takeout,* 16 June 2017, www.intellectualtakeout.org/article/tolkiens-fatherly-advice-his-son-sex-0/.

fatherless children. How will you answer the One who comforted, preserved, and protected your family in your absence? For all your many deeds are now laid bare before you, and nothing is concealed any longer.

How many ways—known and unknown—have you, by your selfishness, led our family away from the Lord and willingly delivered us to the Deceiver? Did you not realize that your poor example would shape the lives of our children, for worse not better, and leave me with many undue hardships?

God bestowed you the great honor of leadership over several of His own precious creations. You were charged with a holy commission by your Creator; when you turned your back on your family, you turned your back on God. The Lord witnessed you bartering for fool's gold His precious gifts. He watched you mishandle and malign your own soul and the souls of your family, in exchange for trifles: only a pitiful man would willingly exchange his soul for temporal indulgences.

Any objective appraiser of your life goes wanting for any article in it which separates men from beasts: self-sacrifice. In that moment of judgment, would you not happily jump at the chance to go back to remedy your grave errors to save yourself from eternal ruin?

You have that choice right now before you, as you read these very words. You still possess a great gift many who have gone before you do not: *the time to change and a woman to embrace you as you cross our threshold.*

You still enjoy the freedom, dear husband, to return to your family and lead us as God commands you! Throw off the bonds with which you have shackled yourself. For, surely, if you do not do so now, your bonds will eventually latch and confine you to perdition, at the end of your days.

God created men with such high esteem that He assigned to man the headship over his woman and their shared children. Our Lord did not give you such an honor for nothing. He expects you, dear husband, to lead us, protect us (even from yourself), support us financially (by keeping me away from the many indignities of the workforce), to teach us by your good example how to live morally, and to love us as Christ loves his Church.

Do not, out of shame, feel like there is no turning back from your wantonness. Turn back you may. I am called by my God to forgive you and rejoice at your return. Being a good Christian woman, I have been praying ceaselessly for your soul and for your return. Daily, I instruct our children to do them same. They want only that which is owed to them: the affections and care of an honorable leader. Please work hard to be worthy of our affections—the great things for which God has created you—and reclaim what is rightly yours: the rightful headship of your family.

No one can take your place in my heart—or in our children's. Until you return, your absence will be a bleeding, open wound to us. If indefinite, your absence will affect the subsequent choices of our children in their adolescence and adulthood. A wife, if she practices her faith, is wholly dependent on a husband to provide for her. I am now at a great disadvantage through having to cover for your duties as I perform my own. This means you have also deprived your children of a mother.

It is not too late. Just as Christ forgives us over and again, so can we, your family, forgive you. One of the hallmarks of masculinity is being able to say, "I was wrong. I will change. Please forgive me." If you can say that and follow through, you can still be a king among men! Indeed, I long to call you *my* king.

Love,

Your Wife

Epilogue

Until now, we have covered many beautiful aspects of a women's role in Christian marriage from Sacred Scripture, the Church's teachings, the early Church Fathers, and the humble insights of this author. Before concluding let us look to a twentieth-century saint who devoted his life to helping couples find holiness in their marriages. St. Josemaría Escrivá's salient advice concerns the purpose of marriage, how to handle disagreements, and the absolute acceptance of the indissolubility of the marriage bond during times of difficulty.

St. Josemaría Escrivá, on the purpose of marriage:

> The majority of the members of Opus Dei are married people, so in this field I can speak from the experience of many years of priestly activity in many countries. For the married members of Opus Dei human love and marriage duties are part of their divine vocation. Opus Dei has made of marriage a divine way, a vocation, and this has many consequences for personal holiness and for apostolate. I have spent almost forty years preaching the vocational meaning of marriage. More than once I have had occasion to see faces light up as men and women, who had thought that in their lives a dedication to God was incompatible with a noble and pure human love, heard me say that marriage is a divine path on earth!
>
> The purpose of marriage is to help married people sanctify themselves and others. For this reason, they receive a special grace in the sacrament which Jesus Christ instituted. Those who are called to the married state will, with the grace of God, find within their state everything they need to be holy,

to identify themselves each day more with Jesus Christ, and to lead those with whom they live to God.

That is why I always look upon Christian homes with hope and affection, upon all the families which are the fruit of the Sacrament of Matrimony. They are a shining witness of the great divine mystery of Christ's loving union with His Church which St. Paul calls sacramentum magnum, a great sacrament (Eph 5:32). We must strive so that these cells of Christianity may be born and may develop with a desire for holiness, conscious of the fact that the Sacrament of Initiation — Baptism — confers on all Christians a divine mission that each must fulfill in his or her own walk of life.

Christian couples should be aware that they are called to sanctity themselves and to sanctify others, that they are called to be apostles and that their first apostolate is in the home. They should understand that founding a family, educating their children, and exercising a Christian influence in society, are supernatural tasks. The effectiveness and the success of their life—their happiness— depends to a great extent on their awareness of their specific mission.

But they mustn't forget that the secret of married happiness lies in everyday things, not in daydreams. It lies in finding the hidden joy of coming home in the evening, in affectionate relations with their children, in the everyday work in which the whole family cooperates; in good humor in the face of difficulties that should be met with a sporting spirit; in making the best use of all the advantages that civilization offers to help us rear children, to make the house pleasant and life simpler.

I constantly tell those who have been called by God to form a home to love one another always, to love each other with the love of their youth. Anyone who thinks that love ends when the worries and difficulties that life brings with it begin, has a poor idea of marriage, which is a sacrament and an ideal and a vocation. It is precisely then that love grows strong. Torrents of worries and difficulties are incapable of drowning true love, because people who sacrifice themselves generously together are brought closer by their sacrifice. As Scripture says, *aquae multae*, a host of difficulties, physical and moral, *non potuerunt extinguere caritatem*, cannot extinguish love (Cant 8:7).[327]

St. Josemaría Escrivá, on how to handle disagreements:

I would advise them to love one another and to realize that although disagreements and difficulties will crop up throughout their lives, if they are solved with ordinary common sense they can even contribute to the deepening of their love.

We each have our own character, our personal tastes, our moods — sometimes our bad moods — and our defects. But we all have likeable aspects in our personality as well, and for this reason, and many others, everyone can be loved. It is possible to live happily together when everyone tries to correct their own defects and makes an effort to overlook the faults of others. That is to say, when there is love which cancels out and overcomes everything that might seem to be a motive for coldness or disagreement. On the other hand, if husband and wife dramatize their little differences and reproach each other for their defects and mistakes, they put an end to peace and run the risk of killing their love.

Couples have the grace of the married state—the grace they receive in the Sacrament of Marriage — which enables them to live out all the human and Christian virtues in their married life: understanding, good humor, patience, forgiveness,

327 Josemaría, Escrivá De Balaguer. *Conversations with Saint Josemaría Escrivá.* New York: Scepter, 2007, no. 91.

good manners and consideration in their mutual relations. The important thing is not to give up the effort, not to give in to irritation, pride or personal fads or obsessions. In order to achieve this, husbands and wives must develop their interior life and learn from the Holy Family the best way to practice the virtues of a Christian home, for both supernatural and human reasons. I repeat again that God's grace will not be lacking.

Anyone who says they cannot put up with this or that, or finds it impossible to hold their peace, is exaggerating in order to justify themselves. We should ask God for the strength to overcome our whims and to practice self-control. When we lose our temper, we lose control of the situation. Words can become harsh and bitter, and we end up by offending, wounding and hurting, even though we didn't mean to.

We should all learn to keep quiet, to wait and say things in a positive, optimistic way. When her husband loses his temper, the moment has arrived for the wife to be especially patient until he calms down, and vice versa. If there is true love and a real desire to deepen it, it will very rarely happen that the two give in to bad temper at the same time.

Another very important thing is to get used to the fact that we are never a hundred per cent right. In fact, one can say that in matters like these, which are usually so debatable, the surer we are of being completely right, the more doubtful it is that we really are.

Following this line of reasoning makes it easier to correct oneself later on and if necessary, to beg pardon, which is the best way of ending a quarrel. In this way peace and love are regained. I am not encouraging you to quarrel, but it is understandable that we should fall out at times with those we love most, because they are the people we are always with. We are not going to fall out with someone in Timbuktu! Thus, small rows between husband and wife, as long as they are not too frequent, (and they should see to it that they are not) are not a sign that love is lacking; and in fact they can help to increase it.

Finally, I would advise parents never to quarrel in front of their children. They can remind each other of this with a certain word, a look or a gesture. If they cannot avoid the argument altogether, they can, at least, put it off till later when they are calmer. The family atmosphere should be one of peace between husband and wife because peace is a necessary condition for deep and effective character training. Children should see in their parents an example of dedication, sincere love, mutual help and understanding. The small trifles of daily life should not be allowed to hide from them the reality of a love that is capable of overcoming all obstacles.

Sometimes we take ourselves too seriously. Each of us gets angry now and again. Sometimes because it is necessary; other times because we lack a spirit of mortification. The important thing is to show, with a smile that restores family warmth, that these outbursts of anger do not destroy affection. In a word, the lives of husband and wife should consist in loving one another and loving their children, because by doing this they love God.[328]

St. Josemaría Escrivá, on accepting the indissolubility of the marriage bond during times of great difficulty:

While understanding their suffering, I would tell them that they can also see in their situation God's Will, which is never cruel, for God is a loving Father. The situation may be especially

328 Josemaría, Escrivá De Balaguer. *Conversations with Saint Josemaria Escrivá*. New York: Scepter, 2007, no. 108.

difficult for some time, but if they go to our Lord and His blessed Mother, they will receive the help of grace.

The indissolubility of marriage is not a caprice of the Church nor is it merely a positive ecclesiastical law. It is a precept of natural law, of divine law, and responds perfectly to our nature and to the supernatural order of grace. For these reasons, in the great majority of cases, indissolubility is an indispensable condition for the happiness of married couples and for the spiritual security of their children. Even in the very sad cases we are talking about, the humble acceptance of God's Will always brings with it a profound sense of satisfaction that nothing can substitute. It is not merely a refuge, or a consolation, it is the very essence of Christian life.

If women who are separated from their husbands have children in their care, they should understand that their children continue to need their loving motherly devotion, and especially now, to make up for the deficiencies of a divided home. They should make a generous effort to understand that indissolubility, which for them means sacrifice, is a safeguard for the integrity and unity of the great majority of families and ennobles the parent's love and prevents the abandonment of the children.

Surprise at the apparent hardness of the Christian precept of indissolubility is nothing new. The Apostles were surprised when Jesus confirmed it. It can seem a burden, a yoke, but Christ Himself said that His yoke was sweet and his burden light.

On the other hand, although recognizing the inevitable hardship of a good many situations, which often could and should have been avoided, we should be careful not to overdramatize. Is the life of a woman in these circumstances really harder than

> that of other maltreated women, or of people who suffer any of the other great physical or mental sorrows that life brings with it?
>
> What really makes a person unhappy and even destroys a whole society is the frenzied search for well-being and the attempt to eliminate, at all costs, all difficulties and hardships. Life has many facets, very different situations. Some are harsh, others may seem easy. Each situation brings its own grace. Each one is a special call from God, a new opportunity to work and to give the divine testimony of Charity. I would advise those who feel oppressed by a difficult situation to try to forget about their own problems a bit and concern themselves with the problems of others. If they do this they will have more peace and, above all, they will sanctify themselves.[329]

Truth Lives

I'd like to sincerely thank those of you who stuck with me right here to the very end of *Ask Your Husband*. That is, I salute and thank those of you who didn't throw this book across the room after you read something you vehemently disagreed with. Or those of you who *did* throw this book across the room but picked it back up and resumed reading it nonetheless.

No matter how many times your copy of *Ask Your Husband* has been tossed, I consider you my sister in Christ. It's my sincerest hope that you run your race well enough—that is, in the service of your family, not yourself—that on your deathbed the eagerness to receive your reward will overcome all fear.

My own marriage has brought me far more joy than these eight chapters could possibly convey. I desire that God-centered happiness for all married women. (Yes, even those women whose only usage of

329 Josemaría, Escrivá De Balaguer. *Conversations with Saint Josemaría Escrivá.* New York: Scepter, 2007, no. 97.

these pages was to kindle a bonfire or to line their birdcage.) Truth lives even if we ignore it, demean it, deny it, suppress it…or burn it.

I'll leave you with this parting shot: God *clearly* outlined what He expects from us, ladies. All we must do is lay down our arms and quit trying to bicker with Him about it.

Made in the USA
Las Vegas, NV
15 December 2023